Children's Games in Street and Playground

Iona and Peter Opie

Children's Games
in Street and Playground

Volume 2: Hunting, Racing, Duelling, Exerting,
Daring, Guessing, Acting, Pretending

Floris Books

First published in 1969 by Oxford University Press
This edition, in two volumes, published in 2008 by Floris Books

British Library CIP Data available

ISBN 978-086315-667-0

Printed in Great Britain
By Bell & Bain Ltd, Glasgow

Contents

9. Daring games   111

Games in which players incite each other to show their mettle

10. Guessing games   124

Games in which guessing is a necessary prelude or climax to physical action

11. Acting games 157

Games in which particular stories are enacted with set dialogue

12. Pretending games 00

Children make-believe they are other people, or in other situations, and extemporize accordingly

5. Hunting Games

Squeak, whistle, holly
Or the dogs shan't folly.
Traditional call, South Molton

In hunting games there are no boundaries (Boy Scouts aptly style them 'Wide Games'), and the feature of games without boundaries is that those being pursued must give some indication of the direction they have taken, which they do, according to the game being played, by shouting, by showing themselves, by showing a light, by leaving a trail, or by providing a guide. A secondary characteristic is that both pursuers and pursued operate as teams under leaders, and ordinarily move in a pack. In hunting games those who are pursued may, and often do, make use of cover; but the game is not over if they are seen, named, or even touched; the quarry has to be effectively captured, sometimes, as in Seeking Games, by ritual action on the body.

Hare and hounds

The general opinion is that the more players there are in 'Hare and Hounds' the better — 'even twenty' says one enthusiast. Sometimes only one or two boys set off as the hares (or 'foxes'), and the rest count to 300 or 400, or 'fifty *very* slowly', to give them a decent start. At other times the players divide into two equal groups of hunters and hunted. 'Hare and Hounds' is essentially a country game, not infrequently played 'on the edge of the dark', and 'to have a good game you want an hour at least because you might run for miles'. 'We go all across the country, round the school, over the rivers, across bogs.' The hares must keep together, have a definite course in mind, and are generally supposed to circle back to the starting-place after a certain length of time. The hounds must catch up with them before they are home. If one of the chasers views a hare he shouts 'Tally-ho', to put the others on the right course. Otherwise the hounds rely on calls. Every now and again they cry out for guidance, their shrill voices sounding across valley and field:

Hollo, hollo, hollo,
The hounds can't follow.
Knighton and Lydney

Hollo, hollo, the dogs won't follow,
Whistle or shout or else come out.
Thirsk

Robinson Crusoe give us a call,
A peeweep whistle or nothing at all.
Luncarty

Faintly in the distance—or startlingly close sometimes if it is dusk—comes the answering 'peeweep' or 'hollo'. 'If the call is not answered,' explains a 10-year-old, 'the hounds are allowed to give up after calling three times.' Usually, however, 'the hounds don't come back until they've caught all the foxes'.

In Radnorshire 'when the hounds catch a fox they tap him on the head three times'. In Burton Salmon, near Pontefract, 'he must be patted three times on the back'. On the Isle of Lewis a player must be held while he is named and his captor says 'One, two, three, caught'. In other places 'you have to catch him in a way that he can't get away. This game is very rough so you have to watch that you don't get caught'. 'If the hounds catch the hares the hounds give them any punishment they like.' 'If we catch the fox,' says a 9-year-old at Dovenby, 'we pretend to eat him. If a boy sulks we just leave him and if he joins again we let him.' 'It is a very sporting game for boys,' added a small male participant, 'but a shade too rough for girls.' The girls deny this: 'We like playing it,' they say, 'because it is very exciting.'

Usual names: 'Hare and Hounds', 'Hounds and Hares', 'Hunts', 'Hollo', and in Wales, 'Fox and Hounds'. Other names: 'Fox Off' (traditional in Yorkshire), 'Robinson and Crusoe' (Luncarty and Stromness), 'Stag Hunting' (Helston), and 'Whistle or a Cry' (Eassie, Angus).

§ The names have had little cause to alter through the centuries. Randle Holme of Chester (born 1627) knew the game as 'Hare and Hound' or 'Hunting of the Hare', so did Edward Moor (born in Suffolk 1771), and William Howitt (born in Derbyshire 1792). George Mogridge (born near Birmingham 1787) knew it as 'Stag Chase'. Thomas Miller (born

Gainsborough 1807) called it 'Stag Out'. John Clare (born 1793) refers to 'Fox-and-Hounds' (*Village Minstrel*, ii. 37); and Strutt states specifically in 1801 that 'Hunt the Hare' was the same pastime as 'Hunt the Fox' under a different denomination. Whether it is also the pursuit to which Hamlet refers, 'Hide fox, and all after' (IV. ii), is impossible to say (see Vol.1 p. 203), but the game seems to have been played before Shakespeare's day. In *The Longer thou livest, the more Foole thou art*, published in 1569, Moros, the simpleton, boasts:

> Also, when we play and hunt the fox
> I out run all the boyes in the schoole.

It may be added that calls in the nineteenth century include:

> Hoot and holloa
> Or my dogs shall not follow!
> *George Mogridge, 'Sunny Seasons of Boyhood', 1859, p. 106*

And the following, apparently from Somerset, the game being 'Pee-wip' or 'Pee-wit':

> Whoop, whoop, and hollow,
> Good dogs won't follow,
> Without the hare cries 'pee wit'.
> *J. O. Halliwell, 'Nursery Rhymes', 1844, p. 104*

Froissart records that in his childhood at Valenciennes, about 1345, he played 'au chace-lievre' ('L'Espinette amoureuse', l. 233).

Jack, Jack, shine a light

'Jack, Jack, Shine a Light' is one of the most played of after-dark games. In some places only one or two people are selected to go off with the light, while the others give them 'the most part of five minutes to get clear away'. In other places the players divide into two teams, and one team sets off with a number of lights. The lights are usually torches, but several children speak lovingly of candles fixed in jam jars, carried inside the jacket until the light has to be shown. Country children are sure the game is best played in the country 'where there is plenty of space and woods to run about in and hide'; town dwellers extol the pleasure of playing in a man-made maze:

> 'It is played on dark nights, down passages and on
> bombed buildings. There are lots of places you can hide,
> on shed roofs, in yards, in doorways, in trees, laying on the
> roofs of cars, inside lorries, laying on the ground in dark
> corners, and sitting on high walls.'
> *Boy, 13, Grimsby*

Usually those who are hunted pick a place from which it is easy to get away, for if they hear a call they must show their light, and point it in the direction of the pursuers. In some places 'Jack' whistles or calls back instead of showing a light. At Allerton Bywater, near Pontefract, the searchers sing out:

> Jack, Jack, shine a light,
> Aren't you playing out tonight?

and the other team taunt their pursuers by chanting the same words back at them. In most places those who are caught join sides with the catchers. 'But if anyone proves tiresome by shouting out of turn or making some kind of noise to give the hiders away,' says a Stoke-on-Trent girl, 'he or she is tied up and left until the hiders are found.' Those not caught eventually make their way back to the den, and if no one is there, they shout out that they are 'Home!' 'There is generally a time limit of an hour, but,' says a 12-year-old ambitiously, 'it may last all night.'

   Alternative names: 'Jack, shine your lamp' (Newcastle upon Tyne), 'Jack, shine your lantern' (Accrington and Tunstall), 'Jack, shine the maggie' (Spennymoor—the traditional name in County Durham), 'Jack, Jack, shiny eye' (Ponders End), 'Shine a licht, Jock' (Langholm),[1] 'Shine a light' (Grimsby), 'Shine the lamp' (Oxford), 'Shine, Jack, shine' (Pontypool), 'Flash the light, Dickie' (Caerleon), 'Dick, shine the torch' (Lydney), 'Dicky, Dicky, show your light' (Liss, and traditional in south-east Hampshire for fifty years), 'Nicky, Nicky, show a light' (Brockenhurst), 'Mickey Mike, show your light' (Brighton), 'Mickey-me-light, show your light' (the name current in Alton for the past sixty years), and 'Midnight Hide-and-Seek' (Sheffield).

§ Boys have probably enlivened the darkness with a game such as this for as long as man has been able to carry a fire box. The game 'Chase Fire', listed by Randle Holme as one of the 'recreations and sports ... used by our countrey Boys and Girls' (*Academie of Armory*, iii, 1688, xvi. 91), was probably this game, although possibly it was 'Will o' the Wisp' below. 'Hunt the dark lanthorn' played at Eton in 1766, subsequently known at both Eton and Harrow as 'Jack-o'-Lantern', was certainly this game; the great point of the sport at both schools being to entice the pursuers into some pool or muddy ditch by showing the light exactly in a line on the other side (W. L. Collins, *Public Schools*, 1867, p. 312). A description of 'Jack! Jack! Show a light' occurs in *The Boy's Treasury of Sports*, 1844, pp. 63–4, the detail being added that 'the hiding party is provided with a flint and steel'. In 1870 when 'Dicky, Dicky, show a light' was described in *The Modern Playmate*, p. 10, the hider or hiders were armed with 'a policeman's dark lantern', and Dicky, when hard pressed, might effect his escape 'by turning sharp upon his pursuers and blazing his bull's-eye in their faces'. In *Cassell's Book of Sports and Pastimes*, 1881, p. 267, the game is recommended under the names 'Sam, Sam, show a light', and 'Nicky Night, show a light'.

Will o' the wisp

This game varies from 'Jack, Jack, Shine a Light' in that the hunters do not have to call for guidance, but are lured along by the 'Wills', who flash their torches in one place, and run quickly to another, endeavouring all the while to keep just out of reach of their pursuers. This is no easy business for the 'Wills', who need to be the best runners amongst the players and to know their territory well; in fact a single good runner on his own usually makes the most effective Will o' the Wisp. The game does not appear to be played often, and has been reported only from Alton and Billericay.

Tracking

In country places tracking can take place only in the daytime; but in towns, where chalk arrows gleam under the street lights, tracking is generally a night game. The children divide into two equal gangs. The 'escapers' set off, equipped with pieces of chalk, and tend to be given a longish start because 'laying arrows' every ten or fifteen yards takes time and inevitably slows down their pace. 'In the country,' says a young inform-ant, 'the arrows may be drawn on buildings, stones, trees, telegraph poles, fences, and any place where they show up. They may also be formed of three sticks or a number of stones in the shape of an arrow.' In Langholm they sometimes make an arrow by placing a small stone in front of a large one. In Manchester a refined method of laying a trail is to squeeze a bad orange, making a track of juice and pips. False trails are made by drawing the arrows back to front, or pointing them 'over walls or shelters', or get-ting one of the party to lay a trail down a side street. If he does this he puts a cross at the end of the trail to show it is false. The real trail usually leads to a hiding-place. When the gang have chosen their hiding place they write HOME somewhere nearby, with an arrow pointing in its direction, or make an Ⓕsign, meaning 'find', or draw the sign ←┤→; to show they are hidden somewhere roundabout and the trackers must now search without further help. The hiders then crouch together waiting for the trackers to come upon them. As the trackers follow their trail they strike out the arrows, sometimes with a different coloured chalk, so that the trail will not cause confusion in the next game when the trackers become the hiders.

Names: 'Arrows', 'Arrow Chase', 'Follow the Arrows', 'Arrow Tracking', 'Find the lost Sheep' (Pontypool), 'Cat and Mouse' (Caerleon and High Green near Sheffield), 'Hares and Hounds', and, since snails leave trails, 'Chase the Snail' (Wilmslow). A variation, in which the hiding party lie in wait and hope to jump out on the trackers is known as 'Tracking and Ambush' (Bristol).

§ In Edwardian London tracking was known as 'Chalk Corners' or 'Chalk Chase'.

Paper chase

Paper chases have generally been school-organized affairs. Even in their heyday, after being extolled in *Tom Brown's School Days* (1857), the amount of preparation they entailed: the collecting of enough newspapers, the tearing of them into innumerable small pieces, the packing of the soft piles of fragments into satchels or bags—fun though it was—was scarcely a procedure which could be undertaken spontaneously. Today, when the unfisting of satchelfuls of litter, however minutely fragmented, is generally looked upon with disfavour, the chasers are bequeathed the dreary sport, as a 10-year-old Welsh girl reports, of 'picking up the paper as they run so as not to litter the countryside'. The paper chase, it seems, will very shortly be a sport of the past. 'Anyhow there is too much litter lying about nowadays to make chases practicable', commented one cynic.

§ Dickens referred to 'paper chases' by name in *Household Words*, vol. xiii, 1856, p. 28; and they were popular enough at the time to be played on horseback by British officers on the plateau before Sebastopol. Sometimes, however, the chase was called 'Hare and Hounds' (e.g. in *Every Boy's Book*, 1856, pp. 10–12, referring to the 1830s), and it is occasionally so named to this day in books for the young.

Stalking

The attraction of 'Stalking' ('Gang Stalking', 'Shadowing', 'Indians') is that the hunters can become the hunted. The aim of the game is to follow the other gang and touch them unseen from behind. However, if the side which went out first becomes aware that it is being followed, it can turn aside into a gateway or clump of bushes, wait until the followers have gone past, and become the stalkers of those who suppose themselves to be stalking. Thus, in this game, unlike the majority of seeking and hunting games, those who follow rather than those who are followed are the ones who most strive to remain unseen.

Clearly the success of the game much depends on where it is played; and it is no coincidence that the time and place most often mentioned for the game is at night round 'the backs', that is to say, down the back alleys and through people's back gardens and back yards.

Other names: 'Polecat' (Street, Somerset), 'Wolves in the Dark' (Accrington).

Hoist the green flag

This curious game, in which the leader of the hiding party traces a cryptic map on the ground showing the whereabouts of the party he has just hidden, has been reported only from Scotland and overseas. Some twenty players gather together at a den where there is 'soft earth or maybe sand'. They choose two leaders who pick sides, and toss to see which side shall go off to hide. The leader of the hiding side takes his team to a place where they can all hide together, but does not necessarily lead them there by a direct route. He may set off in the opposite direction, deliberately lead them into a garden and out again, and unnecessarily climb over a wall. When he has his team well hidden he returns to the den, and draws a map of the route that was taken to reach the hiding-place. Overtly he appears as helpful as possible with the directions: he is under obligation to mark every turning that was taken, every gate that was entered, every wall that was climbed over. However, he uses only straight lines on his map, and the lines do not necessarily point in the direction he took; and, in Aberdeen, he further confuses his account with the word *chocolate*: 'We went through a chocolate garden, over a chocolate fence, round a chocolate corner, through a chocolate door, and flopped under the sky.' The seeking side study the map, decide where the hiding-place may be, and set off with the leader of the hiding side, who usually walks just behind them. This leader is allowed to communicate with his own side, shouting out news and instructions, but in a prearranged colour code, thus 'Green' may mean 'danger, stay quiet'; 'Blue'—'they've gone the wrong way'; 'Red'—'come out'. The crisis in the game occurs when the seeking side catches sight of the hiders, or when the seekers are about to catch sight of them, or when the two sides are far apart but the seekers are so much astray that they are as far from the den, or further, than are the hiders. In the first situation the leader of the seekers shouts to his side to run; in the other two the leader of the hiders gives the order to his side with some pre-arranged signal (as 'Red' or 'Rotten onions'), and they run for the den. The seekers must either try to catch the hiders or reach the den first, where (in Forfar) 'the captain of the side which is back first lifts something up above his head and the whole side call "Hoist the green flag" '; or, in most places, he—or whoever arrives first—rubs out the map. The side which manages to obliterate the map are acknowledged the winners, and have the right to go out and hide next time.

Names: 'Hoist the Green Flag' (Aberdeen and Forfar), 'Hoist the Sails' (Toronto), 'Flag' (Kinlochleven), 'Run, Sheep, Run' (Cumnock and Edmonton, Alberta, and commonly in the United States), 'Sheep Lie Low' (Glasgow), and 'Scout' (Isle of Lewis).

§ The game appears to be well known in the United States. J. H. Bancroft, *Games*, 1909, pp. 6–7 and 170–1, gives it as 'Run, Sheep, Run' in Minnesota, and 'Oyster Sale' (an obvious corruption of 'Hoist the Sail') in New York. W. L. McAtee, 'Indiana in the Nineties', *Midwest Folklore*, 1951, p. 245, describes it under the name 'Go, Sheep, Go'. And Brewster, *American Nonsinging Games*, 1953, pp. 40–1, who reports an almost identical game called 'Figs and Raisins' played in Greece, knew it as 'Run, Good Sheep, Run', in Indiana.

6. Racing Games

Now and again in the playground the urgent concern of the younger children is to organize races. Boys of nine and ten are to be seen striding about, being almost belligerent in their anxiety that nobody shall start running before they do; and it is clear to the observer that something more is astir than recreation, their pride in themselves is at stake. They arrange to run from one end of the playground to the other, or the length of the netball court and back, and the starter, who may be 'someone who is not a good runner', ordinarily says 'One, two, three, go', or 'On your marks, get set, go', or 'One to be ready, two to be steady, and three to be off'. But in Oxford children sometimes say 'One for the money, two for the prize, three to be ready, and four to be off', or 'Ready, steady, get your knives and forks ready, go', or, for some reason, 'Ready, steady, paddle, go'. In Newcastle upon Tyne they say, 'Ready, set, fire, go'. In Canonbie, 'Ready, steady, fire (or fire-engine), go'. In Birmingham, 'One to be ready, two to be steady, three to be perfect, four to be off'. And in Aberdeen, 'One to be ready, two to be steady, three to be balanced, and four to go'. Sometimes the starters cannot resist making themselves unpopular by saying, not 'Ready, steady, go', but 'Ready, steady, grapefruit', or 'Ready steady, *go*loshes', and everyone groans and has to start again. In Helensburgh they use the traditional rhyming start 'Scotch horses, Scotch horses', and in Swansea 'Bell horses, bell horses':

Bell horses, bell horses, what time of day?
One o'clock, two o'clock, three and away.[2]

The winner of a race, says a north London boy, will exult: 'Yah! beechyer', 'Lardy', 'Excelsior', 'Good ole me', 'Lapped yer', 'I'm easy best'. But he (or she) who has not done so well may console himself with a little chant:

First is fussiest,
Second is muckiest,
Third is luckiest.
Oxford and elsewhere

First for fuzzy,
Second for ugly,
Third for lucky.
Aberystwyth

First is the worst,
Second is the next
Last is the luckiest.
Lydney

In Lydney they have, too, the happy saying, 'Last gets luck, finds a shilling in the brook'.

Types of races

It is our impression that children do not really enjoy competitive athletics. The only running-race that comes to them naturally is the one that follows the challenge 'Last one there is a sissy!' (or, as Samuel Rowlands reported in 1600, 'Beshrow him that's last at yonder stile'). The races they have when they are on their own are noticeably ones in which their respective running abilities are not too finely matched. They like races in which ordinary running is made impossible by the nature of the course; races in which they crawl beneath parked cars, edge their way along parapets, and clamber over the roofs of garages. One group of 10-year-olds were not much exaggerating when they named their course 'Devil's Death Ride'. They hold races in which other skills than running are required, such as 'Pat-Ball Races' and 'Spitting Races':

'You spit as far as you can, run to where your spit lands and
spit again, continuing like this to the winning post.'

And they have races in which the competitors have to adopt laborious methods of progression, as hopping, crawling, rolling, skipping, running backwards, running sideways, or blindfold, or with both legs tied together, or one leg tied to a partner (the 'Three-legged Race'), or running or jumping with feet inside a sack (in the eighteenth century sack-races were popular at fairs), or on stilts (quite a number of children have stilts), or with tin cans tied under their feet (called 'Whip Tin

Can' in Accrington), or walking on their hands while someone holds their feet ('Wheelbarrow Race'), or riding on people's backs ('Horse Race', 'Piggyback Race'), or being carried—at no great speed—by a combination of two people, or three, in a 'Camel Race' or 'Chariot Race'.

There are also the races which children markedly prefer, which they engage in when they have means of moving faster than their feet will carry them, races on roller-skates, ice-skates, bicycles, or home-made trolleys.

And there are the race-games in which progress is so severely controlled, as in 'May I?', or in which the start is so elaborate, as in 'Drop Handkerchief', or in which the restarts are so numerous, as in 'Peep Behind the Curtain', that they scarcely appear to be races, although fundamentally this is what they are, as will be seen by the descriptions that follow. Likewise chases are included in this chapter where the chase can equally well be a race: the chase being to a fixed point or over a fixed course, as in a steeplechase, or the chaser having to follow the precise course taken by the one he chases. Indeed, in these games, race and chase are interchangeable, and children will chase each other in one version of the game and race each other in another.

It is to be noticed, however, that despite assiduous cultivation in school-time, relay and team races do not thrive when children are playing on their own.

Hesitation starts

There is one style of race, or manner of starting a race, much adopted in the backstreets, in which the competitors are likely to hesitate before they run. Their hesitation is only momentary, but where space is minimal, and the race is merely across the road, each fraction of a second counts.

The most common of these races is 'Odds and Evens', in which the starter, who is on the far side of the road, calls out either 'Odd' or 'Even', and a number. If description and number agree, for example 'Odd seven', the players run across the road and back again, and the last one back is out. But should he call 'Even seven', no one must move, and anyone doing so is out. Similarly in Newcastle the game is 'Shops'. If the starter says 'I went to the butcher to buy some bread' nobody must move. 'You run only if you can buy the thing at the shop and the last one back to the wall is out.' Likewise in Millwall in 1952 there was a game known as 'King George'. The players stood ready to run with one foot in the gutter and one on the pavement, and the caller took up his position at the far wall and would say, perhaps, 'King George wears medals!' This being true the crowd would rush across the road, touch the wall, and race back. But if the caller said 'King George wears petticoats!' anyone who believed this and ran, or anyone, more likely, who began to run because he was over-eager, had run himself out of the game. In Scotland, where a game with the unlikely sounding name of 'Eatables and Drinkables' is nevertheless popular, one pavement is designated 'eatables' and the other 'drinkables'. The player who is starter, or 'mannie', stands in the middle of the road, and the players line up on one of the pavements ready to run:

> 'If the players are all at the Eatables side the mannie has
> to shout out something to drink and they all run over and
> the first one to say 'over' is mannie. But just to confuse
> the people he can shout something to eat, like bread or
> biscuits, and if you move you are out.'

An 11-year-old lad in Orkney points out, however, that the person in the middle is not to be permitted to call out 'Water (pause) biscuits'.

Other names: 'Fruit and Vegetables' (Spennymoor) and 'Juicy Juicy' (Cumnock).

Races in which the progress of those taking part is dependent on their fulfilling a condition or possessing a particular qualification

May I?

Some children say that this game is, as it certainly appears to be, a silly game. Nevertheless vast numbers of bright children (girls rather than boys) are amused by it, and it is played throughout Britain. One child stands on one side of the road, and the rest line up facing her on the other side. The object of the game is to be first across the road and able to touch the person in front. However, the players can move forward only one at a time according to the instructions they receive individually from the one in front, who employs a terminology more or less peculiar to this game, thus: 'Jean, take one giant and three babies', 'Pauline, do a lamp-post', 'Phil, five pigeon steps'. The player addressed asks 'May I?' and advances as instructed, then waits where she is until her turn comes again. However, should a player forget to ask 'May I?' and advance before receiving permission, she has to go back to the starting-line. The names of the movements which, say the young, 'do not need describing, for we know just what to do', are as follows, and are general throughout Britain unless a particular locality is specified.

Baby Step. A small heel-to-toe step, also known as a 'dolly step' or a 'fairy step'.

Bag o' Tatties. A jump landing heavily on the ground. Langholm.

Banana Slip. A slide forward with one foot as far as possible and the other foot drawn up after it.

Barrel. A spin-around, moving forward at the same time. Cf. 'umbrella'.

Black Pudding. An order to go back to the beginning again, that is fairly widely understood, e.g. at Brightlingsea, Grimsby, and Hounslow; but in some places the equivalent order is 'rotten egg'.

Bob Jump. A big jump from a crouching position. Also known as a 'frog jump' and, in Alton, as a 'chair'.

Box of Chocolates. Five jumps. A 'big box' is ten jumps. Aberdeen.

Bucket. Player steps through own linked hands. Also known as a 'Jackdaw'.

Bunny Rabbit. A hop with both feet together.

Cabbage. A step forward taken in a crouching position, with arms folded round body 'like a cabbage'. At Ellesmere in Shropshire a 'Cauliflower' is similar but with hands placed on the head.

Caterpillar. A movement forward lying face down on the ground, drawing feet up beneath the body and pushing forward. 'You graze your knees horribly doing it.' Petersfield.

Crocodile. 'Person lies flat on the road with his feet touching the kerb and his or her hands out as far as they can go.' Person stands up at the point reached. Aberdeen. Cf. 'Lamp-post'.

Cup and Saucer. One 'bob jump' forward, and one jump with legs apart.

Cushion. A jump while sitting on haunches, hands behind back. Aberdeen.

Dolly Tub. The twirl-around step more often known as an 'umbrella'. In the north children remain familiar with the cross-headed stick turned in a wash-tub, and this step is called a 'dolly tub' as far south as Chester.

Ghost Walk. Progression sideways with feet together, pivoting alternately on heels and toes. Sussex.

Giant Walk or *Giant Stride.* As large a step as possible.

Knock. Player is pushed, and stands where he lands. Aberdeen.

Lamp-post. Player stretches out on ground, and then stands on the spot reached by his finger-tips. In Peterborough the player steps forward with arms upright and body as stiff as possible.

London and Back. Player runs to the person in front, then back to the starting-place, and forward again until told to stop. London suburbs. Known elsewhere as 'train' (q.v.), 'running bucket' (Langholm), 'running river' (Berry Hill), 'trip to fairyland' (Workington). The player in front may have his back turned so that he does not know where the runner is when he says stop.

Long Needle. Running until told to stop. Market Rasen.

Lotus Walk. Walking on knees. Wispers School, near Chichester.

Needle. A heel-to-toe step. North-west England.

Newspaper. Three steps forward. Doncaster.

Pigeon Step. A step the length of the foot, or, in some places, the width of a foot.

Pin. A step the width of a foot. North-west England. In Guernsey a step on the points of the toes.

Poker. Occasional alternative to 'lamp-post'. In Aberdeen a jump while standing stiff.

Policeman's Walk. Both the caller and the walker shut eyes. The walker steps forward until the caller shouts 'stop'.

Posh Lady. A high step, holding head in air. Edinburgh.

Postage Stamp. A number of ordinary steps according to the value of the stamp quoted. Kirkcaldy.

Scissors. A jump forward with feet apart, and a further jump landing with feet together. At Finedon, Northamptonshire, however, and doubtless elsewhere, this is known as 'Open and Shut Bible'.

Soldier, Chocolate Soldier, or *Wooden Soldier.* A step forward with the body held stiff in supposedly military fashion.

Spit in the Bottle. Player spits as far as he can and moves forward to where the spit lands. Liverpool. In Workington 'Spitfire'. In Ellesmere 'Cuckoo Spit'. More often called 'Watering-can' (q.v.).

Squashed Tomato. Both caller and called run towards each other, with arms crossed in front of them. The one advancing remains at the spot where they squash into each other. The caller returns to his place in front.

Tablecloth. Two large steps forward. Barrow-in-Furness.

Train. Player runs round the person in front, back to the start, forward to the person in front, and so on until told to stop. This is sometimes called 'fire engine'. Alternatively he may be told to do 'slow train' (the same course but walking), 'blind train' (walking with eyes shut), or he may have eyes shut and be led, which is 'ghost train'. See also 'London and back'.

Trip round the Moon. Player shuts eyes and is taken to wherever person in front wishes. Norwich.

Umbrella. A twirl-around on one foot with arms extended, a step forward being taken with the disengaged foot as the turn is completed.

Waterbottle. A 'hot waterbottle' is running until told to stop. A 'cold waterbottle' is walking until told to stop, the person in front having his eyes shut. Edinburgh.

Watering-can. Player spits as far as possible and stands where the spit lands. (Spitting races are sometimes called 'watering-can races'.)

Wheelbarrow. One player whose feet are held off the ground, as for a wheelbarrow race, reaches forward as far as he can, and both players go to the spot touched.

Since the movements of each player are under the control of the person in front, the game gives, or appears to give, little scope for initiative, and much scope for favouritism; but this seems to trouble adult observers more than it does the children. In some places the person in front (the 'leader', 'caller', 'outer', or 'on it') has her back turned to the rest, and the racers are allotted numbers, or the names of the days of the week, or of the months of the year, so that the leader does not know whom she is instructing, but this is not usual. The fact is that the players do not care greatly about who wins, but like watching their companions having to do absurd movements, such as 'lamp-posts' and 'watering-cans'. In Scotland, when the one in front has been touched, the game sometimes concludes—as games commonly did in the past—with all the players rushing back to the starting-line, the one who is 'het' chasing them. The player who next goes in front is then not the first to have got across the road, but the one who is caught on the way back.

Names: 'May I?' is the usual name, but sometimes the game is known as 'Steps', 'All Sorts', 'Walk to London', 'Variety', or 'Mother, May I?' It is also quite often known by the name of one of the steps, for instance, 'Fairy Footsteps', 'Giant Steps' (in Inverness, 'Giant Spangs'), 'Banana Slides', 'Scissors', 'Cups and Saucers', 'Squashed Tomato', 'Black Pudding', 'Pins and Needles' (the usual name in the north-west), 'Box of Chocolates', 'Chocolate Boxes', 'Umbrellas', 'Trip to Fairyland', and 'Pigeon Walk'. When players are known by the days of the week the game is called 'Days'.

§ The history of this game is obscure. It has certainly been popular in Britain for the past forty or fifty years, known in Hanley, *c*. 1915, as 'Lankeys and Strides', in Kilmington, Devon, 1922, as 'Granfer Longlegs', but not known to Gomme, 1894–8. It is played in Canada, the United States, and Australia, but Sutton-Smith, *Games of New Zealand Children*, 1959, p. 49, who describes it under 'Steps and Strides', gives a slightly different game under 'May I?' in which the contestants them-selves suggest the steps they should take, for example, 'May I take two banana skins, please?' Since it is not unusual for a component of one game to become attached to another game, it is understandable that new games arise. The present game is certainly an improvement on the one called 'Judge and Jury' described by Mrs Child in *The Girl's Own Book*, 1832, p. 40. In this game a player, when called upon, had to jump up and spin a plate, yet was not to make any movement without first asking leave: 'May I get up?' 'May I walk?' 'May I stoop?' 'May I pick up the plate?' The game 'May I?', as played today in Britain, is, however, well known in southern Europe. It is played throughout Italy, usually under the name 'Regina reginella', the children asking 'Queen, Queen, how many steps must I take to reach your beautiful castle?' and the queen allots to each so many 'lion's steps', or 'tiger's steps', or 'ant's steps' (Lumbroso, *Giochi*, 1967, pp. 291–3). It is well known in Austria under the names 'Kaiser, wieviel Schritte darf ich machen?' or 'Vater, wie weit darf ich reisen?' (Kampmüller, *Oberösterreichische Kinderspiele*, 1965, pp. 199–200). It is played in Yugoslavia under the name 'Gospodicna, koliko je ura' (Brewster, *American Nonsinging Games*, 1953, p. 164). And an observer tells us he saw the game played in Israel, the child in front being called 'Abba', and the steps being given in the same cryptic style, for example, 'ten elephants' and 'eight ants'.

Aunts and Uncles

In this game, as in 'May I?', one player stands alone on one side of the road or playground, the rest line up facing him on the other side, hoping to get across. The player on his own calls out a name such as 'Uncle Leslie', and any competitor having an uncle of this name has the right to take one pace forward. Other names, such as 'Aunt Pat' and 'Uncle Henry', are then called in as quick succession as the caller is capable of thinking of them, and whoever has a relative so named takes a step forward, or if he has two Uncle Henrys or two Aunt Pats, two steps forward. It is clearly an advantage in this game for a player to have, or to suppose that he has, an infinite number of blood relations. Indeed the relatives may be of any kind. As one boy observed, 'This game, although it is called "Aunts and Uncles" includes mothers, fathers, grandfathers and grandmothers', and it is, of course, not improbable that the same name will be called more than once. Whoever crosses the road first wins, and becomes the next 'caller' or 'relationer'.

The game is so slow moving it is remarkable that it should be popular in all parts of Britain, even though chiefly with younger children. Their excuse that the game is 'quite interesting really' scarcely disguises the fact that the 'interest' is less in the action of the game, than in the information it discloses about the number and nomenclature of other people's relatives. Thus, as in 'May I?', the fun lies more in watching other people's progress than in making progress oneself. In consequence little variation in the way the game is played has been noticed between one place and another, except that in Kirkcaldy a player having a relation who has been named, is then told, as in 'May I?', what kind of step forward he should take, for example, a 'baby step' or an 'umbrella'.

The game is sometimes known as 'Relations'.

Letters

'Letters' is much like 'Aunts and Uncles' except that the person in front, instead of calling the names of possible relations, calls out letters of the alphabet. Contestants take a step forward, or in some places a jump, each time a letter is called which comes in their name; and if the letter comes twice in their name they take two steps or jumps. In some places two steps are also allowed if the letter is a person's initial; and an Inverness boy says that they then 'take a spang, that is a lang jump'. Thus the game is simpler, but quicker-moving than 'Aunts and Uncles'; and often seems to be played of an evening by no more than four or five friends having quiet fun together 'in our road'. Occasionally when the person in front is reached there is a chase back to the starting-line.

The game is also known as 'Names', 'Letters in Your Name', and 'Alphabet'.

Colours

This game is similar to 'Letters', but more personal. The child in front calls out a colour, and those who have it 'on their body or on their clothes' take a step forward. When the caller is touched there is usually a chase back to the starting-line, and if the person who was in front does not manage to catch someone he, or more often she, has to 'call' again. Although the game is scarcely more than a poor relation of 'Farmer, Farmer, may we cross your Golden River?' (q.v.) it has a wide distribution, being played in places as far apart as Perth, Spennymoor, and Welshpool. It is also reported from Australia and New Zealand.

Eggs, bacon, marmalade and bread

In this variant of 'Colours', reported only from south-west Manchester, the caller is concerned not with what is on the body, but within it. 'This game is played by two or more persons. One person stands at one side of the road while the rest line up at the other side of the road. The person who is on says, "What did you have for breakfast, did you have porridge? If so take two steps." This keeps on until the person who is asking the questions is took, and they all run back to the other side of the road. If the questioner ticks a player running back he is on' (Boy, c. 12).

Peep behind the curtain

'Peep Behind the Curtain' is the delight of 8-year-olds, for success in it comes not from athletic ability, but from luck and cunning. One player stands on the far side of the road, or somewhere twenty to thirty feet away, with his back turned to the rest, and usually facing a wall. The rest try to be first to sneak up on him and touch his back without his seeing them move, although he is allowed to turn round often and suddenly to try and spot them moving. Usually he is supposed to count ten under his breath before turning round, or to mutter a formula. But he says the words quickly or slowly as he likes, and the other players do not know when he is going to turn round. In some places there is a standard formula for him to say. In the south-west it is generally 'L-O-N-D-O-N spells London', in Monmouthshire 'On the way to London—one, two, three', in Welshpool 'Cat's in the cupboard and can't catch me', at Hoyland, near Barnsley, 'Crack, crack, the biscuit tin', and in Penrith 'One, two, three, four, five jam tarts'.[3] As the person in front turns round, the players 'freeze', for if he sees anyone moving even a hand, let alone a foot, he sends that player back to the starting-line to begin again. He then turns back to the wall, and everyone resumes their advance. Some move cautiously, as if treading on eggs; others dart forward hoping to reach the player in front in one bold dash, but usually are unable to stop moving quickly enough when he next turns round. The player who is first to reach the one in front takes his place in the next game, for this is a game in which, for some reason, the coveted role is that of the player who turns round. 'Sometimes there's an argument who is to be on it first,' remarked a Caerleon boy, 'but we settle it after a while. I don't know why everybody wants to hide their eyes. I would prefer to be with the other boys who creep up.'

'Peep Behind the Curtain' is a quiet game, probably the most-played of 'quiet' street games. But in the north country and in Scotland it is traditional for the game to end with a race back to the starting-line. In the West Riding, and consequently in Guernsey (see Vol. 1, note 24) the player who succeeds in touching the one at the wall shouts 'Black Pudding', and everyone rushes back to the starting-line. On the Isle of Bute the cry is 'Queen Victoria' (and the game is so called); at Annesley in Nottinghamshire the cry and name is 'Queenie'. In other places (see map) the cry is 'Sly fox' or 'White horse'. In some places (e.g. Spennymoor) all the players have to touch the wall, not the player in front, and it is only after the last of them has touched the wall that they run back and are chased. In Aberdeen and Kirkcaldy a player seen moving is sent back only a certain number of paces rather than back to the starting-line; and, as is often the case, the Scottish practice is also that

'Peep Behind the Curtain.' Simplified map showing distribution of principal names.

of the United States (cf. 'Red Light' in Brewster's *American Nonsinging Games*, 1953, p. 35).

Names: There are more than thirty names for this game, sometimes two or more being current in one place. (The distribution map, Fig. VII, shows only the predominant names.) 'Peep Behind the Curtain' prevails in London and the south-east. The name 'London' does not become general until children are a hundred miles from the metropolis, e.g. at Gloucester, Worcester, and Birmingham. The name 'Grandmother's Footsteps' seems to be known mostly in private schools. Other names include: 'Black Peter' (Golspie), 'Black Pudding' (Halifax, since *c.* 1900, and Guernsey), 'Bull's Eye' (Wickenby), 'Carrot, Carrot, Neep, Neep' (Perth), 'Chocolate' (Norwich and Yarmouth), 'Creep Mouse' (Bristol, Wells, New Radnor), 'Creeping' (Wilmslow), 'Creeping Jinny' (Wigan), 'Creeping Up' (usual name in Australia and New Zealand), 'Crystal Palace' (St Helier, Jersey), 'Cuckoo' (Troutbeck, nr. Ambleside), 'England, Ireland, Scotland, Wales' (Helensburgh), 'Fairy Footsteps' (Manchester), 'Five Jam Tarts' (Penrith), 'Foxy' (Carlisle, Scarborough, Peterborough), 'Giant's Treasure' (Helston),[4] 'Granny' (Lockerbie), 'King's Palace' (Castel, Guernsey), 'On the way to London' (Caerleon, Cwmbran, Pontypool), 'One, Two, Three' (Scalloway), 'One, Two, Three, Four, Five' (Aberdeen and Langholm), 'Peeping Tom' (Market Rasen), 'Piggy Behind the Curtain' (Wilmslow), 'Policeman' (Oxford), 'Policeman's Steps' (Wootton Bassett), 'Red Light' (Liverpool, Blackburn, Spennymoor, Peterborough, Helensburgh, and Edmonton, Alberta), 'Statues' (Stamford, Cumnock, Forfar, Kirkcaldy, but in other places 'Statues' is a different game, see pp. 92f), 'White Horse' (Edinburgh, and eastern Scotland).

§ At the beginning of the century the game was generally known as 'Steps', e.g. at Eastbourne, *c.* 1910, Victoria, NSW, *c.* 1915, and in Bancroft's *Games for the Playground*, New York, 1909, pp. 188–9. In Austria it is 'Ochs am Berg', 'Der Hase läuft über das Feld', or 'Küche-Zimmer-Kabinett' (Kampmüller, *Oberösterreichische Kinderspiele*, 1965, p. 199). In Germany it is 'Eins zwei drei—sauer Hering!' (Peesch, *Berliner Kinderspiel*, 1957, p. 32). In Italy and Sardinia it is usually 'Uno, due, tre, stella', though interestingly, at Forenza in southern Italy it is 'Per le vie di Roma' (Lumbroso, *Giochi*, 1967, pp. 289–91).

Games in which only two competitors run against each other at a time, one of them generally being instrumental in the selection of the other

Black magic

Several racing and chasing games have fused, under names such as 'Black Magic' (Hackney and Oxford), 'Black and White' (West Ham and Stockport), 'Flip Flop' (Ipswich), 'Pit-a-Pat' (Titchmarsh), 'Tip Tap' (Walworth and Cwmbran), 'Tip Tap Toe' (Sheffield), and 'Tit for Tat' (Swansea), owing to the singular manner in which the person who is 'on' selects whom he will run against. The players line up, and hold their hands out in front of them, with their palms all facing upwards or all facing downwards. The person who is 'on' or 'dipper' goes along the line tapping or smacking the top of each hand, but smacks the underside of the hand of the person he elects to run against. Alternatively, he walks along the line repeating some hocus-pocus such as 'Black, black, black, black ... *magic*', 'Black, white, black, white ... *red*', 'Black, white, black, white ... *whisky*', or 'Tip, tip, tip ... *tap*', 'Flip, flip, flip ... *flop*', or 'Tip, tap, toe, my first go, if I touch you, you must, must, must ... *go*!' Thereupon the pair race to the opposite wall and back, or to a selected point, or, sometimes, the one who is 'on' is chased to a certain point by the player he has chosen, and, as a 10-year-old explained, 'If he "has" the dipper he is now "it", but if he doesn't the dipper remains the dipper'.

The game 'Kerb or Wall' is also sometimes started in this manner.

Kerb or wall

This game is essentially a street game. One player is made 'on' or 'out' by the ordinary process of dipping (e.g. 'Ickle ockle, chocolate bottle, ickle ockle out; if you want a titty bottle please shout out'). The player then discovers his rival by lining the rest up against a wall on one side of the road, and 'hitting' each of their hands in turn as he repeats the particular rhyme associated with the game in his locality, for instance:

> Peter Pan said to Paul,
> Who d'ya like the best of all—

Kerb stone, or the solid brick wall?
Said Peter Pan to St Paul
Who lives at the bottom of the garden
    wall.

Walworth version. Several others current in London

Bim, bam, boo, and a wheezey anna,
My black cat can play the piano,
One, two, three, kick him up a tree,
Kerb or wall?

*Stockport. Versions in various stages of decomposition
throughout north country*

Two little dicky birds
Sat upon a wall,
One named Peter
The other named Paul.
Paul said to Peter,
Peter said to Paul
Let's have a game
At 'Kerb and Wall'.

*Birmingham. Cf. 'Oxford Dictionary of Nursery Rhymes',
pp. 147–8*

Kob or wall or lucyanna,
Jack and Jill went up the ladder.
Which would you rather have
Kob or the old brick wall?

Newcastle upon Tyne

The player whose hand is struck last has to choose 'kerb or wall'. If he chooses 'kerb' he runs to the edge of the near kerb, back to the wall where he started, then across the road to the far wall and back to the home wall again. If he chooses 'wall' he runs first to the far wall, then to the home wall, then to the near kerb and back. The person who dipped covers the same ground, only he does it the opposite way round. If 'kerb' was chosen he does 'wall'; if 'wall' he does 'kerb'. The dipper always gives the other person the choice of 'kerb or wall'. Whoever wins becomes 'on' or 'dipper' next time. If there is a tie they may be made

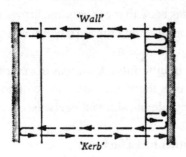

The street game, 'Kerb or wall'

to run again, or to go out of hearing and each choose a similar name, as 'candy rock' and 'candy stick', and the bearer of the name selected by the rest is declared winner.

This game is fast, rough, and sometimes conducted in reckless fashion, especially when played at night, if the older children join in, for the kerb can become a trip-stone sending players sprawling on the pavement, and the runners crash against the wall in their effort to reach it first. Nevertheless—or perhaps in consequence—there seem to be few places where the game is not played.

Names: Usually 'Kerb or Wall' or 'Kerb and Wall', but also 'Crib and Wall' (Stornoway), 'Kerby Wall' (Helston), 'Big Black Wall' (Hounslow), 'Brick, Stone, Kerb, Wall' (Birmingham), and there are three names emanating from the rhymes: 'Peter Pan' (Peckham and elsewhere, not uncommon), 'Ombombay' (Oxford and Spennymoor), and 'Ina Vana Vea' (Wigan).

Time

Two players, chosen by conventional means, go off a little way and agree on a time of day such as 'Half-past six'. They come back to the others, who have lined up, and one of them goes along the line saying 'Half-past what?' and receiving a suggestion from each person in turn. The player who chances to give the right time races, or sometimes chases, the other time-fixer. Usually the race is to an agreed spot and back again. In Barrow-in-Furness the running does not begin until the one who is taking the guesses shouts 'Clock's right'. In Scalloway, Shetland, the one who is standing out has his back to the others and arms outstretched. The player who guesses the correct time runs up to him and touches his arm, and this is the signal for the race to begin. In Aberdeen the time-fixer, whose part in the game is little more than that of referee (although not looked upon as such), takes the two runners to the middle of the road, stands with one on either side of him, and declares:

> My father had a fiddle
> And he broke it through the middle.

When he says 'middle' the two players run round whichever is the nearest lamp-post on their side of the road, then cross the road and run round the other player's lamp-post and back to the person in the middle. The player who wins becomes the referee time-fixer in the next game, and the referee becomes the runner time-fixer.

The game is usually known as 'Time' or 'Timey', although in Swansea it is 'Old Timer', in Barrow-in-Furness 'Clock Time', and in Guernsey 'One o'clock'. In a variant called 'O'Clock', played in Swansea, each player in the line is given a number, while the player who is 'on it' is out of hearing. He then calls out a number not knowing which player this means he will have to run against.

§ The game was current in Fraserburgh in the nineteenth century under the name 'Time' (Gomme, *Traditional Games*, vol. ii, 1898, pp. 293–4), although the game called 'American Times' played in Fraserburgh today is purely a guessing game (see p. 129f). In Argyllshire it was known as 'Time' or 'Polly in the Ring' (*Folk-Lore*, vol. xvii, 1906, pp. 102–3).

Drop handkerchief

They say 'Drop Handkerchief' is best played with twelve people or more. One of them is chosen to be out and the rest join hands and make a big circle. They then loose hands and either remain standing or sit on the ground. The one who is out has a handkerchief or 'something that won't make a noise when it is dropped'. He—or, more usually, she—goes round the outside of the circle singing—perhaps to the tune of *The Jolly Miller* or *Bobby Bingo*:

> I sent a letter to my love
> And on the way I dropped it;
> One of you has picked it up
> And put it in your pocket.

Sometimes everybody sings. Then the one who is running round outside the circle drops the handkerchief quietly behind one of the players and races on. The player who has had the handkerchief dropped behind her must pick it up and race round the circle in the opposite direction, trying to get back to her place before the dropper reaches it. Usually the dropper is first. She can see if she is going to win by the point where they meet on the far side of the circle. Sometimes there is jostling and pushing when they meet, as the one who is losing hopes by force or craft to make up lost ground. The player who arrives back last has to go round the circle with the handkerchief in the next round.

Less often now than formerly the game is a chase not a race, and the player who has the handkerchief dropped behind her runs after the dropper in the same direction around the circle.

In many places in Britain the game is still embellished with actions or imagery from the past, which are sometimes also to be found in versions of the game on the Continent. In Govan, south-west Glasgow, the children crouch down in a ring singing:

> I sent a letter to my lad (*pronounced 'lod'*)
> And on the way I dropped it,
> I dropped it once, I dropped it twice,
> I dropped it three times over:
> Over, over, in amongst the clover,
> Over, over, in amongst the clover.

Here, as of old, the player who is pursued may run in any direction he wishes in and out of the circle, while he who chases 'must go the very same road as the other person, or he is called "a rotten", and he must sit in the middle' (Girl, *c.* 10). In Spalding, Lincolnshire, the one who loses the race for the empty place goes into the centre and is made to suck her thumb until someone comes to replace her. In Aberystwyth, and also at Frodsham in Cheshire, if a girl does not notice that the handkerchief has been dropped behind her she must stand in the centre and, similarly, place her thumb in her mouth. In the neighbourhood of Welshpool, where the game is sometimes known as 'Dummy', the girl who drops the handkerchief aspires to run the full circle before the player notices that the handkerchief has been dropped behind her. If she succeeds in this she shouts 'Dummy', and sends the booby into the centre of the circle to suck her thumb. But should the player who had the handkerchief dropped behind her be a fast runner, and catch the dropper, the catcher shouts 'Dummy', and sends the dropper into the centre to suck her thumb. And so the game continues 'until nearly everyone is in the centre sucking their thumbs'. In Radnorshire, and some other parts of Wales, the procedure is different. When the girl who is outside the ring has finished singing 'I sent a letter to my love', she holds the handkerchief up and calls out 'All see it?' The children in the ring reply 'We see it'. Then the runner says 'You'll never see it again until you find it'. Whereupon the children in the ring shut their eyes, and the runner drops the handkerchief behind one of them, calling out 'All people look behind their back', and the race begins. Across the border, at Upton Magna in Shropshire, the same ritual is adopted, and is expressed in song:

> I wrote a letter to my love
> And on the way I lost it,
> Some of you have picked it up
> And put it in your pocket.
>
> Now is the time to close your eyes,
> Close your eyes, close your eyes;
> Now is the time to close your eyes
> And see (*sic*) if you've got the letter.
>
> Now is the time to look behind,
> Look behind, look behind;
> Now is the time to look behind
> And see if you've got the letter.

Similar words have been reported from County Durham. Other songs, sung to various tunes, among them *A tisket, a tasket* and *Yankee Doodle*, are traditional in other places.

> Sent a letter to my love
> And on the way I dropped it,

> I dropped it once, I dropped it twice,
> I dropped it three times over.
> Shut your eyes, look at the skies,
> Guess where the letter lies.
>> *New Cumnock*

> Lucy Locket lost her pocket,
> Someone must have picked it up
> And put it in her basket.
> Please drop it, drop it, drop it....
>> *Birmingham*[5]

> Who goes round my house at night?
> Nothing but dirty Tommy.
> Who stole all my chickens away
> And left me only one?
> So it's rise up and run, run, run.
> I sent a letter to my love
> And on the way I dropped it,
> I dropped it once,
> I dropped it twice,
> I dropped it three times over.
> Over, over, in amongst the clover,
> Not yet, not yet, not yet. . . .
>> *Paisley*

At Arncliffe, in the West Riding, the handkerchief is not a letter but a pigeon, and the one who is outside the circle sings:

> I've got a pigeon in my pocket,
> I won't tell you where I got it.

In most places, even though the players keep their eyes open, they are not allowed to watch the handkerchief-dropper, nor to look behind them until she has passed. However, the race is more exciting when a player is left in no doubt that it is her turn to run. In Stirling, for instance, and also in Flotta, the player who is about to drop the handkerchief goes round touching each person's head saying 'Not you, not you', until she reaches the player she wishes to compete against, when she says 'but you!' In

Swansea, after the player has dropped the handkerchief she continues her circuit, touching each person on the head, saying 'It wasn't you, it wasn't you, it wasn't you ... it was *you!*' Only then do the two players race round in opposite directions. And in Blackburn, Lancashire, the girl carrying the handkerchief sings:

> I sent a letter to my lad
> And by the way I dropped it,
> I dropped it, I dropped it,
> An old man came and picked it up
> And put it in his pocket, pocket.
> The doggie won't bite you, nor you, nor
>   you, nor you ...

Not only does this song hold an echo of past times, but so does the action, for if the one behind whom the handkerchief is dropped succeeds in catching his challenger—or tempter—he has the right, as of old, to a kiss.

§ A miniature history of deportment could be based on a study of this old and much-loved game. 'I sent a Letter to my Love' is depicted in *A Little Pretty Pocket-Book*, 1744 (earliest surviving edition 1760), where a youth is shown dropping a letter, not a handkerchief, behind one of the maidens in the ring. 'Dropping the Letter' is named, but not described, in *Suffolk Words*, 1823, p. 238, as a Suffolk game of about 1780. 'Dropping the 'Kerchief' is described in the 1829 edition of *The Boy's Own Book*, p. 38, played as in Glasgow today: 'the pursuer is bound to follow precisely the course of the pursued'; and this rule appears, too, in *The Gallovidian Encyclopedia*, 1824, where the game is titled 'Allicomgreenzie', and said to be 'played by young girls at country schools'. The first mention by name of 'Kiss in the Ring' is in *Sports and Pastimes of the English People*, 1801, p. 285, where Strutt says, in a description of 'Cat after Mouse':

'When this game is played by an equal number of boys and girls, a boy must touch a girl, and a girl a boy, and when either of them be caught they go into the middle of the ring and salute each other; hence is derived the name of "Kiss in the Ring".'

Throughout the nineteenth century 'Kiss in the Ring' was a favourite game at Christmas time and midsummer, at rustic weddings, bank-holiday outings, fairs, and flower shows, and it was played by 'grown lads and lassies' as well as by children. Pleasing references to the game in these settings occur in Hone's *Every-Day Book*, vol. i, 1826, col. 692; *Sketches by Boz*, 1835, ch. xii; Chambers's *Popular Rhymes*, 1869, pp. 129–30 (played in eighteenth-century Dumfriesshire under the name 'Pease and Groats'); *Punch*, 16 August 1890, p. 78; and in Flora Thompson's *Candleford Green*, 1943, p. 62; as well as in several of the Opie manuscripts. There are couples who have celebrated their golden weddings (see e.g. *Hereford Times*, 7 October 1960, p. 11, and *Hants and Sussex News*, 7 June 1961, p. 1), who first met when they 'saluted each other' while playing this merry game, in the days when a kiss between young people could still be a light-hearted courtesy.

In *The Girl's Own Book*, 1832, p. 45, the American authoress Mrs Lydia Maria Child describes the game under the name 'Hunt the Squirrel', as also does Newell in *Games of American Children*, 1883, pp. 168–9. In England this name has not been common, although mentioned by Horace Walpole in a letter, 8 October 1742, and known to London elementary schoolchildren in 1910. This personation of a small animal that bites, which occurs today in the Blackburn game, was quite general in the nineteenth century (see Gomme's *Traditional Games*, vol. i, 1894, pp. 109–12, 305–10, and *The English Dialect Dictionary* under 'Hitch-Hatch'). One such version, not uncommon around 1900, opened with lines which belong to the eighteenth century:

> I had a little moppet, I put it in my pocket,
> And I fed it on corn and hay;
> And it won't bite you, and it won't bite
> you ... but it *will* bite you.

(Cf. *Oxford Dictionary of Nursery Rhymes*, p. 313.) The game itself, or something like it, considerably antedates the eighteenth century. It appears to be referred to in a Reichenau glossary, compiled before 1300, where, as transcribed by F. J. Mone, *Anzeiger*, 1839, p. 395, an entry reads:

> 'Circulatorius ludus est puerorum in circulo sedentium, post
> quorum tergum discurrit puer unus, portans aliquid in manu, quod

ponit retro aliquem sedentium ignorantem, vulgariter dicitur:
Gurtulli, trag ich dich!'

The closest parallels to 'Drop Handkerchief', however, are found in the
Romance languages, 'Le Jeu du mouchoir' in France, 'Pan para todo el
año' in Spain, 'Ovo marzo' in Trieste, and 'Bacio nel cerchio' in Sardinia.
In Germany a more robust circle game is usual, in which the person pursued is hit rather than kissed; and it may well be that the medieval monks
at Reichenau were describing the start of the closely related game 'Der
Fuchs geht rum', an account of which appears below under 'Whackem'.

Bump-on-the-back

This is 'Drop Handkerchief' without the handkerchief. The player who
goes round the outside of the circle taps or pushes the back of the person
he wishes to run against, and the race is on. When Brownies or Wolf
Cubs play the game it is the practice, sometimes, for the two who are
racing round the circle to stop when they meet on the far side, and for
them to shake hands and say 'Good morning', before they race on; or
even for them to say 'Good morning' as they shake their right hands,
'Good afternoon' as they shake their left hands, 'Good evening' as they
shake their right hands again, and 'Good night' as they shake their left
hands again. This is usually done at speed although both parties are
being held up for the same length of time. When these formalities are
customary the game is usually known as 'Good Morning'.

§ Gomme, *Traditional Games*, 1894–8, gives the names 'French Jackie'
(Keith), 'French Tag' (Forest of Dean), 'Gap' (Barnes), 'Push in the Wash
Tub' (Crockham Hill, Kent), and 'Tap-Back' (Bitterne, Hampshire).
Correspondents have known the game as 'Pushing in the Buttertub'
(Eastbourne, 1914), and 'Filling the Gap' (Honiton, 1922).

In Germany in the nineteenth century the game was called
'Ringschlagen' or 'Komm mit', or, in Königsberg, 'Guten Morgen, Herr
Fischer', this being the greeting with which the players addressed each
other on the far side of the circle (F. M. Böhme, *Deutsches Kinderspiel*,
1897, p. 589). The game is popular in Italy, being played under a number
of names such as 'Pugno', 'Chi tardi arriva male alloggia', and 'Giorni
della Settimana' (Lumbroso, *Giochi*, 1967, pp. 114–15, 117–19).

Whackem

This ring game, which is similar to 'Drop Handkerchief' but more vir-
ile, is a favourite with boys in Acocks Green, south-east Birmingham.
The players stand in a circle with their eyes closed and their hands
behind their backs, while one of their number runs round the outside of
the circle with a short piece of rope. As he runs he places the rope in
somebody's hands, and the boy who receives it instantly opens his eyes
and belabours his neighbour to the right of him. This neighbour, though
taken by surprise, must set off around the circle as fast as he can, for he
is subject to as many further blows as his pursuer can inflict upon him
until he has completed the circuit and returned to the safety of his place.
The player with the rope then continues round the circle, and places the
rope in another boy's hands. The game is also played in gymnasiums,
and by Wolf Cubs, usually under the name 'Beat the Bear'.

§ 'Whackem' may be compared with the games 'Whacko' and 'Daddy
Whacker' (qq.v.); and is perhaps allied to the game played by Irish girls,
known in County Kerry as 'Burning' (Irish Folklore Commission, MS.
vol. 470, 1938). In this game the player going round the outside is said to
be 'burning', and she strikes the person she means to burn, which is the
signal for the chase to begin. The notion that the one who runs round the
ring is hot or burning is not apparently confined to County Kerry. J. O.
Halliwell, *Popular Rhymes and Nursery Tales*, 1849, p. 113, describes a
game known as 'Drop-Cap' in which the child selecting who shall chase
him makes his progression round the circle chanting:

> My hand burns hot, hot, hot,
> And whoever I love best, I'll drop this at
> his foot!

Halliwell also describes (p. 130) the game of 'Drop-Glove' (a game
listed by Randle Holme in 1688) in which the player whose part it is to
carry the glove cries 'It burns, it scalds!' as he drops it behind a player.
Likewise in the game 'Tartan Boeth', a version of 'Drop Handkerchief'
played at Beddgelert in north Wales (Gomme, vol. i, 1894, p. 112), the
child with the handkerchief says 'Tartan boeth, oh mae'n llosgi, boeth
iawn' ('Hot tart, oh it burns, very hot'), and drops the handkerchief at the
words 'very hot'. In the game 'Black Doggie', a further version of 'Drop

Handkerchief', played at Rosehearty in Aberdeenshire (Gomme, vol. ii, 1898, p. 407), any player in the ring who did not notice that the hand-kerchief had been dropped behind him, while the dropper completed a circuit, was declared to be 'burnt', and had thereafter to kneel down and be out of the game. Similarly in Argyllshire, in the game 'Drop the Napkin', if a girl was unaware that the handkerchief had been dropped behind her, or did not follow exactly the course of the one she was pur-suing, the other children raised the cry 'Ye're burnt' or, quaintly, 'You burned a hole in your porridge' (Maclagan, *Games of Argyleshire*, 1901, pp. 213–14, and *Folk-Lore*, vol. xvii, 1906, p. 102). And in Hungary, where a comparable game is called 'I Carry Fire' (Brewster, 1953, p. 91), the players recite while the handkerchief is being carried round:

> I carry fire; don't see it.
> If you see it, don't tell anyone.

It seems probable that this calefaction by a secretly deposited article, whether cap, glove, or handkerchief, is connected in some way with the childish contention that a hidden object—such as the thimble in 'Hunt the Thimble'—is hot, and that he who approaches is 'getting warmer' or 'burning'.

It appears from Böhme that the usual way boys in Germany played the game 'Fuchs geht rum' in the nineteenth century was little different from the way the boys play 'Whackem' at Acocks Green today. The players stood in a circle, with their hands behind their backs, and none must look round. A player called 'the fox', who was armed with a knot-ted handkerchief (variously termed *Plumpsack, Klumpsack, Plumser, Knötel*, or *Tagel*), skirted round the outside of the circle saying:

> Seht euch nicht um,
> Der Fuchs geht rum.

He secretly placed the *Plumpsack* in someone's hands, and that per-son struck his right-hand neighbour with it, and chased him round the circle back to his place (*Deutsches Kinderspiel*, 1897, pp. 556–7). Further, J. C. F. Gutsmuths, in his pioneer work *Spiele für die Jugend*, 1796 (1802, pp. 232–4) exactly describes the game, under the name 'Das böse Ding', the player who goes round the circle with a knotted handkerchief singing:

> There goes a wicked thing around
> That will properly sting you:
> If anyone looks behind him now
> He'll get it on the neck.

However, Gutsmuths considered that the original method of play was much the same as the way many children continued to play it in Böhme's day, particularly in northern Germany. The players sat in a circle facing inwards, and the player making the circuit behind them intoned 'Die Gans, die Gans, die legt ein Ei':

> The goose, the goose, it lays an egg,
> And when it falls, it falls in two.

He let the *Plumpsack* fall behind one of the players without him knowing. If the person noticed it, he picked it up and chased the dropper round the circle; but if he failed to notice it and the dropper came round the circle again and picked it up, he had the privilege of chasing the inattentive player round the circle. In fact the game was initially the same as 'Drop Handkerchief', but the chaser commonly used the knotted handkerchief (or rope, or belt) to strike the person he was chasing whenever he came within range. In Holland, Böhme added, the game was known as 'De Vlugt of Sackjagen', and while the dropper went round the circle his words were 'Cop, cop heeft ghelecht' (the little hen has laid). In present-day Austria, where the game is called 'Der Plumpsack geht um', the association with the poultry yard is maintained. A player who fails to hit the one who has dropped the knotted handkerchief behind him is obliged to go into the centre of the ring and is jeered at for being a 'rotten egg' (Kampmüller, *Oberösterreichische Kinderspiele*, 1965, pp. 140–1). In Switzerland a version of the game is actually called 'Faul Ei'; and the unsuccessful player is similarly relegated to the centre of the circle, and called a rotten egg (cf. the Govan version of 'Drop Handkerchief'). In Trieste, too, as already reported, a version of 'Drop Handkerchief' is called 'Ovo marzo', the player who fails to notice that the handkerchief has been dropped behind him being dubbed a 'March egg' (Lumbroso, *Giochi*, 1967, p. 118). And in Berlin, where the inattentive player is struck three blows if he fails to run, the striker chants as he delivers them, 'Eins, zwei, drei, ins faule Ei!' (Peesch, *Das Berliner Kinderspiel der Gegenwart*, 1957, p. 15).

There can be little doubt that the game 'Die Gans, die Gans, die legt ein Ei' is descended from the ancient Greek game 'Schœnophilinda', described by Pollux (ix. 115), in which, it appears, one player endeavoured to drop a short rope, without being seen, behind one of the company who were squatting in a circle. If he succeeded the squatter was belaboured round the circle; if detected, the dropper was chased round the circle. And it may be noted that this was also the opinion in Elizabethan times. Adrianus Junius in his *Nomenclator*, Antwerp, 1567, named the equivalent game 'Cop cop heeft geleyt'; and when John Higins prepared his English edition in 1585 he named the equivalent game in his day 'Clowte, clowte, to beare about', and gave, as an alternative name, 'My hen hath layd'. This name has not been found subsequently in Britain, but girls in Scotland still seem to have been echoing it 300 years later in a nonsense song they sang while playing 'Drop the Napkin':

> Drip, drop the napkin,
> My hen's laying,
> My pot's boiling,
> Cheese and bread and currant-bun,
> Who's to get the napkin?
>> R. C. Maclagan, Games of Argyleshire, 1901, p. 213.

Stoney

In 'Stoney' which several girls of eight and nine describe as 'my best game', the others do not know who has been chosen to run, nor when she is going to start. The attraction of this game for small girls is its secretiveness. They stand in a row—perhaps there are only four or five of them—with one girl, 'the outer', who has a pebble or cherry stone, standing in front. They hold out their hands with palms together, 'as if praying', but leave a small hole at the top. The girl with the stone holds her hands in similar fashion and proceeds along the line placing her hands on top of theirs. She drops the stone into one person's hands, and neither of them makes any sign that she has done so. When the person who has the stone thinks the others are not looking, she dashes across the road and back, or runs to an agreed point, having to complete the course without any of the others managing to touch her. If she succeeds she is the 'outer' next time.

This game, popular in London, and sometimes called 'Cherry Stone', has been reported only from the Home Counties, and from Berkshire, Oxfordshire, and Devon.

Games in which the Players Start Running from Different Places

Puss in the corner

The fun of 'Puss in the Corner' is that the players themselves negotiate when they are going to run; its disadvantage is that it is normally for five players, no more and no less. Four of the players stand at four points: lamp-posts, drain covers, or, if indoors, the four corners of a room. The fifth stands in the middle, or where he likes. Those at the corners call to each other: 'Puss, Puss, come here', 'Puss, Puss, come and get some milk', 'Puss, Puss, come to my corner', and change places when they think the one in the middle is not looking. The player in the middle has to try and reach one of the corners when it is empty; and if he is success-ful the player he has raced goes into the middle. Any two corners may change places, and often all four run at once. They keep switching about, even to opposite corners, until one player becomes confused, dashes to the wrong corner, and makes it easy for the middle player to slip into an empty corner. This game is popular. As one youngster remarked, 'I like it because it makes you feel happy and gay and it is very funny'.

Names: 'Puss in the Corner' and 'Puss, Puss' (both common), 'Poor Pussy' (Wigan), 'Puss in Four Corners' (Wolstanton), 'Fox and Chickens' (Market Rasen), 'Bear's in his Den' (Golspie). The name 'Corners' is not uncommon, especially when the players use the corners of a netball court. In Aberdeen the game is known as 'Poles', in Forfar 'Polecat', the players taking their positions at the poles of the washing-lines. Sometimes small circles are chalked on the ground for the corners, and they draw five or six, or however many are required, so that more than five people can play.

A variant game in which more than five children can take part is played in West Ham and called 'Bad Penny'. Each player has a partner, except 'Bad Penny'. They stand in a line with their partners, and 'Bad Penny' just in front of them. At a given word one from each pair races to a certain point and back again, their partner marking their place. 'Bad

Penny' runs with them, and tries to get back to one of the partners first, whereon the player he has displaced becomes 'Bad Penny'.

§ 'Puss in the Corner' was one of the games Randle Holme listed in his *Academie of Armory*, 1688, III. xvi, § 91. It has frequently been alluded to since, e.g. by William King, *Useful Transactions in Philosophy*, no. i, 1709, p. 43; John Arbuthnot, *Memoirs of Martin Scriblerus*, 1714 (Pope's *Works*, vol. vi, 1757, p. 115); in *Round about our Coal Fire*, 1731, p. 9; *The Craftsman*, 4 February 1738, p. 1; by Dorothy Kilner, *The Village School*, vol. ii, *c.* 1785, p. 42; in *The Happy Family* [1786], p. 18; *David Copperfield*, 1850, ch. vii; and by Keats in a letter to Georgiana, *c.* April, 1819:

> 'You may perhaps have a game at Puss in the Corner—Ladies are warranted to play at this game though they have not whiskers.'

Descriptions of the game appear in Strutt's *Sports and Pastimes*, 1801, p. 285; *Juvenile Games for the Four Seasons, c.* 1820, p. 36; and in most other nineteenth-century collections, the player in the middle (unlike today) usually being nominated the 'puss'. Thus a writer in *The Boy's Own Paper*, 12 November 1887, p. 103, recalled:

> 'With us we had "any number of players", and a puss for every five of them. I have played with twenty-eight corners, and then there were six pussies in the centre.'

In the West Country the game was called 'Catch-Corner' (*EDD*). In Furness and Westmorland it was 'Chitty Puss'. A Cartmel Fell schoolboy said, about 1935, that the players shouted to each other 'Chi-chi-chi-chi, come to my den'—'Chi-chi-chi-chi' being the lakeland manner of calling a cat.

In the United States, where the game is often called 'Pussy wants a Corner', the player in the middle is the cat, and proceeds to each corner in turn pleading 'Pussy wants a corner', only to be told 'Go and see my neighbour'. When the cat goes to the next corner, the others move. In Austria, likewise, where the game is called 'Schneider, leih ma d'Schar', the reply is 'Go to my neighbour' (Otto Kampmüller, *Oberösterreichische Kinderspiele*, 1965, pp. 151–2). In Germany, where the game was recorded in 1851 and called 'Die Schere leihen', the player in the middle went round begging 'Tailor, lend me your shears', and was told in reply 'Da läuft sie leer' (E. Meier, *Deutsche Kinder-Spiele aus Schwaben*, p. 111). Brewster states that the game is played in exactly the same way in Hungary, the one in the middle saying 'My sponsor-woman, where are the scissors?' and the player at the corner replying 'I have lent them to my neighbour'. This is also the practice in Czechoslovakia, where the one in the middle says 'Godmother Anne, lend me a sieve', and the player in the corner replies, 'I have lent it to my neighbour' (*American Nonsinging Games*, 1953, pp. 96–7). He also states that in Greece, where the game is very popular, the player without a corner begs 'Light my candle', and gets for reply 'Go to another corner'. In Sicily, similarly, it appears that the player who is *sotto* used to approach each corner on the pretence of having a candle to light (G. Pitrè, *Giuochi fanciulleschi siciliani*, 1883, pp. 272–3). In Sweden and Switzerland, too, the player asks if he may 'borrow fire', and it appears that the game is related to the child-stealing drama 'Mother, the Cake is Burning' (q.v.), especially as in Germany there was a similar game called 'Kinderverkaufens' (Meier, p. 382). In Italy, however, the game is played without these formalities, and known prosaically as 'Quattro Angoli' or 'Quattro Cantoni' (M. M. Lumbroso, *Giochi*, 1967, pp. 295–8). In France, too, it is generally played as in England, and has long been popular as is apparent, for instance, from Lancret's picture 'Le Jeu de Quatre Coins'. A form of the game is also common in Japan, where the player in the middle is termed 'oni' or devil.

'Puss in the Corner' is also closely allied to the party game known variously as 'General Post', 'Move All', 'Stations', and 'King, King, Come Along', or, as in *Rob Roy*, 1817, ch. xxxi, 'Change Seats, the King's Coming'.

Hot peas

In this game the players race on different courses which are assigned to them by chance. 'Everybody assembles together at a certain gate or street lamp,' writes a 13-year-old. 'Whoever has to be out turns his back to the rest of the players and faces the gate or lamp. The rest of the players put their hands on top of each other on this person's back. One by one they pull their hands away and the person who has his back turned tells each one to go to some certain place, as it might be "Go to the bus stop", or "Go two gates down", or "Go across the road". When every-body has gone where they have been told to go, the person who was out turns round.' He shouts 'Hot potatoes', 'Hot soup', 'Hot mackerel', and they must not move; but when he shouts 'Hot peas' they race back to the gate or street lamp, and 'the last one back goes under an arch and the people thump him or her on the back, and he is "het" in the next game' (Glasgow).

This race-game is also known as 'Black Pudding' in Glasgow: the caller shouting 'different colours of puddings before he calls "Black pudding" '. In Cumnock it is 'Hot Peas and Vinegar' ('Hot peas and chips ... Hot peas and sauce ... Hot peas and *vinegar*'), and the same name and formula is reported from Enfield, the last player home being made to go 'through the mill'. In Wolstanton the game and call is 'Hurry Home!', in Perth 'Sheep, Sheep, Come Home', and in Accrington, where the game is played under the name of 'Ralliho', an additional player is employed, and while the first has his face to a wall, he points at the others in turn, chanting:

> North, South, East, West,
> The wind blows the robin's nest,
> Where shall this one go to?

These words not only neatly join the game to its history, but help to show the evolution of the still more popular pastime 'I Draw a Snake upon Your Back' (q.v.).

§ Robert Chambers's description of the game in *Popular Rhymes of Scotland*, 1869, pp. 122–3, shows how little it has altered in the past hundred years:

'One boy stands with his eyes bandaged and his hands against a wall, with his head resting upon them. Another stands beside him repeating a rhyme, whilst the others come one by one and lay their hands upon his back, or jump upon it:

> Hickety, bickety, pease scone,
> Where shall this poor Scotchman gang?
> Will he gang east, or will he gang west;
> Or will he gang to the craw's nest?

When he has sent them all to different places, he turns round and
calls: "Hickety, bickety!" till they have all rushed back to the
place, the last in returning being obliged to take his place, when
the game goes on as before.'

Presumably the boys' sport named 'Pirley Pease-weep', mentioned in
Blackwood's Edinburgh Magazine, August 1821, pp. 36–7, was also this
game, for it had the words:

> Scotsman, Scotsman, lo!
> Where shall this poor Scotsman go?
> Send him east, or send him west,
> Send him to the craw's nest.

And Caleb, in *The Bride of Lammermoor*, 1819, ch. xxvi, refers to 'the
bairns' rhyme —

> Some gaed east, and some gaed west,
> And some gaed to the craw's nest.'

Other references: W. H. Patterson, *Antrim and Down Glossary*, 1880,
under 'Hurly-burly' (Patterson subsequently described the game and
called it 'Capball'—Gomme MSS., 30 January 1915). Northall, *English
Folk-Rhymes*, 1892, pp. 401–2, ''Otmillo', i.e. 'Hot Mill' or 'Through
the Mill' (Warwickshire). J. Inglis, *Oor Ain Folk*, 1894, p. 110, 'Het
Rows and Butter Baiks' (Angus). E. W. B. Nicholson, *Golspie*, 1897, p.
118, 'Cabbage-stock'. *English Dialect Dictionary*, vols. i and ii, 1897–
1900, 'Burn the Biscuit' (north country), and 'Eettie ottie for a tottie,
where shall this boy go?' (Aberdeen, 1853). Maclagan in his *Games of
Argyleshire*, 1901, pp. 215–16, gives 'Hickety, Bickety'; and 'Huggry,
Huggry, Piece, Piece', in which the last back was asked if he would have
'wind' or 'rain'; if he chose 'wind' he was thoroughly fanned with their
bonnets, if 'rain' he was spat upon.

Correspondents played the game under the names: 'Hurly Burly,
Pim Bo Lock' (Midgley, Halifax, *c*. 1900); 'Ickery, Ickery, I Cuckoo'
(Alfriston, Sussex, *c*. 1910); and 'Tally-ho Dogs' (Millom, Cumberland,
c. 1925).

Compare some of the games, but not the conjectures, given by Gomme
under 'Hot Cockles' (vol. i, 1894, p. 229; vol. ii, 1898, pp. 429–30). It

is possible, however, that the names 'Hot Peas' and 'Hot Cockles' are not coincidental.

The game seems to have been well known in Germany in the nineteenth century under the name 'Salzhäring'. One player knelt down and put his hand behind his back. The other players came up behind him in turn and touched his hand asking:

'Tik, Tak, wo schall de Mann hen?'

Each player was sent to a different place and waited there until the one who sent them called out 'Solten Hering, solten Hering, solten Hering!' They then ran back and, as in Britain today, the last back was punished 'with blows and shoves', and became the kneeling player in the next game (H. Smidt, *Wiegenlieder, Ammenreime und Kinderstubenscherze* (Bremen) 1859, p. 60, cited by Böhme, 1897, pp. 581–2).

7. Duelling Games

The games that follow are those in which two children place themselves in direct conflict with each other, yet scrupulously observe the conventions of the encounter. Whether the test be of their courage when steering directly at each other on bicycles, or of the simple ability to choose a more resilient stem of ribgrass, the naïvety of their conduct is generally such that it does honour to Rousseau. Thus in 'Slappies' a boy will continue to accept punishment from a faster mover, blaming only his own slowness for the pain; and in the 'autumnal jousting with horse chestnuts', as Richard Church has observed, a boy's word is always accepted by his fellows when he states that his conker is a 'fiver' or a 'tenner'.

Obviously the most interesting duels are the ones children engage in when away from supervision; and we omit here the contests, or 'partner activities' (to use P.E. jargon) which have now become domesticated in school gymnasiums, such as 'Chinese Boxing' (trying to force opponent to hit himself), 'Chinese Wrestling' (wrestling with one hand), 'Japanese Wrestling' (trying to get an opponent off a mat), 'Chinese Tug' (standing back-to-back and attempting to pull opponent under legs), 'Cock Fighting' (squatting on the floor, or on hunkers, with hands clasped under the knees),[6] 'Knee Boxing' (fighting only with the knees), 'Pulling the Cow to Market' or 'Obstinate Calf' (attempting to pull opponent along by clasping hands behind the back of his head), and 'Uprooting the Slipper' (attempting to remove opponent's shoe while keeping on one's own). Away from school children feel these contests are dull sport compared with a prohibited game like 'Split the Kipper'.

Contests Mainly Requiring Strength

Elbows

When a boy boasts of his superior strength he may be challenged to 'Elbows'. A table is cleared and the contestants sit facing each other, placing their right elbows on the table and clasping the other's hand, so that the two forearms are upright against each other. The boy who suc-

ceeds in forcing back the other boy's forearm on to the table is the victor; and if a lighted candle is placed on one side of the table and a knife
point fixed upwards on the other, it wonderfully increases the interest of
the contest.

§ One instance of this combat occurred at Mulligan's drinking-place
in James Joyce's story 'Counterparts' in *Dubliners*, 1914; another was
between the 'tough' of the class and the new master in John Townsend's
The Young Devils, 1958, p. 56; a third was fancifully depicted between
Khrushchev and President Kennedy in a French cartoon reproduced in
The Sunday Times, 20 August 1961, p. 2.

Knifing

The two adversaries find sticks of the same length and holding them
in their right hands, take their opponent's wrist in their left hand, and
attempt to stab each other, while avoiding being stabbed themselves.
Alternatively they have one long and strong stick or pole, of which each
takes an end single-handed, and tries to stab or jab his opponent with the
other end. ' "Knifing" is a game I like playing,' says a 12-year-old. 'We
kneel down and start fighting and we see who can get the other's throat
first. But there are certain rules, which are, no kicking, and keep your
free hand behind you.'

Divie dagger

A 14-year-old boy writes: 'Divee Dagger is another game I learned at
Langholm. We played it at the age of eleven when we played on the
hillside. We find a flat stretch of ground of about twenty yards long and
two teams are picked. Someone then makes a wooden "dagger" and
places it upright in the ground. The first people from the teams come out
and stand at the same distance from the "dagger" and on the cry "Now"
they both race for the "dagger". One of them gets the "dagger" and one
of them does not. The two people then fight with the dagger until one
of them is hit with the point and killed (in pretence). Then the second
people of each team fight until each person has had a turn, and then the
team with the most people alive is the winner.'

Lifting

The rivals sit on the ground opposite each other, feet to feet, and either hold each other's hands, or both take hold of a short stout stick, held crosswise between them. They then pull against each other as hard as they can, to discover which is the weaker, all the more humiliating for the loser finding himself raised from the ground while the other remains seated.

§ This trial of strength is clearly depicted in the illuminated manuscript 'The Romance of Alexander', 1344 (Bodley MS. 264, fol. 100), and in a French Book of Hours of the fifteenth century (Douce MS. 276, fol. 39v). It is also shown in *Les Jeux et plaisirs de l'enfance*, 1657, under the title 'Le covrt baston', and this was the name of one of Gargantua's games (1534). In more recent times it has been a popular entertainment in Scotland. It was described by Jamieson in 1808, under the title of 'Sweir-tree', and was also known as 'Drawing the Sweirtree'—the 'sweirtree' or 'lazy tree' being the stick with which the contestants sought to draw each other off the ground. Mactaggart, *Gallovidian Encyclopedia*, 1824, p. 26, quotes an old man of nearly ninety boasting: 'I hae seen the day I wad hae pulled ony o'm aff their doups at the sweertree.' Jamieson later reported (1825) that in Tweeddale when persons grasped each other's hands, without using a stick, the sport was called 'Sweir-drauchts'. In Ireland, where the handle of a spade or pitchfork might be used, it was known as 'Sweel Draughts' (O'Súilleabháin, *Irish Wake Amusements*, 1967, pp. 39–40). In Indiana it was 'Pulling Swag' (*American Nonsinging Games*, 1953, p. 175, where Brewster gives several references to northern Europe). And amongst the Turks it is or was 'Quvvet' meaning *strength* (*Folk-Lore Society Jubilee Congress*, 1930, p. 143).

Cock fighting

The two cocks who are to fight each other are often chosen with the rhyme:

> Hop, hop, hop to the butcher's shop,
> I dare not stay no longer,
> For if I do my mother will say
> I've been with the boys down yonder.

Once they have been selected they have to stay on one leg and keep their arms folded. They hop towards each other, and butt, barge, or 'dunt' their opponent, trying to knock him over, or at least force him to put his second foot on the ground. Whoever unbalances the other, without of course putting both his own feet on the ground, is the victor, and takes on someone else.

This contest is sometimes known as a 'Shoulder Fight'. In Scotland it is 'Hopping Davy' or 'Hoppy Dig' ('Humphy Dick' says an Aberdonian); in Dublin 'Hopping Cock'; and amongst Wolf Cubs 'King of the Ring'. Without barging it becomes 'Catch Leg'.

A similar game is called 'Bumpers' or 'Bumper Cars'. In this the antagonists must keep their arms folded, but have both feet on the ground, and the victor is he who knocks the other player over. The feature of this combat is the initial charge and collision, which in itself is liable to prove decisive, one party or the other usually being sent sprawling (Banbury and St Peter Port).

§ The earliest reference found to a fight between two hopping boys is in *Games and Sports for Young Boys*, 1859, p. 4, where, like today, it is called a 'Cock Fight'. In Forfar, *c.* 1910, it was 'Hockey Cockey Fechtie'.

Eggy Peggy

This is a duel between two hoppers, exactly as in 'Cock Fighting' but with a set ritual for determining who shall be the second combatant. One person is named 'Eggy Peggy', and keeps out of hearing, while each of the other children (the players are usually girls) chooses a colour and stands in line. Eggy Peggy, who is supposed to have a bad leg, hops up to them and says: 'Eggy Peggy has broke her leggy'.

> Children: 'What on?'
> Eggy Peggy: 'A barbed wire gate'.
> Children: 'What do you want?'
> Eggy Peggy: 'A pair of stockings'.
> Children: 'What colour?'

Eggy Peggy names a colour. If there is a child who has chosen this colour she hops out, and the duel begins. Whoever wins is the next Eggy Peggy.

Names: 'Eggy Peggy' (Oxford and Lydeard St Lawrence, Somerset); 'Heggy Peggy' (Bristol); 'Heckety Peckety' or 'Hippety Skippety' (Swansea). Compare the games 'Little Black Doggie' and 'Limpety Lil'. In Scotland and the north country the game is often known as 'Cigarettes'. Each of the players, except the 'caller', chooses a brand of cigarettes, for instance, Bristol, Players, Senior Service, Batchelor, Woodbine, Passing Cloud, Piccadilly, Capstan, etc. The 'caller' names a brand, and if anyone has chosen it he hops forward and the barging begins. In Liverpool the game is played in the same way but using the names of 'Comics', and is sometimes so called; or it is known as 'Fighting Cocks', and the winner who remains standing triumphant in the middle of the road on one leg is called 'king cock'.

Dance, fight or windmill

This entertainment has been reported only from Aberdeen. The players are counted out, and the one who is 'out' stands in front and may challenge whom he wishes to 'Dance, Fight, or Windmill'. The player challenged then has the privilege of choosing the form of the contest. If he chooses 'Dance', both contestants must hop on one leg, and keep turning round all the time until one or other of them is dizzy and collapses. If the player chooses 'Fight', they both fold their arms, approach each other hopping, and have a 'cock fight'. And if he chooses 'Windmill', the one who challenges whirls his arms, and the other must twice run under the flailing arms without being hit.

Branch boy

An 11-year-old in St Peter Port, Guernsey, reports:

> 'Two boys climb on to the branch of a tree, clinging on
> with their hands and facing each other. Then they pull and
> push with their legs to get one another off the branch.

> Very often they both fall to the ground, but if one wins he
> shouts "Branch boy!" and jumps to the ground and sits on
> the other, who objects and fights. If he does not object to
> being sat on he is tied to the tree.'

§ This duel is, of course, merely a make-shift version of the old fair-ground sport in which two contestants perched themselves astride a cross-pole, and each being armed with a bag of flour, attempted the not very difficult task of knocking the other to the ground, and the more difficult feat of remaining on the cross-pole themselves.

Bucking bronco

In this exercise the contestants are not on equal terms: one boy allows another to mount his back, and then devotes his energy to bouncing him off. However, when a horse succeeds in throwing his rider, the rider becomes the bronco, and it is the other's turn to be discomfited. Occasionally the mount is made up of two boys, one bending down and holding the waist of a boy in front, as in a pantomime horse. The amusement is also known as 'Shaking Horse' (Alton), and 'Donkey' (south-east London).

§ It always seems to be necessary to the enjoyment of this sport that the person underneath be thought of as other than a playfellow. As long ago as 1824 Mactaggart described a frolic which the Irish 'seem to enjoy' at their wakes, called 'Riding Father Doud', and Father Doud turns out to hold no more elevated office than that of the present-day bronco (*Gallovidian Encyclopedia*, pp. 320–1).

Piggyback fights

Two small boys mount the backs of two 'well-built sturdy lads', usually by taking a good run and leaping on. The challengers, thus mounted, face each other some ten yards apart and charge. The object of the engagement, carefully explained by our informants, 'is to make the rider and horse part company', 'to knock your opponent down', 'to pull the rider off by any possible means or to upset both rider and horse'. 'The rule is that only the person on the back is allowed to fight, the others can only barge.' Sometimes the riders sit on the bigger boys' shoulders instead of their backs, and are then, in the metropolitan area, known as 'flying angels'. 'I prefer the shoulder fights because they are rougher and more falls are seen,' states a north-country boy. 'The shoulder fights usually end up in a flaring temper,' says another, 'because one man can be pulled off and hurt, and he may get up and hit the other man.'[7]

Sometimes more than two pairs fight at once. A 12-year-old Oxford boy writes:

> 'The craze at our school is piggy-back fighting. Every playtime all the boys from our school collect on the field and find a partner bigger than themselves and mount him. ... To have good fun you need about twenty boys, ten mounts and ten horses. Sometimes more than one boy gets hurt and sometimes the injury is quite serious. Some boys' injuries are a cut leg, a broken tooth, a cut ear. Once or twice a boy's jumper gets torn like mine did last week all round the neck. Some nights all the boys collect on the local park to play.'

Sometimes the boys use sticks as swords, and think of themselves as knights. At Knighton, in Radnorshire, where they play 'Knights on Horseback', the one who 'stays on longest' gets carried shoulder high by the rest. They have a king, and carry the winner before the king, and set him down, and the king ruffles the winner's hair. Then the king presents him with a bunch of dandelions or other wild flowers. 'It is a very good game although rather rough.'

In Edinburgh, and doubtless in other places, they practise jousting on their two-footed steeds. Each rider has a buff ('which is a pole with a muff on one end'), and 'the object of the game is to jolt the other person out of the saddle'. 'The only rules are that you can't aim for the head and you can't knock the horse.'[8]

Sometimes the combats are conducted on other types of mounts.

Camel Fighting. The camel is made by one boy standing upright, and another boy bending down behind him holding on to his hands, or, occasionally, clutching his waist. The rider clambers on to the second boy's back: 'Then you charge.'[9] This formation is also known as a 'Donkey' and, in Dublin, as a 'Milk Car'.

Elephants. Two people stand upright, side by side, with their arms behind their backs holding each other's hands, right hand in right, left hand in left, and a third person bends down and grasps their hands. The rider mounts the third person's back.

Chariots. Sometimes made with the same formation as 'Elephants', the two people in front acting as horses; more often made by two people standing beside each other linking their outer hands, and the charioteer using their inner hands as stirrups, and keeping his balance with his hands on their heads.

Battering Rams. Two boys hold a third boy horizontally on their right shoulders with his feet forward, and try their human weapon against other players mounted piggyback.

Rumblin' Rhinos. Three boys are held horizontally on the shoulders of eight others, four linked together in a line in front, and four behind. A Liverpool boy says:

> ' "Rumblin' Rhinos" are used to smash up piggyback fights.
> The boys who are the crosspieces are chosen because
> they have got hard shoes, either leather, or rubber soles
> with studs on. "Rumblin' Rhinos" can have fights between
> themselves, but this usually ends up in somebody getting
> their teeth kicked in. "Rumblin' Rhinos" are known as
> "Icecream Carts" and "Tanks" in other places. Although
> this game is dangerous it is great fun, especially for the
> winners. The loser is the rhino first rumbled. The game
> is mostly played in the playgrounds of schools, and as
> people get hurt, the school usually ban it, although the
> kids still play it.'

Names: 'Piggyback Fighting' (rarely 'Pick-a-back') is also known as 'Horse Fighting', 'Horses and Riders', 'Jockeys', 'Donkey Fights', 'Cock Fights', 'Fighting Cocks', 'Collie-bag Fights' (Aberdeen), 'Collie-buckie Fighting' (Edinburgh), 'Hunch Cuddy Hunch' (Glasgow), 'Jousting', 'Charging', 'Tournaments', and (in Petersfield) 'Humpback Fighting'.

§ Piggyback riding and fighting is presumably universal. Robert Louis Stevenson in Tahiti, 1888, noted that 'the boys play horses exactly as we do in Europe'; and Samuel Marshak recalled bloody 'cavalry battles' in his youth at Ostrogozhsk in which 'the boys would charge into the fray mounted on their class-mates' (*At Life's Beginning*, 1964, pp. 126–7). Such play is certainly ancient. A sarcophagus in the Vatican Museum, Rome, shows boys engaged in a piggyback fight, although with one of the *horses* clasping the hand of the opposing rider and seemingly attempting to pull him down. (Since the rider is seated in the common classical style, merely clinging with his knees to the upstanding mount, his task should not have been difficult.) Medieval artists depict not merely piggyback riding, but duels between the riders exactly as today (see Rutland Psalter, *c.* 1250, fol. 70b; Stowe MS. 17, Hours of the Virgin, Flemish, *c.* 1290–1300, fol. 100v; Yates Thompson 8, Breviary, v I, French, *c.* 1290–1310, fol. 92; Luttrell Psalter, *c.* 1340, B.M. Adds. 42130, fol. 62; Bodley MS. 264, 'The Romance of Alexander', 1344, fol. 91; MS. Royal 2, B vii, Queen Mary's Psalter, *c.* 1320, fol. 161v). In *Les Trente-six figures*, 1587, piggyback is termed 'le jeu de sainct Chretofle'.

Contests Requiring Nerve and Skill

Danger ride

Two boys mount their bicycles and circle round a patch of wasteland. They may do anything they can to separate their opponent from his bike, swerve in front of him, cut across him, and even aim at him, provided only that they do not actually touch him or his bicycle. At Barrow-in-Furness the two riders charge each other, sometimes down the length of a street, and just before they meet they have to apply their brakes and balance motionless. 'The first one to get off, gets scragged by the other lads.' The game becomes unpleasant when, in some places, it is called 'Chicken' and the two riders charge each other with no intention of stopping: he who swerves first being judged a chicken while the other is a cock (see also p. 119).

Split the kipper

In this contest, which, as one boy admitted, 'takes quite a lot of nerve', the two adversaries stand facing each other, a yard or so apart, with their feet together. The first boy throws a knife, preferably a sheath knife, so that it sticks in the ground not more than twelve inches to the left or right of one of his opponent's feet. The other boy, without moving his feet, plucks the knife out of the ground, and moves his nearest foot to the place where the knife went in. In this position he makes a return throw (most boys specify that the knife must be thrown by the blade), and the first boy, likewise, moves his foot to where the knife stuck in. However, should the point of the knife not stick into the ground, or should it stick in more than twelve inches away from the person's foot ('if more than a span', says a Durham lad; 'if over two knife lengths', says a Fife boy), the player does not have to move his foot, and the throw is lost. The object of the game is to force the opponent to stretch his legs so far apart that he cannot move them further, and gives in, or falls over while attempting the stretch. In this form 'it is a short game and suitable for short breaks at school'. But in many places, particularly in the north, a player is allowed to 'split' his opponent. If a person's legs are uncomfortably wide apart, and his opponent's likewise, or at least moderately open, he may attempt to throw the knife so that it sticks between his opponent's legs, and if he succeeds in this, may close his own. Usually 'splitting' is allowed only once, twice, or three times, otherwise the game can 'go on for ages'. Alternatively in Scotland, including the Isles, if the knife sticks between the opponent's legs, that person has to turn round, and thereafter throw less surely, and undoubtedly more dangerously, with his back to the other player.

This game, or ordeal, which is sometimes played with a dart, iron spike, or geometry dividers, has become popular only during the past decade. In our survey conducted in the early 1950s we heard of it only in the vicinity of Manchester, while in the early 1960s it was reported from virtually every contributing school, a number of boys describing it as their favourite sport. Further, the game now seems to be established, and to be developing its own oral lore, despite the fact that it has caused injuries (not to mention cut shoes and split trouser-seams), and has been banned in a number of schools. In Guernsey a doggerel rhyme or threat is now repeated by the contestants, and it will be noticed that it is similar in style to that used by conker players:

Hick, hack, hoe,
My first go.
I'll split you yet
And you'll forget
That it's your go.[10]

In England and Wales the usual names for the game are 'Split the Kipper', 'Splits', and 'Stretch'. In Wigan it is 'Split Leg', in Enfield sometimes 'Slit Jack', and two West Ham boys call it 'Chinese Torture'. In north Lincolnshire it is often 'Black Foot', or occasionally 'Black Jack'. One report from Guernsey names it 'Watch Your Foot'. Throughout Scotland, where the game is rapidly supplanting the older knife-throwing games, it is 'Knifie'. Several informants state that they first learnt the game at Scouts.

In South Wales and East Anglia a variation is appropriately known as 'Nerve' or 'Chicken'. In this contest the players *start* with their legs apart and aim between each other's legs. The player closes his leg to where the knife stuck. 'It goes on like this until one of the boys gets scared and gives in', says an 11-year-old. 'He is then called "Chicken".'

Territories

This game, apparently well known in the first half of the century, now seems tame compared with 'Split the Kipper'. A circle is drawn on the ground, with a line through the middle, and one boy has one half and one the other. The boys throw in turn into each other's territory. When one of them succeeds in sticking a knife into the other's sector, a new line is drawn through the place where the knife fell, and in the direction that it points, and the old line is rubbed out. The other boy then has to throw his knife into the smaller segment in an attempt to regain territory, while the first boy throws to diminish the other boy's land. Alternatively each boy stands in his own territory, and cuts off pieces of his opponent's territory, until he no longer has space to stand on—Manchester and Aberdeen.

§ Cf. Jamieson, *Scottish Dictionary, Supplement*, 1825, 'Cat-Beds'; Maclagan, *Games of Argyleshire*, 1901, p. 144, 'Sgrothan'; E. Meier, *Deutsche Kinder-Spiele aus Schwaben*, 1851, p. 394, 'Ackerles oder Kluvander'.

Knifie

This curious trial between two boys, which of them can first complete a prescribed series of feats with a pocket knife, is another game rapidly being supplanted by 'Split the Kipper', and in Scotland the new game has appropriated the name of the old. 'Knife', so called in Scotland since the beginning of the century, is a game that has apparently held youthful attention for 400 years. It is here described, perhaps for the last time in Britain, by a 10-year-old boy in the Isle of Lewis:

> ' "Knifie" is a game for two people. First you do "Handy" in which you place the knife in the palm of your hand and try to make it stick in the ground by tossing it into the air. The same with "Backsy" except that you place it on the back of your hand. "Fisty" also has the same idea but it is your fist you place it on. Then you try to stick the knife into the ground six times in succession. Then try "Pitch and toss". Stick it in the ground, then try to hit it with the palm of your hand and try to toss it into the air, so that it will land blade first in the earth. First person to reach this point is the winner. This is a very good game, but it can be very dangerous.'

§ In former times it was the victor's privilege to drive a peg into the ground with as many blows of his knife-handle as the loser required additional throws to complete the game; and the vanquished, by way of penance, had to pull the peg out of the ground with his teeth. Hence the game was commonly known as 'Mumble-the-peg', 'Mumbletypeg', or 'Mumblepeg', a name-form which survives to this day among boys in parts of the United States, and in the outback of Australia, where the loser is made to pull a matchstick out of the ground.

'Mumble the pegge' is mentioned, along with 'scourge-top', 'Leape frog' and 'Nine holes' in the prologue to *Apollo Shrouing* by William Hawkins, a drama acted by the boys of the grammar school at Hadleigh, Suffolk (where Hawkins was master), on Shrove Tuesday, 1626. The youth Nehemiah, in Brome's *The New Academy*, 1659 (II. ii), who looks forward to playing games with a young wife, declares 'at Mumbledepeg I will so firk her'. (His mother tells him, 'When y'are married, you'll finde other pastime.') And a hundred years earlier, Moros in *The Longer thou Livest, the more Foole thou art*, written about 1569, speaking of his diversions at school, apparently refers to the sport when he says, 'You would laugh to see me mosel the pegge'.

As is to be expected with so old a diversion, it has a wide distribution. Sutton-Smith, *Games of New Zealand Children*, 1959, pp. 126–7, describes it under the names 'Stagknife', 'Stabknife', 'Jack-knife', 'Knifey', 'Momley Peg', and 'Bites'; Newell, *Games of American Children*, 1883, p. 189, gives it as 'Mumblety-peg'; Brewster, *American Nonsinging Games*, 1953, pp. 142–5, as 'Mumblepeg', and states that it is played in identical fashion in Hungary. The game has also been described to us by a 12-year-old Polish boy as played in Poland:

> 'You get a knife and set the point of the blade on your
> finger and toss it into the air so that it spins. If it stick in,
> you set the point on your foot and toss it into the air to see
> if it will stick, you then do the same on your nose and chin.
> The person who takes the least number of throws to stick
> it in wins.'

It is still played by boys in Trieste, where it is called 'Il Magnatappo' (Lumbroso, *Giochi*, 1967, p. 23). And it appears to be shown, being played with bricks, in Breugel's 'Kinderspiele', painted in 1560.

Our English correspondents recall playing the game with a sequence of up to eighteen tossings, including from nose, shoulder, and forehead. They knew it either as 'Stick Knife' or 'Stickie Knife'. *EDD* describes it under 'Spinny-diddl-um'.

Contests Requiring Fortitude

Knuckles

'Knuckles', in Scotland 'Knucklie', is a kind of conkers with the hands, played for no other reason, it seems, than to test the physical fibre of the players. One boy holds out a clenched fist and the second strikes the knuckles as hard as he can with his own. The first boy then strikes the other's knuckles, and so on, alternately hitting and being hit. 'As the game proceeds', says a 12-year-old, 'the bashing gets more fierce.' Nevertheless 'you mustn't pull your knuckles away, you've just got to take it. The first to cry is a baby'; or, as another youngster put it, rather more sedately, 'the loser is the one who retires earlier'. Yet some lads seem constitutionally unable to give in, and the game (so called) continues long after skin has been torn from their hands. Two 11-year-olds were observed in a playground taking turns at each other; both were in agony, yet they were found to be still at it ten minutes later, and neither had given in when, mercifully, the whistle sounded for the end of playtime. A 9-year-old on the outskirts of Gloucester told us, with a glint in his eye, that thereabouts the game was known as 'Knuckledusters'.

§ British children have no monopoly of this pastime. A fearsome bout of 'Knuckles' is described in Arthur Roth's autobiographical novel *The Shame of our Wounds*, 1962, p. 44, set in a New York Catholic Boys' Institute.

Flat Jack

Reported only from Northumberland. One boy bends down and the other hits him on the back of the head. Then the other bends down and is hit likewise. If a boy dodges when his head is down, the one who is hitting has another turn. 'They take it in turns and the one who gives in or runs away is the loser.'

Bob and slap

More widespread and slightly less primitive than 'Flat Jack' is the contest in which one person tries to duck his head between another's hands, held about two feet apart. The one who bobs his head between the hands may choose his moment to move; and this gives him a certain advantage, for surprisingly he very often slips through without having his head slapped, no matter whether moving upwards or downwards. The exercise is sometimes known as 'Slapping the Duck', especially in the United States.

§ In nineteenth-century rural England this was a public-house sport, in Hampshire called 'Catch the Crow', the only difference being that one player was seated, with his knees apart, and his hands against his knees, while the second player knelt down and attempted to pass his head between them. It was also known as 'Quack'. 'George Forrest' (The

Rev J. G. Wood) described it in *Every Boy's Annual*, 1864, as 'one of the most mirth-provoking games imaginable', and added, 'I have seen ladies nearly ill through continued laughter'. Indeed, in Capri, today, the Tarantella dancers entertain guests in restaurants and hotels with the humours of the contest, which in the Neapolitan dialect is called 'U Scarrafone du Camp'. Urquhart in his list of English games (*Gargantua*, ch. xxii, 1653), names 'Bob and Hit' and 'Bobbing, or flirt on the nose', one or other of which is possibly this sport.

Slappies

This is another test of a player's willingness to absorb pain. One player stretches out his hands palm upwards, and the other player, at first less fortunate, has to rest his hands flat on top of them, with the backs of his hands uppermost. The player whose hands are underneath attempts to slap one or both of the hands placed on his by suddenly withdrawing his hands and whipping them down on the backs of his opponent's. His opponent may attempt to move his hands out of the way, but not until the other has begun to move, or he forfeits a turn. If the one who is slapping misses the other's hands, he has to go on top; but if he succeeds he has another go. Although the person slapping has further to move, he has the advantage of being first to move (cf. 'Bob and Slap'), and in practice, when the players are of the same age, the chances of being hit or missed are about equal. On occasion, however, one player may gain ascendancy over the other, and, on a cold day, the result can be very painful. In Cumnock the game is known as 'Leathery', in Forfar as 'Puir Pussie'.

§ This sport is also reported from Maryland (Howard MSS.), from Ireland, under the names 'Poor Little Pussy' or 'Poor Snipeen' (*Irish Wake Amusements*, 1967, pp. 46–7), and from Belgium under the name 'Leu Tchôde Main' (*Le Pays de saint Remacle*, no. 2, 1963, p. 144). A party game on the same principle, called 'Copenhagen', is given in *The Girl's Book of Diversions*, 1835, p. 10. A Cornish game called 'Scat' in which a player has to pick up a stick from the hand, with which to hit it, is described in *Folk-Lore Journal*, vol. v, 1887, p. 50.

Stinging

In 'Stinging' the punishment befalls the player who is unlucky rather than unskilful, or so it seems to him, for he has failed to guess the other player's mind. The two contestants flash their fingers at each other, usually making one of the three finger formations used in 'Odd Man Out' and 'Ick Ack Ock' (Vol.1 p. 47), thus, fingers clenched ('stone'), fingers flat out ('paper'), and two fingers stretched out and kept apart ('scissors'). In a number of places, however, for example, Edinburgh, Norwich, and Petersfield, they also make the signs 'rain', bunching their fingers and pointing them downwards, and 'fire', pointing their fingers upwards. 'Rain' puts out 'fire', and rusts 'scissors', while 'fire' burns 'paper', and blackens 'stone'. More often the game is played merely with 'stone' beating 'scissors', 'scissors' beating 'paper', and 'paper' covering and thus beating 'stone'. Whoever wins each time wets his first and second fingers by licking them, pulls back his opponent's sleeve, and smacks his bare wrist good and hard, an operation which is more painful than those who have not experienced it might imagine. Play then resumes and continues until one boy or the other considers he has had enough. This game, like 'Slappies', is particularly prevalent in boarding schools. One informant tells us that on occasion it becomes an obsession in a classroom or dormitory, and some people's wrists, after a run of losses, would be 'absolutely bloody red'; yet they will not give in because they hope to start winning and make the other person suffer. When girls play the game they usually agree that a player must win three times before she has the privilege of giving a slap.

Stampers

The two rivals stand face-to-face, placing their hands on each other's shoulders. They may move about and dodge aside as they please, provided they keep their hands on the other's shoulders, but mostly they push each other, since the object of the exercise is to stamp as hard and as often as possible on the opponent's feet.

§ Formerly players used to kick each other's legs, but 'Shinning' or 'Cutlegs'—a rural, hobnail-booted sport of the nineteenth century—has not been reported in the present day.

Duels by Proxy

Soldiers

This gentlest form of combat, conducted with a stalk of ribwort plan-tain (*Plantago lanceolata*), has been a pastime with the young for more than 750 years. One player challenges another and they take turn about striking each other's stalk with their own until one of the plan-tain heads is whipped off, whereupon the victor crows his victory, and the loser feels no loss: another stalk is quickly produced—this is the pleasure of the game—and a new duel commences. During the flower's long summer season the game seems to be played everywhere, usually called 'Soldiers', although the plantains are also known as 'Blackmen', 'Cocks and Hens', 'Fighting Cocks', 'Hard Heads', 'Knights', and, in Perthshire, 'Carldoddies'.

§ In Scotland and the north country the game was long known as 'Kemps' (cf. the Old English *cempa*, a warrior; Middle English *kempen*, to fight or contend with: the Norwegian *kjæmpe*, and Swedish *kämpa*, a plantain). Jamieson's description in the Supplement to his *Scottish Dictionary*, 1825, might well be of today:

> 'Two children, or young people, pull each a dozen of stalks of
> rib-grass; and try who, with his kemp, can decapitate the great-
> est number of those belonging to his opponent. He, who has one
> remaining, while all that belong to the other are gone, wins the
> game. ... They also give the name "Soldiers" to these stalks.'

Jamieson also gives the name 'Carldoddy'; Moor, *Suffolk Words*, 1823, knew the game as 'Cocks'; Brockett, *North Country Words*, 1829, as 'Hard Heads' (Lancashire); Forby, *Vocabulary of East Anglia*, 1830, as 'Fighting-Cocks'; and W. H. Marshall, *Rural Economy of Norfolk*, 1787, knew ribwort as 'Cocksheads', presumably from the game, for it was certainly already well established. In the historical poem *Histoire de Guillaume le Maréchal*, written soon after 1219, the story is told how the boy William Marshal, later to become Earl of Pembroke and Regent of England, but then not 10 years old, was detained as a hostage in the king's camp, while Stephen was besieging Newbury. One day the boy picked out the plantains (*les chevaliers*) from the cut grass strewn on the floor of the tent, and challenged the king, 'Beau sire chiers, volez joer as chevaliers?' The challenge being accepted, William laid half the 'knights' on the king's lap, and asked who was to have first stroke. 'You', said the king, holding out his knight, which the small boy promptly beheaded, greatly to his own delight. King Stephen (strictly in accordance with the rules of the game) then held out another plantain, but the game was interrupted (ll. 595–619). It matters not whether the story is apocryphal; as early as the thirteenth century a poet has shown himself to be familiar with the game.

Mrs Craik, who knew the amusement as 'Cock-Fighting' (*Our Year*, 1860, p. 149) says that in her day children made the tough stems tougher still by twisting their necks round and round.

Lolly sticks

The game of 'Soldiers' is now also played with ice-lolly sticks, the sticks being, in urban surroundings, more available than are plantains. The stick, which is usually about four to four-and-a-half inches long, is held at both ends while the other player strikes it with his own stick held at one end. However, according to a young Mancunian, it is advisable first to examine the opponent's stick as 'some people try to cheat by playing with cardboard lollipop sticks which are a lot harder to break'. Others, it seems, practise one-up-manship by soaking their sticks 'so that they are waterlogged and won't break'. He continues, 'The lollipops, from which the lollipop sticks come, can be bought outside the school for the price of fourpence. They are bought from two or three ice-cream men who come outside the school at dinner time'. One informant states that at his school 'This craze was very popular until the masters ordered some boys to pick up all the pieces of stick in the school. Then it gradually faded away'. Another boy says 'This is a silly game and sometimes a sharp knock can cause blood on the hand'. Nevertheless, spasmodically, it has its adherents. In Liverpool it is called 'Chop Sticks', in Aberdeen, 'Icicle Sticks', in Sheffield, 'Foggy Plonks'.

Conkers

For a brief spell in early autumn this game is as much part of the English scene as garden bonfires, and hounds cubbing at break of day. The boys are out searching for conkers, throwing sticks and stones up into the chestnut trees (the best conkers are believed to be at the top of the tree) and, with or without permission, invading people's gardens. They meet with little opposition. The youthful pleasure of prising a mahogany smooth chestnut from its prickly casing is not easily forgotten; and when a vicar wrote to *The Times* complaining about the depredations of small enthusiasts, readers' sentiment was clearly against him.[11]

'Conkers', always so spelt, are also known as 'cheggies' in Langholm, 'hongkongs' in Grimsby, 'obbley-onkers' in Worcester, and 'cobs' in the area of Welshpool and Shrewsbury. A flat conker is popularly a 'cheeser' or 'cheese cutter'. Some boys bake their conkers for half an hour to harden them, or put them by the fire for a few days, or up the chimney. Some soak them in salt and water, or in a solution of soda; the majority prefer vinegar. An Edinburgh recipe is a teaspoonful of sugar and a little water in a jar of vinegar. A Putney boy puts them in vinegar for an hour, and then in water, explaining: 'If you did not put them in water the smell would keep on the conker and then people would not play you because they would think it was harder than theirs.' Others, more patient, put their chestnuts in a dark cupboard and leave them until next year. This makes them shrivelled and tough, easily recognizable as 'seasoners', 'yearsies', or 'second yearsers'. A boy with this year's conker, plump and shiny, sometimes called a 'straight conker', being straight from a tree, seldom cares to venture his new acquisition against a 'seasoner' and almost certain destruction.

No boys' game is more ruthless or carried out with more finesse than a conker fight. The conker is carefully selected. The hole through it is made with a meat skewer so as not to split the edges, and exactly through the middle. A strong piece of string, or a lace from a football boot, is procured which is long enough to be wound twice round the hand with about eight inches to hang down, and it is tightly knotted at the bottom to ensure the nut does not slip off and smash to pieces on an asphalt playground. It is a tenet of schoolboy faith that a conker is more likely to survive if it is the striker rather than the stricken, hence the conker-player's concern to have the first shot, which he secures by calling out 'First!' or, according to locality, 'My firsy' or 'Firsy jabs' (Bishop Auckland), 'First swipe' (York), 'First donks' (Shenfield), 'First hitsy' (Hornchurch), 'Bagsie first cracks' (Wigan), 'Iddley, idd-ley, ack, my first smack' (Knighton), 'Hobily, hobily, honker, my first conker' (Lydney).

> Conker Jeremy,
> My first blow,
> Conker Jack,
> My first whack.
> > *Boy, 11, Cranford, Middlesex*

> Ally, ally, onker,
> My first conker,
> Quack, quack,
> My first smack.
> > *Boy, 12, Thornton, Yorkshire*

> Iddy, iddy, onker,
> My first conker,
> Iddy, iddy, oh,
> My first go.
> > *Boy, 13, Oxford[12]*

> Obbly, onker,
> My first conker,
> Obbly oh,
> My first go.
> > *Boy, 11, Gloucester[13]*

The other boy then holds up his conker, dangling on the string, at whatever height best suits his opponent, and keeps it still. The first boy sizes up to it, holding his own conker between his thumb and forefinger, or behind his first two fingers, as if they were a catapult, and pulls the conker loose with a swinging downward motion on to his opponent's nut. If he hits it the other player has his turn; if he misses he may be allowed two more tries. If his string tangles in the other boy's string there is immediate cry of 'strings'—or 'clinks' (Manchester), 'clinch' (Ferryhill), 'clenches' (Wigan), 'plugs' (Wolstanton), 'lugs' (Leek), 'tags'

(Hainton), 'twits' (Cranborne), 'twitters' (Newcastle-under-Lyme), or 'tangles' (Bristol); and whoever cries first has an extra shot, or, in some places, two, three, or even six extra shots. Sometimes boys deliberately play for 'strings' so that they can claim extra shots, but this is not popular since the wrench the hand receives when the strings tangle can hurt and even cut the skin.

When one conker breaks another into pieces so that nothing remains on the string, the winning conker becomes a 'one-er', in Plymouth and Cornwall a 'one-kinger', in Sheffield a 'conker one', in Edinburgh, St Andrews, Kinlochleven, Oban, and doubtless elsewhere in Scotland, a 'bull', 'booly one', or 'bully one', in Cumnock a 'bullyanna'. If it then breaks another person's conker it becomes a 'two-er', if a third a 'three-er', and so on. If one boy's conker is a 'tenner' and another boy's a 'fiver', whichever wins will become a 'sixteener'. A conker that is a 'sixteener', and perhaps becoming battle-worn, is unlikely to be matched against anything less than a 'tenner'. It will not be worth the risk. In London, if a player drops his conker, or it is knocked out of his hand, or it slips off the string, the other player can shout 'stamps' and jump on it, and add its score to his own; but should its owner first cry 'no stamps' it cannot be counted as a victory, even if jumped upon and crushed. The worst disaster that can happen is that both conkers break at once, then both scores are lost.

When the conker craze is at its height 'there are pieces of conker flying in every direction, and we have to clean the yard up every day. The bins and wastepaper baskets are nearly full'. And the girls play too. One girl remarks that when boys are not very good at conkers they come to the girls' end of the playground 'because then they think they'll win, but sometimes the girls win'. When there is to be a match between two skilled players, each with a 'hundreder' or more, excitement flows through a junior school, bets may be laid, and the contest attracts as much attention as any sporting event in the school calendar. In 1952 the BBC staged a contest on TV between a 460–er, a 1136–er, a 2385–er, and a 3367–er. The winner became a 7351–er. More recently a conker championship has been arranged annually at the village of Walton-on-Trent in Derbyshire. But happily the season is too short for much adult exploitation. Suddenly there are no more conkers to be had, and the game dies out. Those boys with a treasured handful set aside for next year hug their secret.

It is presumably just part of man's struggle with nature that one local authority (Lowestoft) has planted a commemorative horse-chest-nut which will not bear chestnuts, so that it shall not be a temptation to the young; and that one toy manufacturer has attempted to popularize plastic conkers which, when broken, can be reassembled.

§ The Horse Chestnut tree (*Aesculus hippocastanum*), introduced into England about the beginning of the seventeenth century, does not seem to have been common in the eighteenth century, and children do not appear to have played with horse chestnuts until the nineteenth century. Previously they played with cobnuts, and records of cobnuts as playthings go back to the fifteenth century; although it is difficult to tell the type of play. However, the name *cobnut* itself may come from *cob*, to strike, to top, to excel; and colloquially a cobnut was a large hazel nut that out-matched the others. Dorothy Osborne, in a letter written probably 29 January 1653, speaks of a friend who wears twenty seals 'strung upon a riban like the nutts boys play withall'; and from Hunter's *Hallamshire Glossary*, 1829, p. 24, it is clear that this was how boys strung their nuts for a cobnut fight:

> 'Numerous hazel-nuts are strung like the beads of a rosary. The game is played by two persons, each of whom has one of these strings, and consists in each party striking alternately with one of the nuts on his own string, a nut of his adversary's. The field of combat is usually the crown of a hat. The object of each party is to crush the nuts of his opponent. A nut which has broken many of those of the adversary is a *cob-nut*.'

In the game of 'Cobs', 'Cobblers', 'Cock Haw', 'Conger', or 'Scabby', hazel nuts were hardened, strings which became 'twizzled' were cried at, and victories enumerated, virtually as with conkers today (see *Notes and Queries*, 7th ser., vol. ix, 1890, pp. 137–8). But cobnuts do not provide such a robust game as horse chestnuts. They are lighter, more difficult to obtain, and when obtained are better eaten.[14]

The Oxford English Dictionary (*Supplement*, 1928) suggests that the name 'conker' for a horse chestnut comes from an earlier game played with snail shells, sometimes called 'conkers', and that this stems from *conch*. There is, however, no record of boys calling snail shells 'conches', although they often called them 'conquerors'. Southey, in a letter to John May, 28 December 1821, recalled that in his schooldays at Corston, near Bristol, in 1782, there was a 'very odd amusement', greatly in vogue, in which snail shells were pressed against each other, point to point, until one of them was broken in:

> 'This is called conquering; and the shell which remained un-
> hurt, acquired esteem and value in proportion to the number
> over which it had triumphed, an accurate account being kept. A
> great conqueror was prodigiously prized and coveted, so much
> so indeed, that two of this description would seldom have been
> brought to contest the palm, if both possessors had not been
> goaded to it by reproaches and taunts. The victor had the number
> of its opponents added to its own; thus when one conqueror of
> fifty conquered another which had been as often victorious, it
> became conqueror of an hundred and one.'[15]

This name is confirmed in *The Boy's Own Book*, 1829, pp. 10–11, where the game of 'The Conqueror' is described as being played with snail shells in the west of England, and is compared with a similar game of the same name in which one player threw a stone marble at another, hoping to split it:

> 'A strong marble will frequently break, or conquer, fifty or a
> hundred others; where this game is much played, a taw that has
> become the conqueror of a considerable number, is very much
> prized and the owner will not play it against any but those which
> have conquered a respectable quantity.'

§ This, in turn, appears to be little different from the game described by Ovid, in his poem 'Nux', where one boy, standing, is said to aim his nut at a nut on the ground, and must split it with a single blow.

The game of 'Conquerors' with snail shells, a parallel to the 'dumping' or 'jarping' of hard-boiled eggs that remains part of the Easter ritual in the north country (*Lore and Language of Schoolchildren*, pp. 252–3), was not peculiar to the west. One of John Clare's favourite pastimes in Northamptonshire was gathering 'pooty shells', threading them on a string, and playing 'what we called "cock fighting" by pressing the knibbs hard against each other till one broke'. See also 'Conkers' in *Holderness Glossary*, 1877; 'Fighting Cocks' in *Leicestershire Words*, 1881; 'Cocks and Hens' in *Northumberland Words*, 1892; and 'Cogger' in *Northamptonshire Words*, 1854. Amongst others, a correspondent to

The Athenaeum, 28 January 1899, remembered duelling with snail shells when a schoolboy at Newport, Isle of Wight, in 1848, and he also 'often played conquerors with both horse-chestnuts and wallnut-shells', which is the earliest date we have for a contest with horse chestnuts, there being no mention in juvenile literature of playing 'Conqueror' with chestnuts until *Every Boy's Book*, 1856.

8. Exerting Games

'When you play "Jumping Jack" you keep jumping up and
down. You go on jumping until you can't jump any more and
fall on the ground. The last one who is jumping is the winner.'

Boy, 10, Alton

Some games are little more than statements of vitality. They have
few rules, they offer small scope for subtlety because the options
open to the player are few, and they make correspondingly large
demands on the player's forcefulness. They are games that are the
pleasure of those whose talents lie in their limbs; and they are made
bearable, very often, only by the pride that the young take in the
practice of stoicism. Thus the game of 'Cat and Dog', played in
Peterborough, is a simple trial of endurance: which of two boys can
longest support the pain of bearing a third boy, who has jumped up
between them, and exerts his weight on a shoulder of each, the first
to give way being 'cat'. 'Grippy', at Langholm, amounts to no more
than one person holding a button or coin in his fist, and the others
trying to force his fingers open and gain the object. 'Steps' (otherwise known as 'Fire', 'Letters', or 'England, Scotland, Ireland,
Wales') consists of jumping down a flight of steps in a given number
of jumps, or taking one jump up or down on to a particular named
step. And the game of 'Bundles', at Enfield and Fulham, seems to
be merely an excuse for violence: 'One person is chosen and he is
given ten seconds to run, then the rest run after him. When he is
caught he is thrown on the ground and punched.'[16] In short, these
are games in which the less courageous, or the more civilized, of
the juvenile community are able to endure the part of spectator with
some fortitude.

Tussles

Children's battles scarcely merit inclusion in a catalogue of games
except that 'games' are what the children call them. It is true that some
tussles for high ground, with names such as 'Gain the Summit', 'Taking
the Crown', 'Territories', 'Pull me Down', and 'King of the Castle' ('I'm

the king of the castle, get down you dirty rascal'), retain a few of the conventions of a game, when a single player holds the keep.[17] But when one gang faces another the contestants are liable to be uninhibited, or like to think that they are, and, according to accounts received, this is so even when the battleground is the school steps:

> 'If one gang captures the "fortress", the other attacks it. Each side has a war cry, ours is "Aaarghrghrghaargh". The gang who has captured the fortress shouts out "Repel boarders". The attackers grab them by their legs and pull them down, sit on them, and pulverize them. Then the other gang comes down from the steps, and strives to rescue their friends, while my friend and I nip round the back and claim the steps. "Come on you miserable runts," we say, and one of the runts runs up the steps, only to be thrown over the side of the railing. By then the others from our gang are with us, dragging one or two hostages by the hair. These we rough up a bit. We give 'em one down the cake 'ole or punch up the bread basket, or give them the "knee-arm", and fling them at their friends when they try to "board" us' (Boy, 13).

Such activity, it is alleged, continues to the classroom door:

> 'When the bell rings there are cries of "Skunks", "Cheats", "Useless nits", and a final push or belt as we run into class. Hardly anybody gets away without some rip, bruise, cut, or black eye.'

Accounts like this are not the testimony of disinterested witnesses; and despite their almost monotonous conformity the adult reader is, of course, content to allow for a certain exaggeration. Then he may happen upon a detail that makes him glad nature has arranged he will not again be a schoolboy. Another 13-year-old writes:

> 'If you are lucky to get away without any affliction then your gang bashes you up because you have not fought well.'

Chain swing

'Chain Swing' is almost as unpleasant as a fight, yet children, particularly young ones, seem unable to resist its thrill, and for a season it
becomes a school craze, until banned, or until several players have been
injured, and its attraction becomes less obvious. A number of children
hold hands in a line, sometimes as many as twenty, often girls. They run
forward together, and when they have gathered momentum, the child at
one end, the leader, some say 'the bully of the playground', stops short
and swings the chain round, which means that the ones at the far end
have to go further and faster than the rest, and the endmost one is easily
jerked off his feet, and dragged along the ground.

This sport also goes under the names 'Chain', 'Drags', 'Tally-ho',
'Whizz Bang', 'Stretching Snake', and, especially in London, 'Long
Sausage'. In Canada and the United States it is 'Crack the Whip'.

§ Compare 'Bulliheisle' in Jamieson's *Scottish Dictionary*, *Supplement*,
1825:

> 'A play amongst boys, in which all having joined hands in a line,
> a boy at one of the ends stands still, and the rest all wind round
> him. The sport especially consists in an attempt to *heeze* or throw
> the whole mass over on the ground.'

Gomme, vol. ii, 1898, reports the game under the name 'Port the Helm'.

Tug of war

'Tug of War', whether between two people or two teams, is one of the
more elemental struggles of the playground. 'When some boys start
a tug of war with a girl's skipping rope, it usually ends up with the
girls going to tell the teacher on playground duty and the boys get into
trouble', reports a 9-year-old. However, a skipping rope is not the most
favoured rope for tug of war, merely the most available. 'It is best to
play with bull rope or your father's car rope because it does not snap so
easily', asserts a 10-year-old. Generally two leaders pick sides; the sides
take hold of the rope, with the heaviest person on each side at the end
because he makes the best anchor man, and each side attempts to pull

the other across a line marked on the ground, or, not infrequently, they pull until the other side lets go, for this is noticeably an activity in which short-trousered tempers quickly fray. 'Before long some people get sick and sit down', remarked another 10-year-old. 'The side that gets tired first usually loses. Some people are bad losers and start quarrelling, but others just say "Well it was only a game it doesn't matter".'

'Tug of War' is not as popular as it used to be, except among young children at the end of a singing game such as 'London Bridge is Falling Down', when the opposing leaders grip each other's hands, and the others line up behind them, each taking hold of the waist of the person in front. Only in the north, it seems, does tug of war continue to be an acceptable playground sport, and to be still called by the names of the opposing sides, as 'Rats and Rabbits', 'Soldiers and Sailors', and 'French and English'.

'French and English' was the usual name in England throughout the nineteenth century, being given in, for example, *The Boy's Own Book*, 1828, and *The Boy's Handy Book*, 1863. The significance of the name was that the side which lost were Frenchmen, while the winners considered they had earned the right to be called true Englishmen. The editor of *The Boy's Handy Book* comments:

'The sport was exceedingly popular in our young days, when the belief held by most Britons concerning their neighbours on the other side of the channel, was still embodied in the beautiful lines (*not* by Tennyson) which ran thus:

> Two skinny Frenchmen, and one
> Portugee,
> One jolly Englishman thrash 'em all three!

And all schoolboys used to believe it, too.'

Maclagan in *Games of Argyleshire*, 1901, p. 132, speaks of 'Tug of War, as it is now called, what used to be called "French and English" '; and Chesterton in *All Things Considered*, 1908, pp. 35–6, recalls the game of 'tug-of-war between French and English'. In the eighteenth century the name seems to have been 'Pull Devil, Pull Baker', for this is the title of a picture by William Hamilton, of which Bartolozzi made an engraving.

Yet earlier, in the sixteenth century, the name was apparently 'Sun and Moon'. John Higins in his *Nomenclator*, 1585 (and dictionaries following) defines the ancient Greek game *Dielcystinda* as 'a kinde of play wherein two companies of boyes holding hands all in a rowe, doe pull with hard holde one another, till one side be ouercome: it is called sunne and moone'. (Cf. Pollux, ix. 112.) It is probable that in the sixteenth century the opposing sides were formed by each player being asked privately whether he would be 'sun' or 'moon', in the way players today are invited to be an 'orange' or a 'lemon' in the game of 'Oranges and Lemons'; and it may be noted that a game of this kind, in which the players were asked whether they would be sun or moon to determine their side in a tug-of-war, was still being played in Alexander county, North Carolina, about 1928 (*North Carolina Folklore*, vol. i, 1952, p. 140).

Adders' nest

A bucket, upturned box, tin can, boy's coat, stone, or stick is placed on the ground, and the players hold hands in a circle around it. At a given signal each player tries, without breaking the circle, to force one or other of his neighbours to touch or knock against the object in the centre, while taking good care himself to keep away from it. When a person touches it he has been poisoned and has to retire. The game recommences without him, and continues until only two players are left, which is the 'really exciting part of the game' since these two are usually the strongest players.

A Banbury girl says: 'There is a special way of holding hands, called "the hand grip". You bend your fingers and so does everyone else. Then you grip each other's fingers.' Sometimes, particularly when girls are playing, they first skip round as if unconcerned, and then all of a sudden begin pushing. In Enfield boys stand together in a ring on a large drain. One boy shouts out 'This drain is poisonous!' They leap off, still holding hands, and the struggle starts to force someone back on to it. In London NW2, four or five children have been observed standing on a manhole cover chanting:

> Five little sausages, frying in a pan,
> One went pop, and the others went bang!

On the word 'bang' they jumped off, and instantly set about ensuring that someone other than themselves should be shoved back on to it. In Accrington, when only one player is left, and he has been declared the winner, the rest of the players come back and try to get the winner 'out'. If this player gets the rest out again he is declared 'double winner'. 'This game can last a long time,' remarks a 10-year-old, 'and usually the winner is very exhausted.'

Other names: 'Poison', 'Poison Pot', 'This Drain is Poisonous' (Enfield), 'Smudger' (alternative name to 'Adders' Nest' in Croydon), and 'Herring on a Plate' (Forfar). The game has been taken up by the physical training instructors under such crummy names as 'Poison Circle Tag', 'Knock the Block', and 'Pull them in the Ring'.

§ In the nineteenth century the game was often played with a heap of boys' caps in the centre of the ring, hence the names 'Bonnety' in Keith and Nairn (Gomme, vol. i, 1894, p. 43), 'Dinging the Bonnets' (*Games of Argyleshire*, 1901, p. 1), and 'Chimney Pots' or 'Upsetting the Chimney' (correspondents with London childhoods, *c.* 1910–15).

Bull in the ring

The name aptly describes the game. The players link hands and enclose one boy who has volunteered or, more likely, been manhandled into the centre, and is now obliged to smash his way out, not using his hands, but charging wherever he thinks the link is weakest. He is allowed to butt, barge, turn-about, take by surprise, and generally display the characteristics of a baited bull, bellowing, looking ferocious, and treading on people's feet in an attempt to weaken their resolution; while those forming the ring 'shout and jeer' in return, but must merely use their bodies to stop the bull from getting out, 'not kick'. Formerly, when the bull escaped, he was chased by the members of the ring, and he who caught him became the next bull. This is still sometimes the rule in Golspie, where the game is also known as 'Bull in the Barn'. In Dovenby, Cumberland, where the game is called 'Farmer and Bull', there is a farmer who remains outside the ring, helping to support the circle whenever needed, and when the bull breaks through the bull has to catch the farmer to make him the new bull.

§ This game seems to be less played today than in the nineteenth century, when it was frequently recorded, e.g. in *Suffolk Words*, 1823, 'Bull in the Park'; *Youth's Own Book of Healthful Amusements*, 1845, 'Bull in the Ring'; *Nursery Fun*, 1868, 'Bull in the Barn'; *Cheshire Glossary*, 1877, 'Cry Notchil'; *Folk-Lore Journal*, vol. v, 1887, p. 50, 'Pig in the Middle and Can't Get Out'; *Traditional Games*, vol. i, 1894, 'Tod i' the Faul' ('Fox in the Fold'); and *Games of Argyleshire*, 1901, p. 239, 'Breaking through the Fence'.

A more ritualistic form of the game, known as 'Here I Bake and Here I Brew', is described in *The Girl's Own Book*, Boston, 1832. The girl within the ring went round saying:

> Here I bake, here I brew,
> Here I make my wedding-cake,
> Here I mean to break through.

A yet more formal version was called 'Garden Gate' or 'Have you the Key of the Garden Gate?' It was recorded by Gomme in 1894, and was still being played by children in Somerset in 1922 (Macmillan MSS.). The player in the middle sang:

> Open wide the garden gate,
> The garden gate, the garden gate;
> Open wide the garden gate,
> And let me through.

The players in the circle, forming a 'garden fence', danced round as they replied:

> Get the key of the garden gate,
> The garden gate, the garden gate;
> Get the key of the garden gate,
> And let yourself through.

The prisoner cried:

> I've lost the key of the garden gate,
> So what am I to do?

Still dancing, the others sang:

> Then you may stop, may stop all night,
> Within the gate,
> Until you're strong enough, you know,
> To break a way through.

Only after these time-taking preliminaries, which provide an example of how a basically simple game can be embroidered when it is popular (see Introduction, Vol. 1, p. 19), does the player in the middle attempt to break out.

In another game on the same principle, 'The Wolf and the Lamb', played at Fraserburgh in 1892 (Gomme, vol. ii, p. 399), a wolf is outside the circle, a lamb within, and the wolf has to try and break *into* the circle. According to N. M. Penzer, editor of Basile's *Pentamerone*, 1634, the players in the Neapolitan game 'Rota de li cauce' similarly tried to keep one player from breaking into their circle, forming a wheel of kicks. However, from the text of the *Pentamerone* (the opening paragraph) it appears more likely that the player was inside the circle and attempting to get out.

Red Rover

This game, which is a particular favourite with girls in Scotland, is played with two sides who face each other about five yards apart. The players on one side link hands (sometimes they grip each other's wrists), and advance and retreat chanting:

> Red Rover, Red Rover,
> Please send someone over.

In Cumnock they name the player they want:

> Red Rover, Red Rover,
> We call *Mary* over.

In Aberdeen they issue the challenge:

Red Rover, Red Rover,
We'll bowl *Mary* over.

The player named charges the opposing team, throwing her weight at a weak link, trying to break through (one child is reported to have had her arm broken in resisting the charge), and if she gets through she is free to return to her own side, and, in some places (e.g. Cumnock and Glasgow), she takes someone with her. If she fails she has to join the other side. The sides take turns in naming someone. 'This continues until there is one big line of people instead of two teams.' In England, where the game is only rarely played, they sometimes have a variant (e.g. at Crewe) in which there are two dens. One person in 'on' and the others link hands and run across to the other den. The person who is 'on' tries to break the chain, and if he succeeds the two players between whom he broke join him, until there is only one player left free. Occasionally the game is played with all the members of one side rushing together against the other side.

§ The history of 'Red Rover', which is also played in Canada, the United States, Australia, and New Zealand, is obscure. It is similar to the game 'Il Re di Spagna' played in Calabria, in which the King of Spain and his men oppose the King of France, and the King of Spain dispatches one of his men to break the chain formed by the French (Lumbroso, *Giochi*, 1967, pp. 177–8). It is also much the same as 'Der Kaiser schickt Soldaten aus' played in Austria (Kampmüller, *Kinderspiele*, 1965, p. 151), and the game called 'King' played in Czechoslovakia (described by Brewster, 1953, p. 170). No record of 'Red Rover' has been found in England or Scotland earlier than the Macmillan MSS., 1922, and it would seem to be an importation from the Continent were it not for a Scots game 'Jockie Rover' which possesses certain similar features. Walter Gregor told Gomme (*Traditional Games*, vol. ii, 1898, pp. 435–6) that in 'Jockie Rover', as played at Dyke, one player, the chaser, had a 'den', and before he emerged called out:

Jockie Rover, three times over,
If you do not look out, I'll gie you a blover.

He had then to run, keeping his hands clasped in front of him, and catch someone by crowning him on the head.

'When he catches one he unclasps his hands, and makes for the den along with the one caught. The players close in upon them, and beat them with their caps. The two now join hands, and before leaving the den repeat the same words, and give chase to catch another. When another is caught, the three run to the den, followed by the others pelting them.

During the time they are running to catch another player, every attempt is made by the others to break the band by rushing on two outstretched arms, either from before or from behind. Every time one is taken or the band broken, all already taken rush to the den, beaten by those not taken.'

It will be seen by reference to 'Warning' and 'Widdy' that this is a Scots version of the chasing game once general in England. In fact at Tarry Croys, near Keith, it is still remembered that children used to chant:

> I warn ye once, I warn ye twice,
> I warn ye three times over;
> I warn all you Buckie wives
> To flee from Jack the Rover.

The game was also played by boys in Brooklyn about 1890 under the name of 'Red Lion' (*Journal of American Folklore*, vol. iv, p. 245), with the challenge:

> Red Lion, Red Lion,
> Come out of your den,
> Whoever you catch
> Will be one of your men.

And in addition the boys played a side-to-side catching game they called 'Red Rover' in which the Rover, in the middle of the street, called out a boy by name who had to run from one sidewalk to the other, and, if caught, had to stay and help catch the others (cf. 'British Bulldog', version 2). In Maryland, too, in the 1940s, children ran back and forth across an open space, being challenged by the chaser with the words:

> Red Rover, Red Rover,
> All I catch must come over.

> Red Rover, Red Rover,
> Let's everybody run over.

Those caught joined the chaser (Howard MSS.). This is not dissimilar from 'Red Rover' as played today at Crewe, in which the free players try to break the linked hands of those attempting to catch them. But it does not explain how 'Red Rover' has come to be played in its present form around the English-speaking world. It seems that at some period a game of breaking through people's hands such as 'Forcing the City Gates', described in Bancroft's *Games for the Playground*, 1909, pp. 89–90, and there taken from I. T. Headland's *The Chinese Boy and Girl*, 1901, was grafted on to the old game of 'Jockie Rover'. (Compare also 'King of the Barbarees' below.)

King of the Barbarees

This rhythmic and ceremonious game is much like 'Red Rover' in that the objective is to break apart two linked hands, or two pairs of linked hands. It is played throughout Great Britain with little variation, and is here described by an 11-year-old Bristol girl:

> 'My favourite game is "The King of Barbarees". This is how you play it.
>
> There is a King, Queen, Princess, Captain of the Guard, and some soldiers, also a Castle which consists of two children holding hands. The king tells the Captain of the Guard to march round the Castle singing,
>
>> "Will you surrender, will you surrender,
>> The King of the Barbarees?"
>
> The Castle replies,
>> "We won't surrender, we won't surrender,
>> The King of the Barbarees."
>
> Captain,
>> "I'll tell the king, I'll tell the king,
>> The King of the Barbarees."

Castle,

> "You can tell the king, you can tell the
> king,
> The King of the Barbarees."

The Captain goes back to the King and, stamping his foot,
says,

> "They won't surrender, they won't
> surrender,
> The King of the Barbarees."

The King says, "Take two of my trusty soldiers."
The soldiers follow the Captain and the rhyme is repeated
again,

> "Will you surrender, will you surrender,
> The King of the Barbarees?"

This goes on until all the soldiers have joined the ring, then
the King says "Take my daughter". Next to go is the Queen,
and last of all the King. The King says "We'll break down
your gates," and after the rhyme has been said again with
the King joining in, everybody makes a line with the King
in front. He takes a run and jumps on the hands that are
linked together and tries to break through them, while the
two who are the Castle count to ten. If he does not break
through, he goes back and one of the soldiers has a turn.
They all jump on the Castle, one at a time, and try to break
it down. If they do not succeed the Castle has won.'

In Scotland and Ireland the king is often referred to as 'King George',
and sometimes the game is so named. Other names: 'King of the
Barbarie' (Market Drayton), 'King of the Bambarines' (Cumnock), and
'Gates of Barbaroo' (Blackburn).

§ Alice Gomme, *Traditional Games*, vol. i, 1894, pp. 18–21, gives only
four versions, all from the south of England, which does not indicate
that the game had the popularity or distribution in the nineteenth century
that it attained between the wars, and still largely retains. Her earliest
recording had been printed only the year before, 'The Tower of Barbaree',

in Gurdon's *Suffolk Folk-Lore*, 1893, p. 63. Yet the game seems to have been long known on the Continent. A version called 'La tour, prends garde' is given in Marion Dumersan's *Chansons et rondes enfantines*, 1846, p. 37, which is little different from the English game. Two girls hold hands to form the tower, and the other players are the Duke of Bourbon, his son, and his soldiers. Before the tower is attacked a colonel and a captain are sent to the tower and sing: 'La tour prends garde de te laisser abattre.'

> The tower replies: 'Nous n'avons garde, nous n'avons garde, de
>   nous laisser abattre.'
> The colonel says: 'J'irai me plaindre au duque de Bourbon.'
> The tower: 'Va t'en te plaindre au duque de Bourbon.'

The colonel then complains to the Duke. The Duke gives him soldiers with which to attack the tower, and eventually comes himself. One by one they attempt to break through the girls' hands, and the player who succeeds in invading the tower is proclaimed Duke for the next game.

Honey pots

This is another game in which the pleasantries of feminine play-acting are the prelude to a sharp test of strength. One player is selected shop-keeper, one a customer, and the rest crouch in a row ('bop down' says a Suffolk girl), and clasp their hands under their knees, pretending to be honey pots. The customer arrives, inquires about the price of honey, and pretends to sample the various pots, touching each child on the head and licking her finger. She chooses one of the pots, and she and the shop-keeper proceed to weigh it, lifting the child by the arms, and swinging or shaking her, or otherwise attempting to break her grip, until they are satisfied that she is sound. She is then purchased. But if she 'breaks', the pot is rejected, and the player has to stand out. This continues until all the pots have either been bought or cast aside.

§ The absurdity of this amusement is almost evidence in itself of its antiquity, and it has certainly been one of the joys of childhood for the past 150 years. 'Honey-pots' was described as 'a common game' among girls in Edinburgh in *Blackwood's Magazine*, August (part ii), 1821, p. 36; was listed amongst old Suffolk games by Edward Moor in 1823;

and under the name 'Hinnie-pigs' was described by Mactaggart in his *Gallovidian Encyclopedia*, 1824, as a game for boys:

> 'The boys who try this sport sit down in rows, hands locked be-
> neath their hams. Round comes one of them, the honey-merchant,
> who feels those who are sweet or sour, by lifting them by the
> arm-pits, and giving them three shakes; if they stand these with-
> out the hands unlocking below, they are then sweet and saleable,
> fit for being office-bearers of other ploys.'

The popularity of the game through the years can be gauged by the number of times it has been described or mentioned, e.g. by the editor of *A Nosegay, for the Trouble of Culling*, 1813, who was clearly very familiar with it; by Hugh Miller, *My Schools and Schoolmasters*, 1852, ch. iii (played by the apprentice Francie 'though grown a tall lad'); by Henry Mayhew, *London Labour*, vol. i, 1851, p. 152 (played by a little watercress seller aged eight); by Mrs Valentine, *The Home Book*, 1867; by Alice Gomme, *Traditional Games*, vol. i, 1894 (many accounts); and by Norman Douglas, *London Street Games*, 1916. In some places before the First World War special words were chanted sing-song fashion while the honey pot was being tested, for instance, at Helmsley in Yorkshire:

> Is she rotten, is she sound,
> Is she worth a million pound?
> Toss her up and toss her down
> She is worth a million pound.

It is from the game that a crouched position has come to be known as a 'honey pot'.

The game is also popular amongst little girls in Italy, and is usually played almost exactly as in Britain under the names 'Laveggio', 'Pentole', and 'Pignatte'. The two children who test the pots go round patting the players' heads, and asking 'Sarà rotta, o accomodata?' 'Is it broken, or mended?' The child selected is then swung by her arms and if she holds she is a good pot, but if she does not hold she is a cracked pot, and is put in another place, and may eventually have to pay a forfeit (M. M. Lumbroso, *Giochi*, 1967, pp. 11–13). Signora Maroni Lumbroso also gives an account of the game 'Pignatte' as played at Forenza, near Potenza. Here one of the two players who are standing whispers a colour to each pot. When she has finished the other player approaches and taps her on the shoulder, saying 'tup, tup'. 'Who is it?' 'I am the Madonna.' 'What do you want?' 'I want a pot.' 'What kind?' The Madonna names a colour. If there is a pot of this colour the crouching player is tested, and according to whether she is found to be a good pot or a bad one she is deposited in paradise or hell. (Cf. 'Jams'.)

A similar game, 'Les Pots de Fleurs', was played in Paris in the nineteenth century. A number of little girls crouched down, clasping their hands under their legs, and sticking their arms out like the handles of flower pots. Three further girls stood facing them who represented God Almighty, the Virgin Mary, and the Devil. A fourth player was a flower-seller, and a fifth his helper. Each of the pots of flowers was given the name of a plant, and according to Rolland, *Jeux de l'enfance*, 1883, pp. 134–5, the following dialogue took place:

> Le bon Dieu: Pan! pan!
> Le marchand: Qui est-ce qui est là?
> Le bon Dieu: C'est le bon Dieu qui vient
>   acheter un pot de fleurs.
> Le marchand: Laquelle voulez-vous?

God Almighty named a plant. The flower-seller and his helper lifted the plant up by the handles ('c'est-à-dire par les bras') and brought it to God Almighty. Then the Virgin Mary and the Devil made purchases in their turn. When all the pots had been sold, and successfully carried to their purchasers, those flower-pots acquired by 'le bon Dieu' and 'la Sainte-Vierge' made horns at those purchased by the Devil. It is possibly relevant that when 'Honey Pots' was played in York about 1910, and a girl's grip broke while she was being tested, she was (according to a correspondent) slapped on the bottom with cries of 'Fire and brimstone'. The game clearly has affinity with the latter part of 'Mother, the Cake is Burning' (q.v.).

Statues

'Statues' is a contest to find who can best act and pose under somewhat trying conditions. The players, usually girls, line up at a wall, or on top of the wall if it is not too high, and hold out their right hands. One person, who is out in front and may be known as the 'puller' or 'twister' (in Scotland the 'birler' or 'burreller'), pulls each person from the wall in turn, either pulling as hard as she can, or giving each player a chance to say how she shall be pulled, asking:

'Do you want egg, bacon, or chips?' (*Egg is a slow twizzle, bacon a fast one, chips a very fast one.*)

Or in Bristol: 'Do you want bread, or honey, or wedding cake?' (*Fast or slow or medium.*)

Or in Edinburgh: 'Salt, pepper, mustard, or vinegar?' (*Vinegar is an extra hard pull with a swing to it.*)

Or in Market Rasen: 'Do you want blood, water, pop, or curtsy?' (*Blood you pull the person out fast, water gently, pop you go round in a circle with them, and curtsy you take them out gently and leave them in a curtsy position.*)

When the player has been pulled she must 'stand how she has been thrown', remaining motionless as if a statue. The puller then tells the statues what she wants them to be, for instance, monster, fairy, mouse, clown, or dancer, either giving all the players the same part or each a different one, and commands 'Clockwork begin'. The statues have to come to life, and do the things they think monsters or fairies, or whatever they are supposed to be, would do, until the puller commands 'Clock-work stop', when—as one boy put it—'you've got to take a shape': the players must adopt the posture they think most appropriate to their set character. The puller then commands 'Lights out' or 'Lanterns shut' and they have to close their eyes. It is now the puller's job to judge which statue has the ugliest or funniest or most beautiful or most monstrous face and posture according to the pose that has been ordered. She goes round tapping those she does not think are so good until only one player is left standing motionless with her eyes shut. The rest silently make a circle round this last statue, and then suddenly begin dancing round, and shouting 'Wake up sleeping beauty', 'You're the pretty lady' (in Wigan, 'You're the big soft jelly baby'), and this person is the winner and becomes the puller in the next game.

Names: 'Statues' (the usual name); 'Bread and Honey' (Bristol); 'Clockwork' (Scarborough); 'Clockwork Statues' (Basingstoke); 'Egg and Bacon' (Helston, Norwich, Wolstanton); 'Egg, Bacon, and Chips' (Alton); 'Hot, Cold, or Boiling' (Wandsworth); 'Pepper and Salt' (Isle of Arran); 'Penny in the Slot' (Peterborough); 'Salt, Mustard, Vinegar, Pepper' (Swansea); 'Stookies' (Edinburgh, Forfar, and New Cumnock).

'Statues' is also played in simpler forms in which the test is no more than to try who can keep still the longest (in St Andrews this is known as 'Dead Lions'), or who can keep a straight face the longest despite being laughed at or tickled.

In Glasgow a similar game, usually played on a slope, is called 'What Do You Want?' A player on the top of the slope is asked 'What do you want?' and may reply 'Gun' or 'Arrow' or 'Atom bomb' or whatever he fancies. He is then shot at 'and has to make a good fall, and when he has finished falling he lies very still as if he was dead'. The player whose act of dying was the most spectacular is then declared the winner. In Edmonton, Canada, the game is called 'The Deadest', and after each of the players has been killed the competition is to find which player is the deadest.

§ The present elaborate form of 'Statues' seems to be a recent development and was not known to our correspondents whose childhoods covered the period 1890–1930. In *London Street Games*, 1916, p. 41, the players were merely pulled, and took up a posture 'sometimes pretty but mostly ugly', which was then judged. In Austria, today, players are simply twizzled, freeze where they land, and then perform appropriate actions at command ('Figurenwerfen' in *Oberösterreichische Kinderspiele*, 1965, p. 162). In Italy the children are not even pulled, they merely adopt poses as instructed ('Le Belle Statuine' in *Giochi*, 1967, pp. 193–7).

Leapfrog

They say leapfrog can be played with any number, large or small (even by only one if there are posts or milk churns about), and it is a good game with just two: one bending down and the other vaulting over, running forward a few steps and making a back for the first boy to vault over. In this way leapfrog is 'quite useful', or so an 11-year-old asserts, 'because if anyone has to go a long distance walk it helps one to get along'. But it is more fun if there are more players. They begin by lining up; one person bends down, and the first in the line jumps over him and runs forward a few steps, and makes a back himself; the second in the line jumps over each of these two players and runs forward a few more steps and makes a third back. Each player who follows has one more back to leap over, and makes another back himself, until everyone is stooping. Then the player who first bent down stands up, and himself jumps along the line of backs, and makes a further back at the other end of the line, and the second person who bent down gets up as soon as he has been jumped over, and starts jumping, and so on. In this way the game is continuous. Whoever is last in the line gets up and jumps over those in front of him, and whoever has cleared all the backs makes a new back at the far end of the line. The sport becomes more exciting if the last in the line stands up as soon as he has been jumped over, and straightway follows after the boy who has jumped over him: then there may be almost as many boys jumping as there are boys bending down, and when a boy comes to the end of the line of backs he has to be quick about bending down himself, for the person he first jumped over may be close on his heels ready, in his turn, to complete the line of jumps. Those who can are gasping 'Keep the kettle boiling' to encourage the flow of jumpers which—in theory—may ripple onwards around the playground without stopping until the school bell rings. But the sport is not as simple as it looks.

If a player does not vault properly, placing his hands evenly on the back of the bent figure and leaping lightly at the same time, the result, says an 11-year-old, will be 'an unartistic heap of humans' on the ground. And as another boy remarks, 'There is only one special rule and that is "Do not push people over when you are jumping over them".' In fact, holding oneself steady while being jumped over requires almost as much effort as does the jumping. When a person bends down he presents either his backside to the jumper, placing one leg forward with knee bent, resting his hands firmly on his knee, and tucking his head well in;[18] or, perhaps more often, he bends down sideways to the oncomers, and grips an ankle. The higher the back he makes the more difficult it will be to jump over him, and the more likely he is to be knocked over.

Likewise the nearer he is to the previous person who bent down the more difficult it will be to jump over him; and sometimes they insist that a player runs five or six yards before he bends down, while sometimes, to make the sport more difficult, the rule is that he must take only three or four steps after he has jumped. Sometimes they play 'Higher and Higher', when those bending down make their backs a little higher after each turn, and a person who can no longer get over has to drop out. Sometimes they play in a circle and one person goes on jumping until he falls. Occasionally the rule is that a jumper may use only one hand when he vaults, a feat which needs practice. And sometimes those making the backs are allowed to sink down as the leaper places his hands on their back which, far from making it easier for the leaper 'may mean that he goes flat on his face'.[19]

§ The only evidence that leapfrog was played in the ancient world, according to de Fouquières, is a decoration on a cyclix showing a child crouching down while another child jumps over him (*Cabinet Durand*, de Witte, no. 706). In the Middle Ages, too, the sport seems to have been uncommon, but it had become popular by the sixteenth century. Gargantua played 'a crocqueteste', a name happily glossed in the caption to a woodcut depicting leapfrog in *Les Trente-six figures*, 1587:

> Ils sautent tous, en criant couppe teste,
> L'vn par sus l'autre, est-ce pas ieu honneste.

Bruegel shows six boys playing leapfrog in his picture of children's games painted in 1560. Borcht shows anthropomorphized apes playing it in his picture 'Spelende Apen' about 1580. And Shakespeare's Henry the Fifth seems to have regarded excellence at 'leape-frogge' almost as a token of manliness (v. ii, in the Folio).[20]

Other references occur in Samuel Rowlands, *The Letting of Humours Blood*, 1600, D8b; Thomas Dekker, *The Seuen deadlie Sinns*, 1606, iv; Ben Jonson, *Bartholomew Fayre*, 1614, I. i (1631); William Hawkins, *Apollo Shrouing*, 1626, p. 5; *The Independent Whig*, 1720, no. 32, ¶ 13, 'Hop Frog'; Abel Boyer, *Dictionnaire*, 1727, s.v. *La Poste*, 'Skip Frog'.

The game is depicted in the first children's book of games *A Little Pretty Pocket-Book*, 1744 (1760, p. 44); it is nicely described in Henry Brooke's *The Fool of Quality*, vol. i, 1766, p. 79; and a character in *The Book of Games*, 1805, p. 110, says that although there are many types of jumping 'leap-frog beats all those hollow'. In *The Boy's Country Book*, 1839, p. 219, William Howitt, who went to Ackworth School in Yorkshire around 1805, recalled that he had 'often seen the whole number—180—making one long line at leap-frog'.

Dialect names: 'Hog over Hie' (Suffolk, 1823); 'Hop-Frog-over-the-Dog' (Lincolnshire, 1894); 'Lankister-lowp' (Lancashire, 1882); 'Lantie Lawp' (Cumberland, 1915); 'Frog Jump' (County Cork, 1938); 'Frog-Lope' (Yorkshire, 1892).

In France the game is generally 'le saute-mouton' or 'le coupe-tête', in Italy 'saltamontone' or 'salta cavalletta', in Denmark 'springe buk', and in Holland 'haasje-over'. In Germany, according to Böhme

(*Deutsches Kinderspiel*, 1897, p. 591) it is 'Hammelsprung' when a boy stands sideways to the leapers, and 'Bocksprung' when he is turned away from them, a distinction which is borne out by Kampmüller's description of 'Bockspringen' in present-day Austria (*Oberösterreichische Kinderspiele*, 1965, p. 110).

The leapfrog games which follow were clearly more popular before the First World War than they are today, even if they were not as numerous as appears from Norman Douglas's catalogue in *London Street Games*, 1916 (pp. 24–34).

Gentle Jack

This is leapfrog with additional hazards. In north London they start by dipping and one boy is picked to bend down, and one to be leader. They jump one at a time over the boy who has made a back, and run round ready to jump over him again, the leader coming last. After the leader has jumped he gives a command such as 'kick him', 'pull his hair', 'give him a cauliflower' (twist his ear), and each boy as he jumps, has to do as instructed. Should one of them while vaulting fail to offer his respects to the stooping figure, he himself must make a back and become the object of attention. Thus the game proceeds, needing to stop only when 'we've all had enough of it'.

§ It is apparent from Edmund Routledge's *Every Boy's Book*, 1868, p. 9, that responsibility for devising this amusement is not to be credited to a modern young bully. In this enumeration of the feats that can be performed while jumping over a boy's back, Routledge writes:

> 'The next trick is "knuckling", — that is to say, overing with the hands clenched; the next, "slapping", which is performed by placing one hand on the boy's back, and hitting him with the other, while overing; the last, "spurring", or touching him up with the heel.'

We find that Victorian writers for the young were, on occasion, more considerable realists than those who have succeeded them. Routledge prefaced his description with the remark: 'This game is capable of being varied to any extent by an ingenious boy.'

Spanish leapfrog

'Spanish leapfrog is similar to ordinary leapfrog but requires more skill', says an 11-year-old Dulwich girl. 'You play this with as many players as possible, and while leaping over the person's back the leader places a cap (or any object) on her back. The other players have to leap over the object as well as the person's back, trying not to knock it off. If they do knock it off they change with the person bending down.'

§ This game was formerly known as 'Spanish Fly' (and is so termed in *Games and Sports for Young Boys*, 1859, p. 16; *The Boy's Handy Book*, 1863, p. 6; *The Boy's Own Paper*, 12 November 1887, p. 103). There was a second way of playing the game in which every player as he jumped deposited his cap or rolled-up handkerchief on the person's back, so that the difficulty of surmounting the pile increased with each turn. Sometimes further complications were introduced, particularly regarding the orderly removal of the caps, which might, for instance, be picked up by the teeth as the jump was made.

Other names: 'Accroshay' (Cornwall, *Folk-Lore Journal*, vol. v, 1887, p. 60); 'French Flies' (*Antrim and Down Glossary*, 1880); 'Leap Frog with Bonnets' (Golspie, 1892, and still played there 1953); 'Cappy' (*Northumberland Words*, 1892); 'Cap-it' (*Warwickshire Word-Book*, 1896); 'Hot Pies' (*Games of Argyleshire*, 1901), and 'Chimney Pots' (Vauxhall Bridge Road, *c.* 1905).

Foot-an-a-half

Of the eighty games described by pupils of Spennymoor Grammar Technical School, 'Foot-an-a-Half' was fourth in popularity, after 'Hum a Dum Dum', 'Split the Kipper', and 'Skipping'. This game, an exacting one, needs about eight well-matched players, one of whom is chosen to be 'down' (often 'the last person who arrives at the place where we are going to play'), and he takes up the leapfrog stance, bending over with his back to the other players, while a line is drawn or a stick placed on the ground to mark his position. He chooses one player to be 'foot-an-a-half', and sometimes a second player, designated 'leader', who he thinks is a good jumper; for this second player may be able to relieve him of his position in the game, which is merely that of vaulting-horse. The foot-an-a-half leaps over him, and the player who is down has to move forward to wherever foot-an-a-half's back foot landed. Foot-an-a-half then looks at the distance between the stick or line and the doubled-up figure, and calls the type of step, or steps, which the others may take beyond the line to make their leap.

> 'He may shout a number like "a oner", this means that the
> rest of the team have to jump over the person's back from
> the line, taking only one step. He may say "a standing
> oner", which means that the team has to stand on the
> line and jump. If however he says "a running oner" then
> it is usually a difficult jump, and the persons jumping are
> entitled to a run.'

The players jump in turn, the leader jumping last, and if they all do it successfully, the foot-an-a-half jumps again, and, as before, the boy bending down moves to wherever the foot-an-a-half lands. Since there is now more space between the mark and the boy to be jumped over, the foot-an-a-half probably allows a further step or hop to be taken beyond the line, and this goes on until one or more players fail to do the leap: either funking it, or not getting over, or taking too many steps beyond the mark, or knocking over the bending boy. When this happens the last person in the line to fail makes the new back.

Properly played, the point of the game is that the foot-an-a-half has to call a jump which, he hopes, one of the players will be unable to manage, although it must be a jump he himself is able to do; while should the leader be able to do it with less steps than the foot-an-a-half has decreed, the foot-an-a-half has to become the vaulting horse. Whenever there is a change in this role the game starts at the beginning again.

At Ponders End, Enfield, where the game is known as 'Long Man', the steps which the 'captain' names are customarily fancy ones, similar to those in 'May I?' (q.v.). Thus he may say that the jump should be 'Broad and straight over' (one standing jump from the line, and then leap), or 'a scissor' (a jump landing with feet astride, and another bringing feet together again), or a certain number of 'pigeon toes' (heel-to-toe steps), or 'an umbrella' (a jump landing face-about, always given in pairs so that the player ends facing the right way), or, if the distance between the line and the bending boy (known as 'it') warrants it, he gives instructions for a sequence of movements such as 'One broad, six pigeon toes, and straight over'.

In Forfar, where 'Foot-an-a-Half' is played in much the same way, a 14-year-old says it is a rule that if the person jumping should knock over the one who is bending down, 'It is a "bull" and he is out, but if the person that is "down" collapses under the person's weight, he can cry "Touch Bill" and the other person can cry "No Touch Bill" before the other person can say his part.'[21]

§ Several Spennymoor boys remarked that they could not understand why the game was called 'Foot-an-a-Half'. This was formerly the name of a similar game in which, after each player had had his turn and jumped successfully, the boy bending down moved forward a standard 'foot and a half' (the length of his boot plus its width) and automatically increased the difficulty of the jump for the next round. 'Foot and a Half' was played at Sedgley Park School, about 1805 (Husenbeth, *History*, 1856, p. 106); while in the south of England the game was known as 'Fly the Garter' (referred to by Keats in a letter to John Hamilton Reynolds, 3 May 1818; and by Bob Sawyer in *Pickwick Papers*, 1837, ch. xxxvii).[22] The forerunner of the present game seems to have been 'Foot and an O'er' described in *The Youth's Own Book of Healthful Amusements*, 1845, pp. 35–8:

'This is a famous play in Lancashire; for go where you will on the cold, wintry day, or the clear summer's morning, there are sure to be some employed at "Foot and an O'er". As many may play as please. In the first place, the lads draw lots as to who shall stoop first; and he, you know, who is unfortunate enough to lose, is obliged to set his back. The first youth who jumps over is called the leader, after whom all the rest must follow: the last that leaps is styled the Footer, who when he has jumped, marks with the toe of his shoe the distance he leaped beyond the lad stooping, and the latter has to remove, and put his heel exactly to the mark of the footer ... But great as is the distance, if the leader does it not, and the footer does, the former must put down his back, and take the place of the lad that is now down. If the footer cannot perform what the leader has failed to do, the latter will *not* have to stoop, but may take the leap at one and an o'er, as it is termed; which means that the leader jump once from the mark as near to the boy as he pleases, and then takes a stand jump over: that is called one and an o'er.'[23]

The rule that the first jumper shall decree the steps which the others may take between the line and the boy who is down, appears in the version of the game called 'Last Man's Jump' in *The Boy's Own Book*, 1855, p. 32:

> 'The one who is down ... goes to the spot where the last player, who is called the "cutter", alighted at. The best player is generally chosen by him for the cutter, so that he may, by manoeuvring, or jumping a good distance, cause another to be down, and so relieve him. The one who goes first has the privilege of taking a jump, a hop, and jump,—or a hop, stride, and jump between the garter [the starting mark] and the back, before going over; but whichever he does, the others must follow, except the cutter, who is allowed to run to the back, so as to enable him to take a better spring.'

Brewster, *American Nonsinging Games*, 1953, p. 106, gives the name of the game in Illinois as 'One and Over'; and Culin, 'Street Games of Boys in Brooklyn', *Journal of American Folklore*, vol. iv, 1891, pp. 227–8, gives the name 'Head and Footer'.

Jumping games

There are several competitive jumping games, on the principle of 'Foot-an-a-Half', for which sudden crazes will arise, and then, when it has become clear who the best jumpers are in the school, everybody becomes sick of the craze, and the games seem to be forgotten, only to reappear afresh two or three years later.

One a Foot. This might be described as the girls' version of 'Foot-an-a-Half'. 'Out of the people playing a leader is chosen, usually a volunteer. The girl puts two sticks together, then she runs and jumps from the front of the sticks, and where her heel lands the second stick is placed. Then she says whether it is a "noner" or "oner" or "twoer". The people following must jump as she did. If it is a "oner" the people jumping are only allowed to put one foot once in between the two sticks. The game goes on until one person is left in. This person is the leader for the next game' (Girl, 13, Spennymoor).

Fly. ' "Fly" is the name of a game where you use six sticks and place them about a foot apart, and have to jump over each stick without touching it and without jumping over a space between two sticks. The last girl to jump over takes a long jump and calls the number of a stick. They put the stick of this number where she jumped to, and the game goes on until the spaces between the sticks get so big that people can't jump them. The person who can jump furthest is the last girl next time' (Girl, *c.* 11, Portsmouth). 'Fly' appears to be well known in Australia, but there only the last stick (or stone) is moved forward.

Leapers. 'You get a piece of chalk and draw an oblong square, draw a line across two inches past the middle, get a dice, and throw on to the line. You stand about two feet back from it and try and leap over the dice. If you can leap over the dice you are a leaper and have one point. You keep moving the chalk line back and see how many points you get in half an hour' (Girl, 9, Wolstanton).

Baby Leapfrog. 'A lot of people lie down with their backs up in the air. The very last person who is at the end jumps over the others' backs. When she has jumped over the last one she lies down. The first person she jumped over, gets up and starts to jump over the others and so on till they have all had a shot and then they begin again' (Girl, 10, Kingarth, Isle of Bute).

§ This trivial amusement might be passed over as the artless invention of a group of little girls seeking an afternoon's diversion, were it not that the following report, from nearby Argyllshire, appeared in *Folk-Lore*, vol. xvi, 1905, p. 78:

> '*Leum Maighiche.* (Hare's Leap.) Several take part in this. One lies down on the ground on his back; another jumps over him and lies down where he has landed parallel to the one already down. Another leaps over both and likewise lies down till all are down, or the distance that can be leapt is covered. The first to go down then rises and leaps over the party, followed in rapid succession by the remainder, the fun largely consisting in the rapidity in which they follow each other. If one is slow in clearing the way for his successor, he is said to be "run down", and must retire from the game. This was also played in Orkney.

This, in turn, may be compared with 'Loup the Bullocks' in Mactaggart's *Gallovidian Encyclopedia*, 1824, p. 320, in which the players plant themselves in a row on 'all fours' about two yards from each other, and are jumped over in similar fashion.

Hi Jimmy Knacker

Of all street games this is the one grown men recall most readily, and with the greatest complacency, possibly because it is the toughest of the games, the one in which players are most frequently hurt, and which requires the greatest amount of stamina, *esprit de corps*, and indeed fortitude.[24] Two sides are chosen with four to six boys, or sometimes girls, on each side ('It's best to get the big hefty ones on your side'), and they toss to see which side shall jump first. The side which loses has to be the 'down' side and 'make a back'. One boy, variously known as the 'pillar', 'pillow', 'cushion', or 'buffer', stands with his back against something firm, as a tree, wall, or lamp-post, and sometimes interlocks his fingers in front of him to form a cup. The next in the team, usually one of the smaller boys, stoops down placing his forehead in the cup, with the crown of his head against the cushion's stomach, and holds on to the cushion's waist or legs. The next boy in size comes behind him, placing his head under the second boy's legs and gripping his thighs; the rest of the side follow behind, interlocking in similar fashion to present one long back, the biggest boy taking last place, since he generally has to support most weight, and makes a higher and more awkward back for the other side to jump over.

The other side have now to jump on to the backs of the 'down' side, an obligation for which they show no reluctance, rushing forward one at a time, placing their hands on the back of the end boy, and leaping with as much force and weight as they have in them, for if they crush the backs of those they jump on, and bring them to the ground, they can command another turn. Usually the best jumper in the side runs first, for he must jump over three or four backs, landing far enough forward to leave room for the other members of his side to mount behind him. This they attempt to do, among 'many angry shouts and groans' from those underneath, and often try to concentrate their weight on one of the weaker boys who they think can be made to collapse. Thus a boy who has not tucked his head in properly may find himself with another lad far heavier than himself sitting on his neck. Arguments start, and retribution may be taken if a jumping boy lands with his knees on someone's back, or if anyone starts edging forward (known as 'creeping') to make room for those who are to follow, or when anyone takes a long time before he jumps. In some places those about to jump give notice of their approach with cries such as 'Olley olley' or 'More weight' or 'Warnie, I'm a-comin' (London), or

'Two stone heave-ho!' (Wigan), or 'Weights coming on' (Accrington), or 'Rum-stick-a-bum, here I come' (Nottingham). But it is not wholly a joy-ride for the mounting side. Should one of them fall off, or put a foot on the ground to steady himself, the whole side pays forfeit, and has to dismount and make a back for the others to jump on.[25] Frequently there is little room for the last player to jump on and he clings precariously to the backs of the riders in front of him, while those underneath shake and bounce to intensify his discomfort. Usually the team has to stay mounted for a given length of time. A Croydon boy claimed that they must remain seated for five minutes while those underneath strove to dislodge them. In general they have to remain seated (or at least keep their feet from the ground) for twenty seconds after the last boy has mounted, or while the player at the back counts up to ten, or while the mounted team give vent to a chant of local prescription, for instance in Stepney and Poplar:

> Hi Jimmy Knacker, one, two, three,
> Hi Jimmy Knacker, one, two, three,
> Hi Jimmy Knacker, one, two, three.

In Enfield:

> Onk, onk, horney, one, two, three,
> Onk, onk, horney, one, two, three,
> Onk, onk, horney, one, two, three.

—All over!

In Grimsby, 'Bung the barrel, bung the barrel, one, two, three'. In Newcastle, 'Mountikitty, mountikitty, one, two, three'. In Warwick, 'Mollie, Mollie Mopstick, all off! all off!' In Nuneaton:

> Mopstick, mopstick, bear our weight,
> Two, four, six, eight, ten.

At Meir, in the Potteries:

> Badger, badger, badger, one, two, three,
> All off and have another go.

At Tunstall, where girls are notable enthusiasts, 'One, two, three, four, five, six, seven, eight, nine, ten—Cock Robin!' And in Forfar:

> Huckie duck, huckie duck,
> Three times aff an on again.

Alternatively, in Manchester and Birmingham, and in places generally where the game has an equine name, victory is claimed by the under side, who declare themselves 'Strong horses' if they manage to support the 'up' side for a prescribed length of time; while if they collapse the mounted side cry 'Weak horses' or 'Weak donkeys' or, in Scotland, 'The cuddy's broke'. In Scotland, too, they are particular about the conduct of the jumping side. Sometimes no talking is allowed, or no talking or laughing, or, in Kirkcaldy, 'no tickling, talking, laughing, or kicking'. In Wigan, according to a young informant, he who stands with his back to the wall acts as a kind of umpire, and should he see any rider show as much as his teeth, he shouts 'Lall-i-ho!' and the riders have to dismount and become the under team.

The game is in fact remarkable not only for being played throughout Britain,[26] but for the almost royal burden of names it bears, sometimes several known in one district. For instance, Croydon boys call it not only 'Hi Jimmy Knacker', but 'Bung the Barrel', 'Hi Cockalorum', 'Jump Teddy Wagtail', and 'Trust Weight'. In Kirkcaldy it has no less than seven names: 'Cuddy's Wecht', 'Cuddy gie Wecht', 'Loup the Cuddy', 'Leap the Horse', 'Hunch, Cuddy, Hunch', 'Camel's Back', and 'All Aboard'. Some names are clearly regional: 'Mountikitty' on Tyneside, 'Bumberino' in south Wales, 'Pomperino' in Cornwall. Other names, such as 'Hi Cockalorum' and 'Bung the Barrel', can be described as standard names; but even setting these aside, the nomenclature is so mixed, regionally, it has not been found possible to produce a distribution map. Thus the north-country 'Muntikitty' is found in East Anglia where it is meaningless ('Muntikitty' becomes 'Mad-a-kiddy', 'Mud-a-giddy', and even 'Mother Giddy'), while in Ayrshire 'Bung the Barrel' has taken the place of 'Hunch, Cuddy, Hunch' which was the name there half a century ago. The fact is that the game is much played by Boy Scouts, and enthusiastic Scoutmasters have probably assisted in disrupting the traditional terminology.

The following are the names known to be current: 'All Aboard', 'All on the Horses', 'Apple Bombers' (Weymouth), 'Badger' (general around Stoke-on-Trent), 'Bucking Bronco', 'Buckle Up' (Petersfield, for past fifty years), 'Bull Rag' (Manchester), 'Bumberino' or 'Bomberino' (south Wales, especially Cardiff for past sixty years), 'Bump a Cuddy' (Gateshead), 'Bung Billy Barrel' (Camberwell), 'Bung the Barrel' (London since 1900, and elsewhere especially Surrey, Hampshire, and Oxfordshire), 'Bungle Barrel' (Hampshire, west of Winchester), 'Carabuncle' (Stirling), 'Cock Robin' (Tunstall), 'Cuddie Backs' (Portpatrick), 'Cuddie Hunkers', 'Cuddie's Loup', 'Cuddie's Weight' or 'Cuddie gie Way' (Edinburgh and around Firth of Forth), 'Donkey' (Morpeth), 'Funking Cuddie' (Ballingry), 'Hi Cockalorum' (Croydon and Sittingbourne—see below), 'Hi Jimmy Knacker' (East London since 1890), 'Hi Johnny All On' (Nuneaton), 'Hacky-Duck' (Teignmouth), 'Huckie-Duck' (Dundee, Forfar, Helensburgh), 'Huckey Buck' (around Ipswich), 'Hunch, Cuddy, Hunch' (Glasgow, Stirling, and Lanarkshire), 'Jackerback' (Peterborough), 'Jimmy Knacker' or 'Jimmy, Jimmy Knacker' (predominant in north London since nineteenth century), 'Jockeys' (Brixton), 'Johnny Knacker' (Greenwich), 'Jump Jimmy Knacker' (predominant in south London, e.g. Camberwell and Kennington), 'Jump the Cuddie' (Aberdeen), 'Jump the Long Horse' or 'Jump the Long Mare' (Lydney), 'Lall-i-ho' (Wigan), 'Leapfrog' (Wimborne, boys emphatic this was the name), 'Loup the Cuddie' (Kirkcaldy), 'Lumps' (Wareham), 'Marching Army' (Pontefract), 'Mollie Mollie Mopstick' (Warwick), 'Mont-a-kiddy', 'Mudikiddy', 'Mountikitty', or 'Munt-a-cuddy' (general in Cumberland, Northumberland, Westmorland, Durham), 'Onk, Onk, Horney' (Enfield), 'Piecrust' (Bootle and Pontefract), 'Pig's Whistle' (Norwich, for past seventy years), 'Piggy 'gainst the Wall' (Nuneaton), 'Polly on the Mopstick' (Birmingham and Nuneaton), 'Pomperino' (Cornwall), 'Rum-stick-a-bum' (Nottingham), 'Strong Horses' (various places), 'Strong Horses, Weak Donkeys' (Glamorgan and Monmouthshire), 'Trust' (Luton), 'Trust Weight' (usual name, Sale, Manchester), 'Weak Horses' (Camberwell, Leicester, Manchester, Swansea), 'Weights' (Accrington), and 'Wooden Horse' (Manchester).

One boy in Camberwell called it, graphically, 'Jump Jimmy Knockerbone'; a boy in Liss swore the name was 'Squashed Guts'. In Guernsey it is known as 'Lamp-Post' or 'English Jumpbacks', formerly it was 'Saute Mouton'—in Jersey rendered 'Saltey Mayou'. In New York it is 'Johnny on the Mopstick' or 'Johnny on the Pony'.

§ The early history of the game is bound up with 'Buck, Buck, How Many Fingers do I Hold Up?' (q.v.). Urquhart renders Rabelais's *Cheveau fondu* as 'Trusse', a name seemingly common in the seventeenth century, being known to William Hawkins in 1627 ('The Waues in the sea play at trusse and at leapfrogge on one anothers backe'), and to John Cleveland, about 1658 ('Or do the Iuncto leap at truss-a-fail?'). In *The Daily Advertiser*, 7 November 1741, a writing-sheet was offered to schools having pictures of youthful diversions including 'Truss-Fail'. The present-day 'Trust' and 'Trust-Weight', known to have been current for three generations, presumably stem from this, a truss being a measure or weight of hay or straw, and on the Cheshire-Lancashire border the game was still known as 'Truss and Weight' in the 1920s. Another name in the seventeenth century seems to have been 'Leaping the Nag', since this is given in a contemporary manuscript annotation to 'Le Cheval fondv' in a copy of Stella's *Jeux de l'enfance*, 1657, pl. 23.

The earliest account of the game, which is in *School Boys' Diversions*, 1820, under 'Leap-Frog', is not satisfactory. But it is adequately described in the fourth edition of *The Boy's Own Book*, 1829, p. 23, under 'Saddle My Nag'; and very fully in the 1855 edition under 'Jump, Little Nag-Tail' together with the formula for the mounted side:

> Jump, little Nag-tail, one, two, three,
> Jump, little Nag-tail, one, two, three,
> Jump, little Nag-tail, one, two, three,
> —Off, off, off.

The details are given that boys about to jump should shout 'Warning', and that those who cannot bear their burden are dubbed 'Weak horses'. However, the best-known name for the game in the nineteenth century seems to have been 'Hi Cockalorum': indeed this name became almost proverbial, and the Great Macdermott had a song about it.[27]

The following names are also known to have been current: 'Agony Oss' (Midlands, *c.* 1910), 'Backs' (Staffordshire, 1920s), 'Bom Bom the Barrow' (Stratton-on-the-Fosse, Somerset, 1922), 'Blind Rabbit' (Windermere, 1937), 'Bring the Basket' (Christ's Hospital, *c.* 1850), 'Broken Down Horses' (London, 1908), 'Bull Loup' (Crosby Ravensworth, Westmorland, 1937), 'Bum Bum Barrel' (Newark, *c.* 1900), 'Bumeroo' (Weymouth, 1920s), 'Bumsy Barrels' (Oxford, *c.* 1910), 'Bung the Bucket' (Barnes, 1894), 'Bungs and Barrels' (Oxford, *c.* 1912), 'Challey

Wag' (East Anglia, *c.* 1890), 'Charley Ecko' (Paddington, 1910), 'Charley Nacker' (London, 1903, Hampstead, *c.* 1910), 'Char char Wagtail' (south Devon, *c.* 1915), 'Churchy' (Belfast, *c.* 1900), 'Cockit' (Wellingborough, 1920s), 'Donkey Jump' (Askam-in-Furness, 1937), 'Dumb Weight' (Bradford, *c.* 1910), 'Gipsy Bunker' (Leicester, 1930), 'Heavy on Ton Weight' (Liverpool, *c.* 1912 and *c.* 1925), 'Here Come I, Ship Full Sail' (Southampton, *c.* 1915), 'Here Comes My Ship Full Sail' (*London Street Games*, 1916), 'Hi Bobberee' (East London, *c.* 1900), 'Hi Diddy Jacko' (Beckenham, 1914–16), 'Hipperay-Ho' (Swansea, 1930), 'Hopopop' (Bembridge, Isle of Wight, *c.* 1905), 'Horney-Dorney' (Surrey, 1927), 'Horny Winkle's Horses' (*Living London*, vol. iii, 1903, p. 267), 'Hotchie Pig' (Scottish Border country, *c.* 1925), 'Huckaback' (North Walsham, Norfolk, 1880s), 'Hunching Cuddy' (Coalburn, Lanarkshire, *c.* 1915), 'Hunk, Cuddy, Hunk' (Dalkeith, *c.* 1900), 'Iron Donkeys' (Chardstock, Devon, 1922), 'Jack upon the Mopstick' (Warwickshire, 1892), 'Jacky, Jacky, Nine Tails' (Alton, *c.* 1906, *c.* 1920, Medstead, *c.* 1935), 'Jimmy Wagtail' (*London Street Games*, 1916), 'Jump Jimmy Wagtail' (Gloucestershire, 1902), 'Johnny on the Mopstick' (Worcester, *c.* 1930), 'Kicking Donkey' (Crosthwaite, Westmorland, *c.* 1910, 1935), 'Lanky Lowp' or 'Lancaster Lowp' (Kirby Lonsdale and neighbourhood, *c.* 1900, 1937), 'Lip-Toss Coming In' (Redruth, *c.* 1900), 'Long-Back' (East Yorkshire, 1890), 'Long-Tailed Nag' (Devonshire, *c.* 1920), 'Mopstick' (Kettering, *c.* 1915), 'Mount Nag' (*Every Boy's Book*, 1856), 'Piggy-Wiggy-Wagtail' (Framlingham College, *c.* 1915), 'Ride or Kench' (Lancashire, 1920s), 'Sally on the Mopstick' (Broadway, Worcestershire, *c.* 1901, Birmingham, *c.* 1930), 'Ships' or 'Ships a-sailing' (Huddersfield, 1883, Henfield, Sussex, *c.* 1930), 'Three Ships' (Huddersfield, *c.* 1910), 'Thrust' (Pendlebury, *c.* 1910), 'Tick-Tock-Tovey' (south Devon, *c.* 1915), 'Ton Weight Coming' (Newton-le-Willows, 1930s), 'Trusty' (Kidsgrove, 1920s), 'Warnie I'm a Coming' (*London Street Games*, 1916), 'Weak Horses' (Bradshaw, Birkenhead, and Wandsworth, *c.* 1910), 'Weights On' (Worcester Cathedral Choir School, *c.* 1925).

Our information about the game in other countries is less extensive than about 'Buck Buck' but seems to show that its hardihood (or fool-hardiness) appeals to the youth of all nations. Certainly in France 'Le cheval fondu' has long been played in this exacting form. It was not only one of Gargantua's games, but was mentioned by Calvin's teacher, Mathurin Cordier, in his *De corrupti sermonis emendatione*, 1531, ch.

38, and many times depicted by French artists in the seventeenth and eighteenth centuries. A detailed description appears in Belèze's *Jeux des adolescents*, 1856, pp. 15–18. In Belgium, Pinon records 'Plus fort cheval', and in Holland 'Bok-sta-vast' (*La nouvelle Lyre Malmédienne*, vol. ii (pt. 3), 1954, pp. 98 and 103). In Germany, Böhme gives 'Das lange Ross' and 'Baumhopsen' (*Deutsches Kinderspiel*, 1897, p. 591). In Moscow, or anyway in the Vnukovo district of Moscow, the game is known as 'Sloná' (Elephants). In Italy it is played with splendid enthusiasm, by youths as well as boys, and is known as 'Il cavallo lungo', long horse, or in Capresi dialect 'U' cavall luong'. Here each player before he jumps shouts the warning 'Mo' vir che me ne vengo', and when the team are mounted they endeavour to remain seated while calling '1 - 2 - 3 - 4 - 5 - 6 - 7 - 8 - scarica a' botta!' The game seems to have been played in Naples for centuries. According to Penzer 'cavallo luongo' is mentioned in Del Tufo's MS. *Ritratto di Napoli nel 1588*; while Basile refers to it as 'travo luongo' in *Il Pentamerone*, 1634 (1932 edition, p. 133, note 23). At Massafra, in the heel of Italy, the game is known as 'Pes u chiumm', weigh the lead (Lumbroso, *Giochi*, 1967, pp. 13–14). Thomas Hyde described the Turkish version, 'Uzun Eshek', long donkey, in *De ludis Orientalibus*, ii, 1694, p. 242; and mention of this name, as we have found, instantly produces a gleam in the eyes of Turkish youth today. A correspondent informs us he saw the game played in India. And a Japanese boy told Howard Spring that a similar game 'Uma-Nori', restive horse riding, is 'one of the most popular winter games of Japanese boys' (*Country Life Annual*, 1958, p. 128).

Skin the cuddy

This variation of 'Hi Jimmy Knacker' is traditional in the north-east of Scotland, and is also played in Wandsworth as 'Jumping Jupiter'. All the boys except one, sometimes two, bend down and make a cuddy or long-back against a wall, in the manner of 'Hi Jimmy Knacker', although the back they make is longer, as more boys are bending down. The player who is out, who is sometimes called the 'bronco buster', has to jump on to the line of backs and attempt to work his way along the line and touch the head or take the cap of the boy who stands at the far end as 'post' or 'pillar'. Since the chain of boys is constantly heaving about, and each player in turn feels it an indignity to be sat upon, the rider is not always

successful in his object. In fact edging along the line of backs is a peril-
ous undertaking; and the determination of the players to make it so can
be judged by the displeasure expressed when a rider manages to reach
the other end and wins a second turn. 'This game is very rough,' confided
an 11-year-old, 'but I enjoy it.'

§ The game has been known as 'Skin the Cuddy' in Aberdeenshire for
three generations. In Argyllshire it was 'Bull the Cuddy' (*Folk-Lore*, vol.
xvi, 1905, p. 346). At Dyke in Morayshire it was 'Saddle the Nag', the
players in one team trying in turn to wriggle along the backs of the other
team; and at Banchory in Kincardineshire it was 'Skin the Goatie', a
single boy on the back of another trying to 'crown' the player who stood
upright supporting the boy giving the back (Gomme, *Traditional Games*,
vol. ii, 1898, pp. 147 and 199–200).

9. Daring Games

'All the games that are played are all harmless (in a way) and
very good fun.'
Boy, 14, St Peter Port

Children seem to be instinctively aware that there is more to living than doing what is prudent and permitted. In a boy's world, trees are for climbing, streams are for jumping over, loose stones are for throwing, and a high wall is a standing challenge to be mounted and walked along. To a child it is more interesting to hang out of a window than to look out of it, to jump down a flight of steps than to walk down it, to defy a park-keeper than to hide from him. Exuberance and curiosity lead him into many of his scrapes; yet a boy's love of daring must arise from something still deeper. The glory he sees in danger is that it seems to be linked somehow with his becoming mature. If he did not do what was forbidden how could he be sure he was a person with freedom of choice? So it is that the juvenile tribe holds ritual games, almost as part of the process of growing up, in which the faint-hearted are goaded into being courageous, and the foolhardy stimulated to further foolhardiness. On the face of it little can be said for these entertainments. Nevertheless, if juvenile folly sometimes takes the unhappy forms it does owing to children's inability to appreciate the consequences of an action until they occur, it may be that these sports serve a purpose. In these games fixed procedures are generally adopted: the dares are proposed and accepted, the feats are closely watched by the rest and appraised; and it may be that these games, by their very formality and emphasis on daring, help the majority of children to understand the nature of risk-taking.

Truth, dare, promise, or opinion

No game is more revealing of the childhood community than this sport, apparently known everywhere (descriptions from forty places), which they impose on themselves 'when we want to play something lively'. Any number may take part, although normally not more than five or six of them are in it together; and the severity of the ordeal varies with the occasion and the players. Sometimes a group of girls go off to the park, find a dry place, and sit down in a circle, as if nothing more was intended than a picnic; at other times the participants are a mixed group of boys and girls ('It is much better if you play with girls,' declares a 14-year-old boy, 'then you have more scope'), and they meet after dark in a disused air-raid shelter, or in somebody's backyard or home.

One person is named 'leader', 'master', or 'questioner', and turning to the player nearest him asks, 'Will you have truth, dare, promise, or opinion?' If the person's choice is 'Truth', he has to answer truthfully any question (usually personal) that the leader may ask: 'Is it true that you love Betty Matthews?' If the choice is 'Promise' he is safe for the present, but has to bind himself to something in the future: 'Will you promise to give me six sweets next time we meet?' If the choice is 'Opinion' he is likely to be assigned the delicate task of giving his opinion of somebody present. And if the person's choice is 'Dare' (the usual choice with boys and hoydens), he is liable to be instructed to knock at a front door and run away, or to punch a passer-by on the back, or to ring up the telephone operator and tell him to 'get off the line as a train is coming', or to engage in some other provocation of the adult world, for there is a curious feeling in this game of having to respond to the challenge 'Are you one of *us*, or one of *them*?' Thus a 13-year-old Scots girl, telling how they meet in the street after dark and play 'Truths and Dares', says:

> 'Sometimes you [are dared to] go to a lady's house and ask
> for a "jellie piece".
> 'Sometimes the question master tells you to go to a wifie's
> window and knock on it and cry "Are you in Nellie?" and
> then run along and knock at the wifie's door and act as
> you're walking up the street, and say that a boy did it and
> went away round the corner.
> 'Then the question master says you have to throw water
> on the wifie's doorstep and she threatens you "I'm going
> awa for the Bobby," and she shammies she's going away for
> the police. Then you play your game on another auld wifie
> until the other wifie come back.
> 'Then sometimes you're dared to go and tie the wifies'
> doors together (of course its the wifies you do not like) and

> knock on them and run awa, and the auld wifies come out
> both together. What a laugh you get when they come out
> and discover the string tied to the door.'[28]

Each player in turn is asked his choice, and having made it, has to comply with the demand which follows. If he refuses he is jeered at ('Called
a coward until we next play the game'), or expelled from the gang, or
in some places, what may seem to him providential, he is made to pay
a forfeit, usually a piece of clothing 'like a belt or a shoe', which he has
subsequently to redeem by accepting a new challenge. Sometimes the
temper of the game hardens, almost accidentally, and without realizing
what is happening the players have become hell-bent on extending themselves, encouraging dares to remove more clothes or to jump from yet
higher places. Then on some desperate occasion, the invisible line may
be crossed beyond which there is no stepping back, and a dare ends sadly
as a court case or newspaper story. In Swansea a 13-year-old schoolboy who had been dared was found to have swallowed eight two-inch
nails (*Yorkshire Post*, 31 October 1960, p. 3). At Ossett an 8-year-old
schoolboy admitted setting fire to a stack of unthreshed oats for a dare
(*Yorkshire Post*, 10 November 1960, p. 14). At Frimley a 7-year-old boy
woke up in the middle of the night screaming that he had seen a body.
He had been dared to peep through the window of the public mortuary
adjoining a recreation ground (*The Times*, 13 December 1963, p. 9).
And in Portsmouth a particularly unfortunate game of 'Dare, Truth, or
Promise' ended with two boys of twelve and thirteen being prosecuted
for improperly assaulting two young girls (*News of the World*, 14
February 1954, p. 7).

   It seems too, from the varying names of the game, that in different
places, or on different occasions, different types of challenge are predominant. On the Scottish Border the game is sometimes called simply
'Finding Out' and the demands are purely (or impurely) for factual
information.[29] In other districts the emphasis is on their relationships
with each other. In Kidderminster the game is occasionally called 'Truth,
Dare, Promise, or Kiss'; in Peterborough and Swansea, 'Do, Dare,
Kiss, or Promise'; in Gloucester, 'Truth, Dare, Warning, Love, Kiss, or
Marriage' ('If you choose kiss you must kiss whoever is named'), and
in West Ham it is 'Dare, Truth, Love, Kiss, Promise, or Demand' ('If he
picks "Love" you must tell him to do something with love'—Girl, 10). In
some places there are degrees of enforcement, thus in Inverness, 'Truth,

Dare, or Got to'; in Watford and Orpington, 'Truth, Dare, Promise, or Must'; in Aberdeen, 'Truth, Dare, Force, or Promise' ('If it was "Dare" I would dare her to climb a lamp-post, ring a bell, or kiss a boy, but she can refuse. At "Force" it goes the same as "Dare" but one is forced to do it'—Girl, 12). At Spennymoor, where the game is called 'Truth, Dare, Will, Force, and Command', three of the choices seem indistinguishable, for with each of them the dare is enforceable. In Edinburgh, where the game is 'Truth, Dare, Promise, or Repeat', the player who chooses 'Repeat' has to repeat his task a certain number of times, the task usually being to make a statement such as 'I'm my ma's big bubblie bairn', which a 14-year-old boy confessed he found exceedingly embarrassing. And in some forms of the game there are no alternatives to accepting the dare, as in 'Got to' in north London, 'Dare, Double Dare' in Plymouth ('After the person has done one dare he has to do another'), and 'King's Command', 'Get the Coward', and 'Chicken' (see below).

§The forerunner to this game seems to be 'Questions and Commands', otherwise known as 'King I am', a popular social sport in the seventeenth century, mentioned by Burton, Wycherley, Herrick, and Randle Holme. It seems to have been as audacious a game as 'Truth, Dare, Promise, or Opinion', and, since it was played by adults, decidedly more witty. Thus in *Gratiae Ludentes*, 1638, p. 65, 'a question proposed to a gentlewoman at the play of *questions and commands*' was:

> 'Suppose you and I were in a roome together, you being naked,
> pray which part would you first cover?' *An.* 'Your eyes, sir.'

In the eighteenth century 'King I am' was looked upon as a childish amusement. It was included in the juvenile *Little Pretty Pocket-Book*, 1744 (1760, p. 30), and was played by the children in Brooke's *The Fool of Quality*, vol. i, 1766, p. 72. Probably its formula was that quoted in *The Craftsman*, 4 February 1738, p. 1:

> 'King I am, says one Boy; another answers, I am your Man; then
> his Majesty demands, what Service He will do Him; to which the
> obsequious Courtier replies, the Best and Worst, and All I can.'

The author of *Round about our Coal Fire* (1731, p. 10), who considered the game suitable for Christmas, suggested that the forfeit should be fixed at a certain sum, or that the face should be smutted, so that he who did not wish to comply with a demand could be 'easy at discretion'. Strutt, in 1801, also termed 'Questions and Commands' a childish pastime, and noted, as earlier writers had done (e.g. William King and John Arbuthnot), that the game appeared to be related to the 'Basilinda' of the Greeks, in which a king, elected by lot, commanded his comrades what they should perform (Pollux, ix. 110). The name 'King's Command' seems to have survived to the present time among certain teenagers, being referred to in a British Medical Association report in 1964.[30] Mention should also be made of 'Roi qui ne ment' played by Froissart about 1345; 'Questions' mentioned by Drayton in 1598; 'Wadds and Wears' in *The Gallovidian Encyclopedia*, 1824; and the game 'Truth' played by the party at Camp Laurence in *Little Women*, 1868, ch. xii. However, in the United States a boy is liable to be 'stumped' instead of dared, as in W. M. Thayer's *From Log-Cabin to White House*, 1881, p. 73, where Edwin holds up a pullet's egg and challenges James Garfield, the future President, 'I stump you to swaller it'. In Edmonton, Alberta, the game is called 'Hot Box', the penalty for failing to comply with a demand being to crawl between the commander's legs and be hit while doing so.

Follow my leader

'Follow my Leader' can be a mere nursery game with a line of little players walking wherever the leader walks, jumping when he jumps, hopping when he hops, dancing, turning somersaults, making faces, crowing, and very often—in accord with the first child's lead—acting like silly-billies. Amongst older children the sport is more testing.

In some versions of 'Truth, Dare, Promise, or Opinion', the challenger has himself to be prepared to carry out the dare if the other refuses, and fundamentally 'Follow my Leader' is the same; but the leader always performs the feat first, and then by implication, and sometimes in so many words, challenges the rest to do likewise. If any follower is unable to perform an action he either goes to the back of the line, or is sent out of the game and has to stay in the den. Sometimes the actual point of the game is that the leader should go on doing difficult things 'until all the followers are in the den. Then the game starts again'. Quite often the game is played on bicycles, the leader choosing the most slippery paths he can between trees and up banks, and the others having to follow: 'If you fall off you're out.' And sometimes the game becomes a test of nerves. The leader, chosen because he has a stout heart, leads them along the top of the parapet of a railway bridge, through the narrow gap between two lime kilns when they are burning, across a weir, or over the roofs of buildings; and sometimes the expedition does not end happily. 'An 11-year-old boy ... was leading four other boys who had walked along the side of a stream and climbed on to the roof, playing "follow my leader" ', reported *The Yorkshire Post*, 12 April 1960, p. 12. The leader 'stepped on to a glass panel on the roof and disappeared into the works ... He landed on the only space on the floor which is clear of machinery. At the hospital late yesterday the boy was stated to be "comfortable" '.

Other names: 'Jack follow my Leader' (Leeds), 'Pied Piper' (Swansea), 'Cappers' (Penrith).[31]

A variation is 'Leading the Blind' (Slough) or 'Guide me with Guilt' (Wilmslow), in which those who follow are blindfolded or must keep their eyes shut, and hold on in a line each to the one in front. Their guide looks for as many obstacles as he can find to lead them over or under, and put them in disarray. 'This game is best to play in a park or in a wood,' explained a 10-year-old, 'where you can fall into bushes or trip over trees.'

§ 'Follow the Leader' is often referred to in children's literature, usually in an admonitory manner, e.g. in *Youthful Recreations*, 1789, p. 122, 'If Tommy Heedless had any fault, it was that of his being too fond of a game we call Follow the Leader'; *Dangerous Sports*, 1801 (1807, p. 85), 'Follow the leader is a game which, as generally played, is full of danger'; *School Boys' Diversions*, 1820, pp. 26–7, 'Follow the Leader ... certainly affords occasions to display courage, and even temerity; but such excesses will ever be shunned by prudent lads.' However, the editor of *The Boy's Own Book*, 1829, p. 24, remarked that 'Without a bold and active leader this sport is dull and monotonous'.

In Brockett's *North Country Words*, 1829, the game is styled 'Jock and Jock's-man'.

Get the coward

This game ('the game I like best', says a Wigan 10-year-old) is a form of 'Truth, Dare, Promise, or Opinion' but without the options and without a leader. 'It is a game for five or six players. You start off by putting the boys' names in a cap. When you have done this you hold a council of boys who decide what to do with the boy who's been picked out of the cap. Sometimes the council might say that he has to ring a doorbell or knock off a policeman's helmet. If he does not do it you shout:

> Iggly piggly poo,
> Put the coward in your shoe,
> When you're through let him go,
> Inny tinny let him know.

Then you run at him and start fighting him, but you don't hurt him. I like it', adds the 10-year-old, 'because it is a rough and very daring game.'

Last across

'Last Across' is the game in which, to the consternation of motorists, children line up on a pavement, wait until the leader has selected a particular car or lorry, and then 'when it gets rather close you all run across the road and the one who gets nearest to the front bumper wins'. Another name for the game is 'First to the Cemetery'.

The question whether there are deeper motives for this game than mere devilment is touched upon in the discussion on play in the street in the Introductory chapter (see Vol.1, p. 19f). Certainly when children take part in street games it is not they who are afraid of the traffic, it is the traffic that is terrified of them; and the children are aware of this, and willing to take advantage of it.

The game of 'Last Across the Railway Line', however, the pleasure of which is even less comprehensible to the adult mind, might seem to dispose of the theory that children are in part giving vent to a frustration, or making a form of protest, when they run in front of cars, for children are not ordinarily thought to be antipathetic to trains. Nevertheless railway property with its untrodden railroad, its quiet green slopes, trees, and bushes, its tantalizingly exposed machinery, must often appear to a child, and in fact be, the most attractive playground in the district; and any investigation into juvenile trespass on the railway might well start with a study of the geography of the places where trespass most frequently occurs. Certainly in some districts the game of 'Last Across' in front of trains is almost normal child's-play. In 1957 the sport was reported to be so common on the stretch of line between Devons Road and Poplar Station that engine drivers were threatening to refuse to drive trains along it for fear of being involved in an accident (*The Times*, 12 March 1957, p. 4). In 1961 the secretary of the Derby branch of the Associated Society of Locomotive Engineers and Firemen stated that playing 'Last Across' the line was 'prevalent throughout the whole of the Midlands', and he added that a new variation had been observed, which intensified juvenile rashness: 'A group of children put pennies into a hat and put it down on the side of the track. They dash across at the last possible moment in the path of the train and the last one to move picks up the cap and claims the pennies' (*Yorkshire Post*, 28 April 1961, p. 9). In 1964 a British Railways spokesman stated that during that year, in Essex alone, three children had been killed and seven injured while playing 'Last Across the Line' (*Daily Express*, 11 December 1964, p. 11). In 1968 at Fryston, near Castleford, where 'the trains go very fast ... and some of the children play a game in which they dare each other to get out of the way at the last minute', eight children saw two of their friends killed by a train (*The Times*, 5 April 1968, p. 1). And in Plymouth, the Western Region became so concerned by the number of incidents, that in July 1968 they launched a 'Rail Safety Campaign', emphasizing the danger of children playing 'Last Across' and 'Chicken', although well aware that such publicity can be self-defeating.

§ Both Norman Douglas in *London Street Games*, 1916, p. 142, and Newell in *Games of American Children*, 1883, p. 122, refer to playing last-across-the-road, but under 'Follow the Leader'. Norman Douglas called it the 'only really dangerous game we have', dangerous because the bravest boy was chosen leader 'who crosses the road just in front of some heavy van'; and it is worth recalling that in the days of horse-drawn traffic crossing the road was scarcely less hazardous than it is today. (In 1865, for example, no fewer than 232 people were killed by carriages in the streets of London alone.) In America, Newell reported, the game was played in a peculiarly reckless fashion in the southern states, 'the leader will sometimes go under a horse's legs or between the wheels of a wagon', whereupon the driver knowing what to expect, would find himself having to stop for the rest of the players to follow.

Chicken

'If you want something done and you are too scared to do it yourself you go up and "Chicken" somebody. You tell them what to do, and if they don't do it you call them "Chicken" and you dare them again, and if they don't do it you call them "Double chicken". And they go off and everybody calls them a chicken, and you call them all names, "Quack quack" and names like that. The sort of thing you tell them to do is to go and hit somebody, or to go and tell a boy you like him.'

Thus two girls of 13 and 14 in Petersfield. Unhappily, by undefined degrees, the practice or threat of 'Chicken' can lead to less innocuous impositions.

A 13-year-old boy in Grimsby says that if two boys are fighting one of them may challenge the other to a 'Chicken Run'. They take their bicycles and go to some traffic lights, and 'when the lights change to red they both go straight through the lights, and the first one to stop is "Chicken", but if one of them keeps going he is the winner of the game'.

Sometimes the duel in which two boys charge each other on bicycles is called 'Chicken'; whoever swerves first as they come at each other is tagged with the odious name, and is even likely to feel he deserves it for his faint-heartedness.

Sometimes 'Last Across' is called 'Chicken', hence the schoolchild joke (current 1963): 'Why didn't the *cock* cross the road?—Because he was chicken.'

And sometimes the game takes yet more senseless forms. In Halifax a boy was caught playing 'Chicken', swerving his bicycle in front of a car and then jumping off and lying on the ground. When the car stopped he jumped on his bicycle and rode off, and he and his friend had a laugh about it. Unfortunately for him (or perhaps fortunately) the fourth and last time he did this was in front of a police car (*Daily Express*, 2 August 1961, p. 4).

In Liphook, Hampshire, a youth playing 'Chicken' with a mixed group of younger children, lay down in the middle of the road at night, deliberately staying there until a car came, but another car which was following overtook it, ran over his head, and killed him. 'The idea of the game,' a 14-year-old boy told the Coroner, 'is to frighten the motorist' (*Hampshire Telegraph*, 12 November 1964, p. 9).

When a group of 11 to 14-year-old boys at Harold Hill in Essex were playing a game to see who dared stay longest on the railway line before an oncoming train, two stayed too long and were killed, and a third was only saved by being knocked off the line by the bodies of the others. The fourth boy, who said he was alive because he had lost his nerve, added, 'This has been going on most nights since a gang of us started going over to a railway bridge on Harold Court road a few months ago. Another test of courage was to lie at the side of the track and let the overlays of the train pass over your head' (*Daily Express*, 21 and 25 November 1960, pp. 5 and 16).

In 1957 an official of the London Midland Region of British Railways reported that they had instances 'where boys lie on the track and put their heads on the line. When the train stops they jump up and run away' (*The Times*, 12 March, p. 4).

In 1966 when thirteen boys and two girls were arrested for trespassing on railway property at Glen Parva in Leicestershire, one boy, aged 13, was caught while actually lying between the tracks, with his feet over one track and his head over the other (*The Times*, 27 May 1966, p. 13).

It is also not unknown for children to lie flat in the middle of the tracks and allow trains to go over them. An express driver on the London to Leicester line was reported in *The Times*, 4 May 1966, p. 10, as saying that at Newton Harcourt, 'I came round a bend at 80 m.p.h. and saw a boy lying face down between the lines with his hands behind his head. I braked, but it was too late to pull up. The train passed over the boy and afterwards I saw him get up and disappear on his bicycle.' A railway spokesman, stating that this was not the only case that had been reported, added that fortunately the train was a diesel, 'any other type would have cut his head off'. Indeed children sometimes seem to be as unaware of danger as the first-day fledglings in one's garden. One boy of 6, who showed his headmistress how to lie under a train, commented: 'All you have to do is lie still with your arms stretched out and keep your eyes closed as the train goes over. It doesn't hurt a bit.'

§ The term *chicken* for the faint-hearted, although old, was not found among children in our survey in the 1950s (when 'yellow' and 'windy' were the popular expressions), but was suddenly known to everyone in 1960, even as the name for the game (see, e.g., *Yorkshire Post*, 24 September 1960, p. 4). Apparently the term came from the United States, where it had been current anyway since 1935; yet it was a return export.

In 1707 in *The Beaux' Stratagem* (IV. iii) Gibbet says 'You assure me that Scrub is a Coward', and Boniface replies, 'A Chicken, as the saying is.' And in 'The Prisoners' Van', in *Sketches by Boz*, 1836–7, a young girl criminal upbraids her still younger sister, who is showing distress, with the words, 'Hold up your head, you chicken. Hold up your head, and show 'em your face.'

Misplaced audacity

In children's games as in other departments of life, the player who takes no risks can expect little admiration; and few children have the ability to judge whether a particular game is worth playing, let alone whether it is worth playing courageously. In a diversion such as the 'Knife Game', which is commonplace among boys in the north country, the sport has little interest if not played with a certain *élan. Sine periculo friget lusus.*

'You need a knife, preferably a large one with a sharp edge and a good point,' reports a 13-year-old.

> 'First of all you spreadeagle your left hand. Then you take the knife in your other hand and as quick as you can stick the knife in the spaces between the fingers without cutting your finger. When you are experienced enough you make it harder, for instance you thrust the knife between the third and fourth fingers, then between the first and second, then between the second and third fingers, and then between the thumb and first finger.'

Likewise on the swings in the park, children do not merely sit on the seats and see who can swing highest, but try who can climb furthest up the chains while swinging, and who can best twizzle the swing while swinging, and who will jump off his seat from the greatest height, and who, by swinging hard, can leap the furthest off the swing, a sport sometimes called 'Parachutes'. ('It is very dangerous for I have fallen off and cut my arm and had to have it in plaster for two weeks'—Boy, 12.) In County Durham, a person is pushed as high as he dare go, and then the pusher stops pushing and cries:

> The cat dies once,
> The cat dies twice,

The cat dies three times over.
If you don't get off I'll give you a knock,
It's time your swing was over.

The person has then to jump. Jumping off the swing is also part of the game called 'Countries' (Liverpool) or 'All Over the World' (Glasgow), where several children go on swings beside each other, and a player on the ground calls out 'England', 'Scotland', 'Ireland', or 'Wales', the names given to the several concrete slabs on which the pushers ordinarily stand, and the swingers must attempt to land on the particular slab that has been named. If there are protecting bars to prevent the swings going too high they also play 'bumps', swinging higher and higher until the chain or rod hits the bar; and one 13-year-old Stoke Newington girl was killed while attempting actually to jump from the swing and catch hold of the crossbar (*The Times*, 14 June 1960, p. 15).

Yet roller-towels, when children make free with them, can be as dangerous as swings. They put their head in the loop of the towel and wind themselves up until they can lift their feet off the ground. They play 'Dangling Man', a game of extraordinary attraction, twisting the towel tight and letting their neck take the weight of their body until they go blue in the face. At Southwell, an 11-year-old boy had a go in the towel after his companions had left, and took twelve hours to regain consciousness (*Yorkshire Post*, 13 October 1961, p. 1). In New Romney a 9-year-old died while playing the game, which his classmates described as one of their favourites (*Daily Express*, 10 December 1963, p. 11). In Islington a 9-year-old died at his school, apparently also while playing this game with a roller-towel, which was there referred to as a 'Spinning game' (*Daily Express*, 7 October 1966, p. 18).

Frequently, as we have observed, it is not bravado that occasions foolishness so much as wonder and curiosity, those twin attributes of inexperience which, for instance, prompt a child to turn round and round until he is giddy and can 'see the world going round'. So it is, when a rumour sweeps through the school that a person who stands on wet blotting-paper, or who puts wet blotting-paper in his shoes, is likely to faint, repeated trials are made; and although the experimenters may be encouraged by the thought that anyone who faints will miss the next lesson, this is undoubtedly not the mainspring of their research.

In 1961, for instance, when a craze for making people faint broke out in a Lancashire primary school, the boys were eager to demonstrate even to their headmaster. 'We can make a boy faint for a minute, sir,' they declared.

'Oh yes?' said Sir, tolerantly.

They sat on their hocks, knees bent, arms outstretched, and took ten deep breaths, then stood up holding the tenth breath, and someone from behind squeezed them round their waist. One boy was flat out for a minute. ('Every thing went all white, sir, and the next I knew I was on the ground.') As the headmaster remarked later, this was another craze that had to be killed as soon as it was born. 'There was a lump the size of an egg where the boy's head had hit the ground.' But five years later the 'Faint Game' was reported in *The Times*, 27 June 1966, p. 11, as newly current amongst schoolboys in north Kent. The procedure was precisely the same as in Lancashire, and apparently equally effective. One boy, *The Times* stated, had already been taken to hospital with a suspected fractured skull.

10. Guessing Games

Children's preference for exercizing their bodies rather than their minds is obvious enough, and their participation in intellectual guessing games, even of the humble order of 'Coffee Pots', 'Animal, Vegetable, and Mineral', and 'I Spy With My Little Eye', is apt to be limited to occasions when they are restricted, and unable to play anything else. Out in the street or playground their guessing games are little more than preludes to action: the means of starting a race or initiating a scrimmage. Even in the simplest of their out-door guessing games, such as 'Squeak, Piggy, Squeak' (or 'Puss, Puss, Miaow'), in which a player has to identify a disguised voice; or 'Guess Who', in which a person is obliged to name whose hands have unexpectedly been placed over his eyes; or 'Leading the Blind' or 'Dumping', in which a blindfold child must guess where he has been led or dumped, the appeal is to the senses rather than the intellect. The fact is that in their guessing games children do not greatly care whether a person guesses correctly or not; no scores are kept, as in gambling games; and, quite often, the games have a dramatic or ritualistic form in which the guesser is happily guessing in the guise of somebody else.

Film stars

'Film Stars' is the most popular guessing game in Britain. It is played anywhere out of doors, often across a road, and sometimes at night. One girl goes to the far side of the road (the game is played mostly by girls), and calls out the initials of a film star or singer, for instance 'C.R.' for Cliff Richard. As soon as a player thinks she knows who the initials stand for she races across the road and back again, and then shouts out the name. If her guess is right she changes places with the person in front; but if her guess is wrong—this is the fun of the game—she has run for nothing. In some places the guessers have to run across the road and back again, and then across the road a third time, and whisper their suggestion to the person in front so that the others cannot hear it. Sometimes several children will be racing as fast as they can against each other, and all of them find that they have thought of the wrong name. ' "Film Stars" is marvellous,' said an 11-year-old, 'I play it as often as I can.' And she is typical. Almost everywhere, it seems, the game becomes an obsession with one group after another of little girls who have recently become starry-eyed, but are still athletic.

Other names: 'Initials', 'Pop Stars', 'TV Stars', and, in Liverpool, 'Filmy', a typical scouse apocope. In Edmonton, Canada, and doubtless elsewhere in the New World, it is called 'Movie Stars'.

Variants of 'film stars'

A game such as 'Film Stars' which is in the ascendant may not only out-shine and eventually replace its progenitor, it can cast its glamour over similar games, and five of them are now played under the name 'Film Stars'; or, to put it the other way round, 'Film Stars' is now played in five variant forms.

(i) The girl who chooses the initials stands only just in front of the others, and as soon as someone guesses correctly she starts to run, but must stop immediately the person who guessed right shouts 'One, two, three, stop!' The guesser then attempts to reach the caller with a certain number of strides, usually three, but sometimes with as many 'pigeon toes', or other specified steps, as there are letters in the film star's name. The guesser does not change places with the caller unless she manages to reach her. This game is surprisingly popular, particularly in the London area.

(ii) In some places, for instance Knighton and Forfar, the chase is more energetic. All the players line up against the wall except the caller, who stands on the kerb. When a player thinks she knows the film star's name she chases the caller. If she catches her before the caller reaches the wall on the other side of the road, she gives her the name of the film star, and if right, becomes the new caller. In Forfar, if none of the guessers can think of the name of the film star, the caller says 'Steppie for the first time', and is allowed to take a step into the road before she gives the star's Christian name.

(iii) This version, which is little more than a way of starting a race, is particularly common in Scotland and the north country, and also

in Guernsey, and is played by boys as well as girls. The caller
stands on the kerb on the opposite side of the road, and as soon as
someone names the film or TV star correctly, he runs across the
road and back, while the guesser does the same in the opposite
direction. Whichever of them arrives back first is the next caller.
(Cf. 'Time' in Race Games.)

(iv) Sometimes, as reported from Aberdeen, Accrington, Netley, and
Liverpool, there is no running, only guessing. The initials called
are usually for difficult names, and the caller has to give hints
when requested, such as the sex of the star, the names of films in
which the star has appeared, and sometimes must even adopt the
characteristic stance of the hero or heroine. 'If' says a 9-year-old,
'the people want to know the first or last name, the person who
has ask them has to tell them otherwise the person who has ask
them is not allowed to play any more that day.'

(v) In Guernsey they have a hybrid variety, called 'Step for a Hint',
which seems to be descended from both the foregoing game and
the race game 'Aunts and Uncles'. In this game it is the player in
front who guesses the name. The others decide who the film star
shall be, line up, and call out the initials. The one in front asks
each player in turn a question about the film star: 'Is he a man?'
'Is he tall?' 'Is he fat?' 'Is he dark-haired?' and each time if the
answer is 'Yes' the player addressed takes a step forward. The
player in front tries to guess the name of the star before somebody reaches her.

I sent my son John

This is the principal game from which 'Film Stars' seems to have
evolved, and it is perhaps remarkable that it continues to retain a separate
identity.

One person stands out, usually some distance away, and thinks of
an article that is sold in a particular kind of shop, for instance, as a 10-
year-old West Ham girl suggested, 'If she was thinking of Bird's Eye
frozen peas she would say "I sent my son John to the grocer to buy some
B.E.F.P." ' When somebody thinks she knows what B.E.F.P. stands for,
she runs to an agreed place and back to the person in front, and tells her
what she thinks it is. 'You go on like this till someone gets it.'

Known as 'I Sent My Son John' in West Ham, Brighton, Orpington, Plympton St Mary, and Forfar (where it has been played under this name for fifty years), it is also called 'My Son John' (Oxford and London, SE7), 'My Mother Works' (Old Kilpatrick, Glasgow), and 'Shops' (Banbury).

§ In the nineteenth century this game was generally known as 'I Apprentice My Son', e.g., in *The Girl's Book of Diversions*, 1835, pp. 51–3, and *Cassell's Book of Sports*, 1888, p. 775. It stems, apparently, from a game called 'Two Poor Tradesmen', played in Regency days, and described in *School Boys' Diversions*, 1820, pp. 15–16. In this, two boys addressed the rest, 'We are two poor men, come out of the country, and want to set up a trade.' 'What's your trade?' they were asked. They named a trade and gave the first and last letter of the article they required. Guesses were then made in rotation, and the person who guessed the article, or anyone who named an article not belonging to the trade, was 'buffeted by the rest to an agreed distance' for his trouble.

Cf. 'Three Jolly Workmen' (p. 130).

Shop windows

This game is hardly to be distinguished from 'I Sent My Son John' except that it is played in front of a shop window, and the object which has to be guessed is chosen from the window. Usually one person studies the window while the others line up on the kerb. He chooses an object such as a tin of salmon, and says 'I see T.O.S.' If someone guesses right he may have to run to the wall the other side of the road without being caught (Abertillery), or race the person who gave the initials; or, when a person thinks he knows, he may have to run to the other side and back before he makes his guess (Kirkcaldy). In Birmingham, where the game is called 'In the Window', all the players choose the object, except one, who has to guess the item they have chosen before he can give chase. In Colne, Lancashire, where the game is known as 'Hot Peas', the children standing on the kerb chorus 'Try again' each time a wrong guess is made, but when the guess is correct they shout 'Hot Peas', and dash to the other side of the road, hoping to get there without being caught.

Anything under the sun

This, too, is basically 'I Sent My Son John', but the caller may choose any subject she likes. 'You can have towns, rivers, counties, countrys, seas, capitals, birds, ships, children's names, plants, and trees.' The caller may say ' "It's a girl's name beginning with G," and if any of the players think they know it,' says a 10-year-old Ipswich girl, 'they run up to the person and back to their place and up to the person again, and if they guess right they are "in". If two people guess right at the same time they choose colours, flowers, or vegetables, for instance, Kingfisher Blue and Lavender Green, not saying who has chosen which. The other players pick one of the colours, and the person whose colour has the most votes is "in".'

In Oxford and Banbury the game opens with the set formula, 'John Peel's favourite animal's name begins with A', and is known as 'John Peel', or sometimes 'John Bull'. In Aberdeen the game is called 'Odds and Ends'. And in a number of places children are insistent that the game is known only as 'Flowers' or 'Animals' or 'Cars' or 'Footballers' or 'Soap Powders' because these alone are the permitted subjects of the initials, as if TV and film stars had never existed.

In Edinburgh, and some other places, the game is played under the name 'Advertisements', and the clues are not initials but slogans such as 'The Sunshine Breakfast Food', and the players have to guess the product sold with the slogan.

Capital letter, full stop

'Capital Letter, Full Stop' is the distinctive name in Ipswich of the form of playing 'Film Stars' in which the caller runs away as soon as a correct guess is made, and the guesser shouts 'Stop' (variation i). The person who guessed correctly then spells out the name she guessed, taking a 'pigeon step' for each letter. She then does 'capital letter', 'full stop', and jumps. 'Then she tries to touch the person's toes.' The game is played in precisely the same manner in Plympton St Mary, but is there known as 'Colours'; and it is played in a very similar manner in Market Rasen, where it is called 'Hop, Skip, and Jump'.

Birds, beasts, fishes, or flowers

In this game every player is physically involved whether or not he himself makes a guess. Two sides are chosen of equal size, and line up on opposite sides of the road, facing each other. One side thinks of a bird, beast, fish, or flower (or, sometimes, the name of a film star, famous person, or 'child in the school'), and advances line abreast to the other side and gives the initial (or initials). If the guessing side makes a wrong guess the callers stand fast. But if the guess is correct they sprint back to the safety of their own side of the road, for any who are caught on the way back have to join the opposing side, whose turn it becomes to give the initial of a subject.

The game is particularly popular in Scotland and the Isles under the name 'My Father' or 'My Father's Occupation', when the subject of the initial is not an object but a trade, or a worker in some trade.

§ In the nineteenth century the game was known as 'Flowers' or 'Bird Apprentice' (Gomme, *Traditional Games*, vol. i, 1894, pp. 33 and 129).

American Times

'American Times' is here described by a 12-year-old girl in Fraserburgh:

> 'You play on the pavement with this one because it is
> mostly played outside. You have to get about six children
> and they all stand against a fence or a wall except two
> children. The two children that are out, they have to
> whisper to themselves the time that they choose and
> when they have thought of a time they go and ask the
> children "What time is it?" and they go right through them
> all and if they still can't answer it, well they go right back
> to the beginning until a person gets it right. When the
> person gets the time right she has got to choose names
> of things. She gets to pick her own choice between girls'
> names, boys' names, colours, fruit, car names, schools, and
> cigarettes. When she's picked what she wants, well she
> tells the two girls. Then they go away and whisper again.
> If she had picked colours then the two girls have to pick

> two colours. One girl takes red and the other takes blue,
> and they go up to the girl who got the right answer to the
> time and say "What colour do you want, red or blue?" and
> if she says "red" well the girl who picked blue has got to go
> in that girl's place and the girl has to go with the other girl.
> When they have changed places they start all over again
> and they play until everybody gets a chance to be the
> "man".

Appallingly tedious as this game may seem, it is nevertheless popular in Scotland, reports coming particularly from Ayrshire and Lanarkshire, and it is not unknown in England.

§ It is possible that the game is American in more than name, for it is described by Charles F. Smith, of the Teachers College, Columbia University, as a 'favourite after-supper game', in *Games and Game Leadership*, 1932, p. 267. However, Matizia Maroni Lumbroso, in her excellent collection of *Giochi descritti dai bambini*, 1967, pp. 230–1, although she has no records of the game in Italy, reports it being played in Sardinia (under the name 'Corochè') exactly as it is played in Scotland.[32]

Three jolly workmen

Even if the pedigree of this pavement 'Dumb Crambo' was unknown, its age would be apparent from the old-fashioned language children continue to use while playing it. In Walworth two or three in a group of youngsters, and sometimes all but one, go to the other side of the road and decide what trade they shall mime. As they come skipping back across the road they call, 'We're three jolly workmen come to do some work.' 'What work can you do?' demand the other side. 'Anything to please you', reply the workmen. 'Pray let us see you do it', say the employers. The workmen then mime the trade, and if one of the employers guesses correctly what it is they turn and run, with the employers after them. If one of the employers manages to catch them before they reach the wall on the other side of the road they change roles and the guessers become the mimers.

This game seems to be played almost everywhere. In Swansea and Welshpool, and other parts of Wales, it is usual for one player to stand alone, while the others, perhaps three players, go away 'to think'. The mimers then return chanting: 'Three jolly Welshmen come to look for work.'

> Foreman: 'What can you do?'
> Welshmen: 'All sorts of things that you
>   can't do.'
> Foreman: 'I'll show you one.'
> Welshmen: 'We'll show you two, that's
>   more than you can do.'
> Foreman: 'Do it then.'

In West Ham, where the game is known as 'Here we come to London Town', the workmen are equally cocky. One person is chosen 'It', and all the rest are the workmen, and retire out of hearing to choose what action they shall mime, 'for instance' (says a 10-year-old) 'robbing a bank or dress-making'. When they have chosen they walk towards 'It' and announce themselves: 'Here we come to London Town'.

> 'What to do?'
> 'Eat plum pudding as fast as you.'

'Set to work and do it', says 'It', and they start their mime. If 'It' guesses right he chases them, and whoever he catches takes his place; but if he cannot guess they think of another mime, and 'It' has to guess again.

In Kirkcaldy the mimers announce themselves: 'We're the men from Buckley Bane, guess what we are doing today.' In Forfar they say, 'Here we come to knock at the old man's door.' In Caistor: 'We're three wise witches come to work.' In Alton: 'We're three men in the workhouse, don't know what to do.' And the dialogue continues: 'What's your trade?'

> 'Monkey Moses.'
> 'How do you work it?'

In Accrington: 'We're three jolly sailor boys out of work.'
> 'What is your cargo?'
> 'Anything but workship.'

In Glasgow: 'Here are two broken matchsticks.'
> 'Where from?'

'Hong Kong.'
'What's your trade?'
'Lemonade.'
'How do you work it?'

And each time, when a correct guess is made, the actors are chased back across the road.[33]

Names: 'Three Jolly Workmen' (Walworth, Bermondsey, Manchester, Runcorn), 'Three Jolly Welshmen' (Swansea, Knighton, Welshpool, Bristol, Lydney), 'Three Jolly Watchmen' (Guernsey), 'Three Wise Men' (Garderhouse, Shetland), 'Three Wise Witches' (Caistor), 'Three Jolly Sailor Boys' (Accrington), 'Two Broken Matchsticks' (Glasgow, Cumnock, Stornoway), 'Matchstick Man' (Inverness), 'Buckley Bane' (Kirkcaldy), 'Here we come to London Town' (West Ham), 'London Town' (Ipswich and Poplar), 'Here comes an Old Woman to do some Work' (Brighton), 'Old Woman in the Wood' (Wells), 'Come to Knock at the Old Man's Door' (Forfar), 'Come to Learn a Trade' (Birmingham), 'Learn a Trade' (Enfield), 'Jack of All Trades' (Market Rasen), 'Chinky, Chinky Chinaman' (Perth), and 'Cobbler, Cobbler' (alternative name, Accrington).

Also, with activities rather than trades, and a king or queen guessing: 'Queen' (Birmingham); 'Queenie, Queenie' (Aberdeen); 'Good Morning, O King' (Bristol), and 'King and His Subjects' (Inverness).

In Whalsay, Shetland, the game is known as 'Aggie Waggie', which is the actors' retort when a wrong guess is made.

§ In *The Folk-Lore Journal*, vol. vii, 1889, p. 230, under the name 'Dumb Motions' or 'An Old Woman from the Wood' (the same name we learnt from a girl in Wells, Somerset, in 1964) the game is said to have been played for several generations in Dorset: 'Here comes an old 'oman from the wood.' 'What cans't thee do?' 'Do anythin'.' 'Work away.' In Sussex the game was known as 'A Man Across the Common'. In *Traditional Games*, vol. ii, 1898, p. 305, three versions are given under the name 'Trades', including one from Ogbourne, Wiltshire, beginning:

Here are three men from Botany Bay,
Got any work to give us today;

and one from Fraserburgh in which the performers proclaimed themselves 'Three poor tradesmen wanting a trade'. It will be noticed that
the workmen in the nineteenth century described themselves as 'poor' or
'broken', while those today are 'jolly' and generally pleased with themselves. In *London Street Games*, 1916, p. 40, the game appears under
the names 'Dumb Motions', 'Guessing Words', and 'Please we've come
to learn a trade'; and the performers not only mime the trade but give
its initials, as 'P.H.' for picking hops. In the 1855 edition of *The Boy's
Own Book*, pp. 51–2, where the game is styled 'Trades and Professions'
('sometimes called "Dumb Motions" in London'), the guessers are similarly assisted with initials and mime. But the 1872 edition says: 'It may
also be played without giving the initials of the trade represented.'

Clearly the game is another offshoot of 'Two Poor Tradesmen', played
in George III's time, and described in Halliwell's *Nursery Rhymes*, 1844,
p. 108, where the performers claim to be:

> Two broken tradesmen, newly come over,
> The one from France and Scotland, the
> other from Dover.

In this game 'played exclusively by boys' the tradesmen told their trade,
and what had to be guessed was the implement they required. 'The fun
is, that the unfortunate wight who guesses the tool is beaten with the
caps of his fellows till he reaches a fixed goal.' (Compare 'Wadds and the
Wears' in Mactaggart's *Gallovidian Encyclopedia*, 1824, pp. 460–2.)

The game is also well-known on the Continent, and has apparently
long been so. Otto Kampmüller gives four versions played in present-day
Austria. In one, 'Es kommen zwei Damen aus Wien', a trade is imitated
and its initials given. The player who guesses correctly then chooses
either 'apple' or 'pear' (as in 'American Times'), and takes the place
of whichever of the principals the choice denotes (*Oberösterreichische
Kinderspiele*, 1965, pp. 67–8). In another version, 'Meister und Geselle',
there is no miming, and the players have to guess what tool is needed
for a given trade, which is precisely as Halliwell described the game in
Britain more than a century ago. The game is also popular in Berlin,
where the children say or sing, 'Meister, Meister, gib uns Arbeit', or
'Wir kommen aus dem Morgenland, die Sonne hat uns braun gebrannt'.
Here, if the master guesses the activity being mimed, the performers
run, and the master tries to catch one of them, who becomes master for

the next turn (Reinhard Peesch, *Berliner Kinderspiel der Gegenwart*, 1957, pp. 35–6). Further versions are given by F. M. Böhme. *Deutsches Kinderlied und Kinderspiel*, 1897, pp. 667–9, and it seems clear from one of them called 'Botschimber, Botschamber', recorded in 1891, that this is the game Goethe's mother was referring to when she wrote to her grandchildren in Weimar in 1786:

'Wenn ich bei euch wäre, lernte ich euch allerlei Spiele:
Vögelverkaufen, Tuchdiebes, Potzschimper, Potzschemper und
noch viele andere.'

Further A. de Cock and I. Teirlinck, *Kinderspel in Zuid-Nederland*, vol. iv, pp. 7–10, give a version, 'Stom-en-ambacht', in which two children perform a trade while the rest guess its nature. It thus seems possible that this was one of the games Bruegel depicted in 1560, where he shows a row of little girls sitting against a wall watching two others who are standing in front of them. Certainly the game was current about this time for not only did Fischart list 'Das Handwerck ausschrenen' and 'Handwerksmann, was gibst dazu', in 1590 (*Geschichtklitterung von Gargantua*), but the game is well documented in France. 'Les métiers' is described in Rolland's *Jeux de l'enfance*, 1883, in *Les Jeux de la jeunesse*, *c.* 1814, p. 71, and in *Les Récréations galantes*, 1672. In Cotgrave's *Dictionarie*, 1611, appears the entry:

'*Mestiers*, a certain Game wherein all trades are counterfeited by signes.'

And Rabelais listed 'mestiers' among the games played by Gargantua (1534). Indeed there is a pleasant story that Louis XIII, as a child, showed 'une imagination singulière' when playing the game, by suggesting that his side should imitate the trade of pickpockets. (Compare the West Ham 10-year-old today.)

In Italy, where the game is also widespread, there are versions called 'Nonnina' and 'Buon giorno re', although usually it is 'Mestieri muti' (M. M. Lumbroso, *Giochi*, 1967, pp. 198–9, 329–30). Here two children act a trade and, as in the Austrian game of the two ladies from Vienna, when a girl guesses correctly she becomes instrumental in determining which of the two actors she shall replace. She is asked whether she will have 'flowers, fruits, cats, actresses, singers, cars, name-plates, or sweets'. If her choice is 'flowers' the pair decide privately the kind of flower each shall be, and then ask her, for example, 'Will you have a rose or a violet?' and she takes the player's place according to the one she has named. In Sardinia, however, the game is 'La regina delle api'. The players perform before a single child, the Queen, who, when she guesses their occupation correctly (for example 'ironing'), chases after them and tries to catch one of them. It is curious that this is how the game is played in Sweden in the present day, where a single player, the King, must guess the occupation of his sons (not daughters); and, as our own survey has shown, it is also one of the ways the game is played today in Britain, particularly Scotland, where a single player, usually designated 'King' or 'Queen' has to guess the *activity* rather than trade which the other players are miming.

Fool, fool, come to school

In this game the guesser, who is styled the 'fool' or sometimes the 'little dog', moves out of earshot while each of the others assumes a fancy name. The guesser has then to decide which person has acquired a given name, and, if, as is most likely, his guess is incorrect, they laugh at him for his trouble. Thus a 10-year-old girl in Hanley writes:

> 'A popular game in our street is "Fool, Fool, come out to play". First of all somebody goes to the other side of the street. Then someone names the others such things as the golden ring and the purple peacock. Then the girl that told them what they were shouts "Fool, Fool, come out to play, and find the golden ring." And if the Fool picks the wrong one they all shout "Go back and learn your lessons." But if the person picks the right one she takes her and puts her in her den.'

Similarly, a 12-year-old girl in Cumnock, where the game is called 'Little Black Doggie', states:

> 'To begin with there are about half-a-dozen players. Two of the players are picked to be what we call the "man" and the "little black doggie". The "man" gives each player a romantic

name, for example "golden moon", "tiger lily", etc. When
everyone has received a flattering name they chant "Little
black doggie come a hop, hop, hop, and pick out the
golden moon", or whatever name they happen to chant.
The "doggie" then hops up in the hope of picking out the
right one, which is very difficult to do. If she doesn't pick
the right one, the players shout at the "doggie", "Away you
go you horrible man", and the poor little "doggie" hops
back in disgrace to let somebody else take her place. If on
the other hand the "doggie" does pick the right one, the
"man" tells her to take the player by the nose or the ear,
etc., thus upholding her position of "Little Black Doggie".

§ Both these forms of the game are traditional. *The Folk-Lore Journal*, vol.
v, 1887, pp. 49–50, gives 'Fool, Fool, come to School' from Cornwall.
Gomme, *Traditional Games*, vol. i, 1894, pp. 330–1, has 'Little Dog I call
you' from Sheffield. The Macmillan MSS., 1922, contain a description of
'Dunce, Dunce, Double Dee', played at Kilmington in Devon. Further,
J. M. McBain in *Arbroath, Past and Present*, 1887, p. 344, describing
the game as it was known in his youth about 1837, shows it to have been
played in essentially the manner it is in Cumnock today. (The players even
adopted golden names such as 'Golden Rose' and 'Golden Butter-plate'.)
He adds that the player who guessed did so in the guise of 'a weird wife
hirpling on a broomstick', to whom the children called, 'Witchie, witchie,
warlock, come happin' to your dael'. Thus it appears that the absurd hopping of the 'little black doggie' at Cumnock today is not the product of a
modern schoolchild's imagination, but a deep-rooted memory of a limping night-hag; and this is apparently confirmed by reference to the game
'Jams' which follows. See also 'Goldens' in *Games of Argyleshire*, 1901,
pp. 236–7 (players named 'Golden Slipper', 'Golden Ball', etc.); 'Golden
Names' in *Folk-Lore*, vol. xvii, 1906, pp. 224–5, where the guesser
is 'Ruggy Dug'; and—a possible relative—'William-a-Trimbletoe' in
American Nonsinging Games, 1953, pp. 177–8.

Jams

The distinction between this game and 'Fool, Fool, come to school' is
that the guesser, who is here openly an old woman or witch, knows the

kind of names the children have adopted (usually varieties of jam), and has to guess precisely what ones they are. The game, which is apparently exclusive to Scotland and the Isles, ends in one of three ways. In Stornoway, it takes the form of a playlet akin to 'Mother, the Cake is Burning':

> 'The witch comes and knocks at the door and asks if there is any jams today The maid says yes, and the witch tries to guess the names of them. If she does not guess the names of them she does not take them.'

On the other hand, should the witch, who 'has to live in a creepy corner', succeed in guessing the names, she gains possession of the 'jams', takes the children away, and hides them in her house.

> 'The mother comes to the witch's house and asks her if she has seen her children. The witch says she saw them at a house or somewhere and when the mother goes to see, the witch sends the children home. The mother comes back and the witch says she saw them running into her house, so the mother goes home and asks the children where they have been. They tell their mother something like they have been eating all the sweets in the house' (Girl, 11).

At Westerkirk in Dumfriesshire, where the game is known as 'Limpety Lil', the guesser is summoned with the words 'Limpety Lil come over the hill and see what you can find'. At Langholm, where the game is called 'Limping Jenny', a 12-year-old reports:

> 'Old Jenny comes into the shop and asks for something. If she asks for lard and somebody is lard she takes that person away with her. When she gets home if she likes the product she puts it in the pantry, and if she doesn't in the dustbin. She then goes for more. At the end of the game all the products that were put in the bin and Jenny all chase the shopkeeper and "bash" him.'

In Scalloway, however, the game becomes a form of 'Honey Pots' (q.v.). When the witch has guessed someone's identity:

'that person is then swung ten times by the other two,
being held by the arms (the "jam" clasps her hands below
her knees). If the "jam" falls before the end of the swinging
then she is rotten and is out' (Girl, *c.* 12).

§ Such details as the division of the products between the pantry and the
bin, and the declaration that some of the jams are rotten, indicate that the
players were formerly divided into two sides. In fact this game is significant not only for its relationship to the latter part of 'Mother, the Cake is
Burning' (p. 172), but is central to the appreciation of child-lore in Europe,
with its ancient dramatization of the conflicting forces of good and evil. In
Gomme's *Traditional Games*, vol. i, 1894, p. 8, appears a version called
'Angel and Devil' from Deptford, Kent, in which the angel comes to the
door seeking ribbons. The angel is asked what colour she wants; and if
there is a child in the house of that colour, the angel leads her away. This is
akin to the game 'Colors' in the United States, where the chief characters
are an Angel, Devil, and Mother. The angel and devil each seek to acquire
children (under the guise of colours) for their respective sides which, at
the end of the game, have a pulling-match, members of each side lining
up behind each other, and holding on to the waist of the player in front. In
Newell's *Games of American Children*, 1883, pp. 213–14, the Good Angel
or 'Angel with the Golden Star' opposes the Bad Angel or 'Angel with the
Pitchfork'. Newell suggested that the game had come from Europe only
recently, since German children in New York used the same imagery, 'Der
Engel mit dem goldenen Strauß' and 'Der Engel mit dem Feuerhaken'.
Indeed the game 'Farbe angeben' was well known in Germany at this time
(Böhme, *Deutsches Kinderspiel*, 1897, p. 636). Newell also pointed out
that the game was played in Austria, where the practice was for the children to be taken to Heaven or Hell according to who guessed their colour,
while the division between these places was marked by a piece of wood,
called 'Fire', over which the subsequent tug-of-war took place. According
to Kampmüller versions of this game, with Angel and Devil alternately
choosing colours, continue to be played in Austria, and are called 'Engel
und Teufel' or 'Das Farbenaufgeben' (*Oberösterreichische Kinderspiele*,
1965, p. 166). The game is also much played today in Italy, where it is
known simply as 'Colori', although the Madonna or an Angel likewise
take turns with the Devil to ask for colours, and the side wins whose
leader guesses the most colours correctly. However Signora Lumbroso
in her *Giochi*, 1967, pp. 222–9, adds the interesting information that in

Umbria the children are not just colours, but 'coloured pots'; and that at Pesaro, near San Marino, each child whose colour has been guessed correctly is tested (as she is in the Shetlands), by being made to put her hands round her knees while the Angel and the Devil swing her a certain number of times according to the number of years old she is. If the player passes this test she goes with the Angel to 'Paradiso', but should her feet touch the ground while she is being swung she goes with the Devil to 'L'inferno'. The game has not only long been played in Italy (described by G. Bernoni, *Giuochi popolari veneziani*, 1874, p. 51), it is traditional in Spain, where the protagonists are likewise an Angel and the Devil (F. Maspons y Labrós, *Jochs de la Infancia*, 1874, p. 91); and it is said that 'Los Colores' was mentioned by Alonso de Ledesma Buitrago in 1606. It is remarkable that when Eugène Rolland reported the game in France the principal players were 'la Sainte-Vierge' and 'le Diable', and the third player was 'une marchande de rubans' (cf. Deptford, 1894). In Germany, as long ago as 1827, a version was recorded called 'Blumen verkaufen' in which the principal players were a Gardener and a Buyer, and the players adopted the names of flowers (H. Dittmar, *Der Kinder Lustfeld*, 1827, p. 270). From this it appears that even the minor variations of this game can be traditional, for in Piedmont, in the present day, Signora Lumbroso reports that children play a game called 'Fiori', in which the principal players are, similarly, a gardener and a buyer, and the children adopt the names of flowers, only here, if the buyer guesses incorrectly three times in succession the gardener becomes the buyer (*Giochi*, 1967, p. 224).

Compare 'Coloured Birds', which follows, 'Honey Pots', and 'Eggy Peggy'.

Coloured birds

The strangeness of the two preceding games is not lessened by the coexistence of the following drama, known as 'Coloured Birds' or 'Coloured Eggs', which is particularly popular in Bristol. One child becomes a mother, one a wolf or fox, and the rest are birds or eggs and choose which colours they will be. The wolf, who has not been a party to their variegation, comes to the door and knocks. Sometimes in Bristol the mother also acts the role of the door, which opens and shuts in keeping with the story. Thus the wolf taps on her head, and the door turns round and says 'Go away'. The wolf taps again, and the door says 'Come in'. In Wolstanton, Staffordshire, instead of knocking at the door, the wolf seeks admittance apparently by pulling a door bell, for he tugs the person's hair. He is asked, 'What do you want?'

> 'Have you any coloured birds?'
> 'What colour?'

The wolf names a colour. If there are no birds (or eggs) of that colour everybody stands firm, and the wolf has to go away and try again; but if one of the players has assumed this colour she runs for her life, either across the road to safety, or in a circle round the playground, or runs until caught. When she is caught she has to go 'to a place' until the catcher has caught the rest of the colours.

This game (which several children describe as 'my favourite game') might be cited as an example of the shallowness of modern juvenile fantasy, were it not that in *The American Anthropologist*, vol. i, 1888, p. 281, W. H. Babcock noted it being played by children in Washington D.C. The visitor was there an angel, and the game called 'Birds'. The angel came up to the other principal player (the 'namer') and touched her on the back.

> Namer: 'Who is that?'
> Angel: 'It's me.'
> Namer: 'What do you want?'
> Angel: 'I want some birds.'
> Namer: 'What color?'
> Angel: 'Blue' (for example).

The angel, having guessed one of the colours, chased the person, exactly as in England today. In France, Belèze reported, the Devil sought animals in the same fashion, his dialogue with the seller commencing, 'Pan, pan.'

> 'Qui est-ce qui est là?'
> 'C'est le diable avec sa fourche.'
> 'Que veut-il?'
> 'Un animal.'
> 'Entrez.'

In this version, if the Devil guessed an animal's name correctly, he had first to buy it, with so many taps on the dealer's palm, before he could set off in pursuit; and if he caught the animal he made it captive with three blows on the head and tail (*Jeux des adolescents*, 1856, pp. 43–4). At Ottensheim in Austria, according to Kampmüller, the game is 'Vogel verkaufen', and the buyer has first to count a certain number before he chases the bird (*Oberösterreichische Kinderspiele*, 1965, p. 165). 'Vogelverkauf' or 'Vögelausjagen' has often been recorded in Germany (Böhme, *Deutsches Kinderspiel*, 1897, pp. 587–8); and it seems to be another of the games Goethe's mother spoke of in 1786 (see previous, under 'Three Jolly Workmen'). It was fully described by Gutsmuths in his deservedly renowned *Spiele für die Jugend*, 1796 (1802, pp. 271–2):

> 'The leader of the company is the Seller. All the little ones are birds, except one who plays the role of Buyer. The Seller stands in front of his birds and gives each a bird-name: you are a citril-finch, you a starling, you a finch, etc. The Buyer must not hear this. Then he comes and asks the Seller: "Have you birds for sale?"—"Yes!"—"Have you a raven?"—"No!"—"A sparrow?"— "No!" Always "No!" until the buyer asks, for instance, for a starling which is amongst the number. Then they all cry "Yes!" and the bird so-named flies off as quickly as possible; that is, he runs hard to get away from his new master. To allow him a start, the Buyer must first pay the Seller a certain number of gold pieces, by tapping his hand. Then he starts off. If he catches the bird, it is his: otherwise the bird goes back to the Seller: so he belongs to the Seller again and he gives him a meal, apples, pears, plums. The party which is the strongest at the end has won.'

It is apparent that this game has also a long history in Britain. In 1825 Jamieson reported it being played at Abernethy under the name 'All the Wild Birds in the Air'. Here, after the players had been given the names of birds, 'the person who opposes tries to guess the name of each individual. When he errs, he is subjected to a stroke on the back. When his conjecture is right, he carries away on his back that bird, which is subjected to a blow from each of the rest. When he has discovered and carried off the whole, he has gained the game' (*Scottish Dictionary, Supplement*, vol. ii, p. 681). Furthermore, the game 'All the Birds in the

Air', so named, is poetically described, and clearly depicted in *A Little Pretty Pocket-Book*, 1744, the first book of games for children, and one of the first books to be published for juvenile entertainment. The description, on p. 47 of the 1760 edition, reads:

> Here various Boys stand round the Room,
> Each does some favourite Bird assume;
> And if the *Slave* once hits his Name,
> He's then made free, and crowns the
>   Game.

The accompanying woodcut, despite the rhyme, shows the game being played out of doors. Five boys, clad in skirted coats, breeches, and tricorn hats, are to be seen standing against a wall, with one lad out at the side conducting the game, and there is one in front, 'the slave', who is apparently guessing.

Queenie

'Queenie' is the perpetual delight of little girls aged eight and nine, for it has the great recommendation of combining the mysterious pleasure of guessing with the ball-play to which they are so much addicted. One girl is selected 'Queenie', given the ball, and stands with her back turned to the rest. Without looking behind her, she throws the ball back over her head, and the other girls scramble for it. They then form up in a row, with their hands behind their backs so that the girl in front will not know which of them has the ball; and they let 'Queenie' know they are ready, sometimes addressing her in doggerel verse:

> Queenie, Queenie,
> Who has the ball?
> I haven't got it,
> It isn't in my pocket,
> Queenie, Queenie,
> Who has the ball?
>> Scarborough, Lincoln, Plympton St Mary, Ruthin, Penrith.
>> In Scotland the verse begins 'Alabala, alabala, who has
>> the ball?'

Queenie, Queenie, on the wall,
Who has got the golden ball?
Welwyn and St Peter Port

Queenie, Queenie,
Who's got the ball?
Is she big or is she small,
Is she fat or is she thin,
Or is she like a rolling pin?
Chiswick, West Ham, Alton. In Norwich they ask 'Or has she got a double chin?'

Queenie, Queenie,
Who has got the ball?
Cashee loo, throw it away,
Boney's behind the wall.
Stockton, Co. Durham

'Queenie' then turns round, and picks out the player she thinks is concealing the ball. If her guess is correct she usually remains Queenie; if she is wrong, the girl who has been successful in concealing the ball takes her place. If a girl manages to catch the ball when Queenie throws it, that girl takes her place in front, provided that she says 'Caught ball' or whatever is the term locally prescribed. (In Liverpool it is 'Copper', in Lincoln 'Kings', in Welshpool 'White Horse', in Swansea 'Cabbage', in Stoke-on-Trent 'Fish'.) Should the ball, by chance, roll back to the person who threw it, they pick it up and return it to Queenie to throw again, although in Norwich they must first cry 'See ball', in Lincoln 'Carrots'. When Queenie turns round to guess who has the ball she need not make up her mind immediately; she can ask one girl, and then another, to stretch out an arm, or to open her legs, or even to do 'a twist' (a quick half turn). And this is considered part of the sport. The girls pretend they have the ball when they have not got it; and the girl who has it feels safe, as long as she does not giggle, because 'we usually hide it under our jumper'.

Names: From Pendeen to Penrith the usual name is 'Queenie', although in Bristol it is 'Queenie-ball', in Liverpool 'Queenie-i', in Preston 'Queenio', and in some places 'Queenie-o-co-co' especially in north Wales and the Potteries. In Scotland and north-east England it is

'Alabala' or, in Helensburgh and Inverness, 'Ali Baba'. In Lincoln it is 'Ellabella Cinderella'.

§ In the nineteenth century the game seems to have been less active and more poetic. The girls divided into two sides. One side had the ball or a similar object, the other side sat with the Queen on the grass. The first side advanced line abreast singing:

> Lady Queen Anne, she sits in the sun,
> As fair as a lily, as white as a swan;
> We bring you three letters, and pray you
> read one.

The Queen answered:

> I cannot read one unless I read all
> So pray, Miss ... (guessing who has the
> ball) deliver the ball.

If the Queen guessed correctly the two sides changed roles; if incorrectly, the one who had the ball replied:

> The ball is mine, it is not thine,
> So you, proud Queen, may sit on your
> throne
> While we poor gipsies go and come.

The side with the ball then retired, chose a new player to hold the ball, and advanced again, while the others kept their seats for what must have seemed eternity.

There are accounts of the game being played in this way in *The Girl's Book of Diversions*, 1835, pp. 2–3; Halliwell's *Popular Rhymes*, 1849, pp. 133–4; Chambers's *Popular Rhymes of Scotland*, 1869, p. 136; Newell's *Games of American Children*, 1883, p. 151, 'My Lady Queen Anne'; Walter Crane's *Little Queen Anne and Her Majesty's Letters*, 1886; Emmeline Plunket's *Merrie Games in Rhyme*, 1886, pp. 14–15; Gomme's *Traditional Games*, vol. ii, 1898, pp. 90–102 and 453; and Norman Douglas's *London Street Games*, 1916, p. 43, 'Queen Mab', and p. 65, 'Queen Anne, Queen Anne, she sits in the sun'. Today the old verses appear only in nursery rhyme books. Our correspondents state that the game was already being played in its modern form in London during the First World War.

Stroke the baby

> 'One boy turns his face to a wall. Then one child strokes his back while the other children say:
>
>> Stroke the baby, stroke the baby,
>> I will tip it.
>
> Then the boy turns round, and points to the one he thinks stroked him. If he points to the right boy, the boy he has pointed to turns his face to the wall and he is the baby. But if the boy points to the wrong boy he is still the baby'.
>
> *Boy, 12 Welshpool*

Guessing who touched one is common today in the opening phase of 'I Draw a Snake upon Your Back' (q.v.), but is sometimes, as above, a game in itself. A student recalls that in Darlington three or four children together would often play the game in the school yard 'in the short time between the whistle and lining up to go in'. One child would turn his back while the rest chanted:

> Strokey back, strokey back,
> Which hand will you tak':
> Be you right, be you wrong,
> Which hand stroked you?

'Then you had to guess who poked you, which hand was used, and what finger.' And she adds that the first person to be 'on' was usually the least popular person in the group: the term 'strokey back' apparently being somewhat euphemistic, for the players would take the opportunity to give the person a hard poke, and 'occasionally there would be vicious punches with clenched fists'.

Names: 'Hot Cockrel' (Ipswich), 'I Draw a Snake upon Your Back' (Windermere), 'North, South, East, West' (Bradford), 'Stroke the Baby'

(Welshpool), 'Strokey Back' (Darlington).

In the United States, where the game is not uncommon, two of its names are 'Bore a Hole' and 'Punchboard'.

§ It is almost an axiom that the more insignificant a game appears, the more remarkable is its history. The sport of giving a person a clout and having him guess who did it, has been popular in England for anyway the past three or four centuries, usually under the name 'Hot Cockles'. It appears to be referred to by Coverdale in 1549 (*OED*); and it is named in Sidney's *Arcadia*, 1590; Rowlands's *Letting of Hvmovrs Blood*, 1600; Marvell's *Mr Smirke*, 1676; and Arbuthnot's *Memoirs of Martinus Scriblerus* written 1714. Traditionally the game was played at Christmas, the guesser being blindfolded and kneeling on the floor, the other players in turn slapping him with some force on his head or back, and hoping that their blow would not be identified. Steele in *The Spectator*, 28 December 1711, and Gay in *The Shepherd's Week*, 1714, are characteristically witty about the game's possibilities when played by simple folk. Brooke in *The Fool of Quality*, vol. i, 1766, p. 72, describes the guesser holding out his hand behind him to be 'well warmed' by the other players until he makes a correct guess. Indeed in France the game is generally known as 'La Main chaude'. In *Les Trente-six figures*, 1587, the caption calls it the 'jeu de frappe main, Où deviner il fault celuy qui frappe'. In Froissart's boyhood, *c*. 1345, the game was simply 'Je me plaing qui me feri' ('L'Espinette amoureuse', l. 223). In Italy today it is 'Mano calda'. In modern Greece the sport is so popular among sailors that even tourists notice it: one player puts his right hand round to the left side of his waist, and shields it from his view by extending his left hand against the side of his face; the others gather round in a group and repeatedly strike or pretend to strike his hand, until he guesses correctly who last hit him. In ancient Greece the game was 'Kollabismos'. Pollux says that one player covered his eyes with the palms of his hands while another hit him and asked him (as do children today in Darlington) to identify which hand it was that dealt the blow (*Onomasticon*, ix. 129). It seems more than likely that this sport was familiar to the men guarding Jesus, when they blindfolded him, and 'smote him with the palms of their hands, saying, Prophesy unto us, thou Christ, Who is he that smote thee?' (Matthew xxvi: 67–8; Mark xiv: 65; Luke xxii: 64). Indeed the game was possibly already old. One of the pictures on the wall of a tomb at Beni Hassan, *c*. 2000 BC, shows a player on his knees while two others, unseen by him, thump or pretend to thump his back with their fists (J. G. Wilkinson, *Ancient Egyptians*, vol. ii, 1878, p. 61). It is difficult to think what kind of game they are playing if it is not one like 'Kollabismos' or 'Stroke the Baby'.

Other names in the British Isles have been 'Slap-of-the-Ear' (north country, *EDD*, vol. v, 1904), 'Buaileadh Am Bas' (= Striking the palm of the hand, *Games of Argyleshire*, 1901, pp. 130–1), 'Bosuigheacht' (= Hitting on the palm, Co. Mayo, *Béaloideas*, vol. viii, 1938, p. 134), 'Soola Winka' (*Irish Wake Amusements*, 1967, pp. 51–2, where several related games are given), 'Handy-Croopen' (*Shetland and Orkney Glossary*, 1866), and 'Pick the Craw' (Miss Jean Rodger, Forfar, *c.* 1910). This last name may be compared with the Austrian 'Krähenrupfen', the name of a similar game in which the players gather round the one who cannot see, who must guess which of them is plucking his hair (*Oberösterreichische Kinderspiele*, 1965, p. 66). It is possible that this game was depicted by Bruegel in 1560 where, in his picture of children at play, he shows a group with their hands on one boy's head, but with only one of them, it seems, actually pulling his hair.

Husky-bum, finger or thumb?

This curious game survives chiefly in the north and midlands. At Wednesbury in Staffordshire, where it is known as 'Bugs', one child leans forward putting his hands up against a wall, and the child playing with him leaps on to his back, holds up a certain number of fingers, and shouts 'How many bugs?' The one underneath makes a guess. If his guess is correct the two change places; if incorrect, he stays underneath, and his rider holds up a different number of fingers. In Wigan, and also in Peterborough, Pontefract, and Bishop Auckland, three or four boys may play at once. One boy makes a back, and the boy who jumps on calls 'Finger or thumb?' If the one underneath guesses correctly he stands up, and the rider bends down in his place. If he guesses incorrectly, another boy jumps on his back and holds up a finger or thumb. 'So we carry on with the game as long as we like.' In Bishop Auckland the one on top calls 'Hum, dum, dum, finger or thumb?' At Retford in Nottinghamshire the cry is 'Finger, thumb, or dum', and either two boys play together, or two teams. When two teams are to play they toss a coin to see which side shall have first jump, and the boys who have to bend down shout 'Baggy front man', because the one in front gets no weight on him, but stands with his back against the wall supporting the second in the team, who bends down and hangs on to him.[34] The others in the team line up, each putting his head between the legs of the boy in front, and his arms around his thighs, so that they present one long close-knit back. The members of the other team jump on to the 'down' side, one at a time, until all are astride. If the bottom side collapses, the players have to form a new back, and the jumpers have another turn; if they stay steady, the leader of the mounted team calls 'Finger, thumb, or dum?', and holds up a finger, a thumb, or a clenched fist. If the down side guesses correctly they become the jumpers, if incorrectly, they are jumped upon again. But if one of the riders' feet touches the ground while he is mounted, there is a cry of 'Touch!' and the ones underneath become the jumpers, as in 'Hi Jimmy Knacker' (q.v.). At Holmfirth in the West Riding, when all are mounted, the cry is 'Finger, thumb, or rusty?'—'rusty' being a clenched fist; at Elsecar, near Barnsley, it is 'Finger, thumb, or rusty bum?'; in Nottingham City it is 'Husky-bum, finger or thumb?'; at Brinsley, north-west of Nottingham, it is 'Husky fusky, finger or thumb?'; at Nelson in Lancashire it is 'Thumb, stick, or roger?'—'stick' being the index finger, and 'roger' the little finger; while at Barrow-in-Furness it is 'Stick, roger, or dodger?'—'stick' being the thumbs pointed upwards, 'roger' pointed sideways, 'dodger' pointing downwards. At Spennymoor, where this 'rough and exciting' game is immensely popular (fifty-six accounts received), they play with as many as ten boys on each side. Since they allow 'no creeping', that is to say, no creeping forward once a boy has jumped on to the line of backs, the first boy to mount has to make a terrific jump along the line of backs to leave room for the others to mount behind him, and 'it is the job of the "pillar" or "cushion" to stop the players from hitting their heads on the wall'. Moreover the jumping side, says a 14-year-old, will try to make the 'down' side collapse. 'This is done either by jumping high into the air and landing with force on their backs or, when everybody except one is mounted, the last boy will run hard and try to push his team-mates forward, this sometimes results in the boy at the front being nearly bent double, and he has to give way to prevent injury.' It is only then—if the side which is down does not collapse—that the point of the game is reached. 'The last man or the jumping side shouts,

"Hum a dum dum,
A finger or a thumb,"

and he holds either a finger or a thumb up in the air.'

As we have said the game is now played mostly in the north and midlands. In other parts of the country it has been progressively overlaid by 'Hi Jimmy Knacker' (q.v.), a game in which victory comes only to the strong, not to successful guessers; but it continues to be played in Penzance (1961) where the leader of the mounted team holds up a certain number of fingers and cries:

Willy, Willy Whiteman,
How many fingers do I hold up?

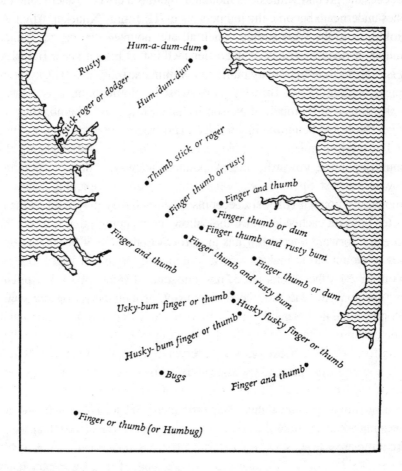

Names for 'Husky-bum, Finger or Thumb?' in northern England.

§ Local journals, and our older correspondents, give general confirmation of the dialect terms used by boys today. In the *Leeds Mercury Weekly Supplement*, 5 June 1897, the leader of the mounted side is said to hold up a digit and exclaim 'Dick, Prick, Anawny, Cherry, Berry!' (Thumb, first finger, second, third, fourth). In York, around 1915, he cried 'Dick, Prick, Polony'. In Forfar, *c.* 1890, the cry was 'Big Dick, Little Dick, and the Bozer' (a circle with the thumb and forefinger). In Barrow-in-Furness, in the 1930s, it was 'Stick an' Roger'. In the Scottish Border country, *c.* 1925, the game 'which involved a wee bit of second sight' was called 'Pinkie, Finger, Thoomb, or Knuckle' (*Southern Annual*, 1957, p. 28). In parts of Derbyshire, *c.* 1900, the cry was 'Husky, fusky, finger or thumb'. In general in Derbyshire, Nottinghamshire, Lindsey, and Sheffield, the game was called 'Rusty' or 'Rustibum, Finger or Thumb'. In Morpeth, 1912, it was 'Kittyback, Kittyback, finger or thumb'. In the neighbourhood of Halifax, up to the 1920s, the leader of the mounted team challenged the boys underneath with the words:

> Inkum, jinkum, jerry mi buck,
> How mony horns do I hold up?

And if their guess was incorrect he responded:

> *Two*, tha ses, an' *three* it is;
> I'll leean thi how to play
> At Inkum, jinkum, jerry mi buck.

At the Calder Ironworks, near Glasgow, about 1855 (*Rymour Club*, vol. i, 1906, p. 5), one boy used to 'make a back' and the others in succession jumped astride of him singing:

> Bairdy, Bairdy, buckety-buck,
> Hoo mony fingers stan's up?

A remarkable feature of this game is that its oral formula, including the meaningless word 'buck', appears to have survived from classical antiquity. Although the name 'Buck, Buck' has not been found amongst English children in the 1960s, both the name and the challenge 'Buck, Buck, how many fingers do I hold up?' are recollected by some of our adult informants, e.g. in Leeds in 1920, and in Launceston, Cornwall, in 1915 ('Bucksebuck, how many fingers do I hold up?'). It is also reflected in the names 'Buckle Up' and 'Huckey Buck' current today amongst the boys of, respectively, Petersfield and Ipswich, for the related game 'Hi Jimmy Knacker'.[35] And it survives in the sidewalk rhyme picked up by Dr Howard in the United States:

> Buck, buck, you lousey muck,
> How many fists have I got up,
> One, two, or none?[36]

Indeed, 'Buck, Buck, how many fingers do I hold up?' seems to have been the standard formula in London up to the First World War (*Living London*, vol. iii, 1903, p. 269; *London Street Games*, 1916, p. 31). In Randle Holme's list of sports 'used by our countrey Boys and Girls' (*Academie of Armory*, Book III, 1688, ch. xvi, § 91), appears the entry:

'Runing or Leaping, Hoping, Skipping, Buk or Runing Leaps.'

This is presumably a reference to the game, whose popularity in eighteenth- and nineteenth-century England is attested by notices such as the following:

c. 1781 *Nancy Cock's Pretty Song Book*, p. 37 (almost certainly first printed 1744):

> Buck, buck, How many horns do I hold up?
> Three.
> Three you say and two there are:
> Buck, buck, How many horns do I hold up?
> One.
> One you say and one there is:
> Buck, buck, rise up.

1796 Introduced into a caricature by Gillray on 17 June.
1819 Keats, in a letter describing the production of Charles Bucke's tragedy *The Italians* at Drury Lane on 3 April: 'It was damn'd— The people in the Pit had a favourite call on the night of "Buck Buck rise up" and "Buck Buck how many horns do I hold up".'
1820 *School Boys' Diversions*, pp. 48–9, 'Any number of boys may play this, if half of them are bucks, and half riders; or, if when

either buck guesses right, another rider will take his place.'

1829 *Boy's Own Book*, pp. 38–9. ' "Buck" ... a sport for two boys
only ... It is usual, but, we think, quite unnecessary, for the player
who gives the back to be blindfolded.'

1856 *Every Boy's Book*, p. 9. 'The boy who plays the Buck gives a
back with his head down, and rests his hands on some wall or pal-
ing in front of him.' The boy who mounts him then cries 'Buck!
Buck! How many horns do I hold up?'

§ In *The Satyricon* of Petronius Arbiter, written about AD 65, in the time
of Nero, there is an incident at Trimalchio's feast involving his favourite
serving boy:

> 'Trimalchio, not to seem moved by the loss, kissed the boy and
> bade him get on his back. Without delay the boy climbed on
> horseback on him, and slapped him on the shoulders with his
> hand, laughing and calling out "Bucca, bucca, quot sunt hic?" '

The coincidence that the same amusement should be played with the
same word-sound in the first century AD and in the twentieth, can, it
seems, only be explained by admitting the stamina of oral tradition.
Thus investigations show that the game is international. It is played, not
only throughout the English-speaking world, but in, for instance, France,
Germany, Switzerland, the Netherlands, Scandinavia, Spain, Portugal,
Italy, Yugoslavia, Albania, Greece, Turkey, Russia, India, and Japan.[37]
Furthermore the word *buck* or *bock* (Old English *buc* or *bucca*) is recur-
rent. In Germany a common name and formula is 'Bock, Bock, wieviel
Hörner hab ich?' In Sweden (according to Eric Gamby, *Kråken satt på
tallekvist*, 1952, p. 71) it is:

> Bulleri bulleri bock
> Hur många horn står upp?

The response is similar to that in the West Riding in 1920:

> *Fyra* du sa, *tre* det var

And in South Africa, where 'Bok, Bok' is almost a national sport, it is

> Bok, Bok, staan styf,
> Hoeveel vingers op jou lyf?[38]

Moreover the game did not go unnoticed on the Continent even in the sixteenth and seventeenth centuries. In *Il Pentamerone*, Day II, 1634, one of the games the Prince played to pass the time till dinner was 'Anca Nicola'. In Bruegel's picture of children at play, dated 1560, five boys are shown playing the game, two making a back, two mounted (one holding up his hand), and the fifth seated, acting 'pillow'. It is also probably the game 'Peertgen wel bereyt' mentioned by Adrianus Junius (*Nomenclator Octilinguis*, 1567); the game 'Pferdlin wol bereit', and perhaps 'Eselin beschlagen', named by Fischart (*Geschichtklitterung*, 1590); and Roger Pinon makes out a good case for it being Froissart's 'Charette Michaut' alluded to in 'L'Espinette amoureuse', written *c*. 1380.

There is also a form of the game, played indoors among women and small children, in which the child who is to guess, kneels down and buries his or her face in the lap of a second player who is seated. This gentle form of the game, consisting purely of guessing the number of fingers held up, is described in the American *Girl's Book of Diversions*, 1835, p. 8, under the name 'How Many Fingers?'

> 'This is a very simple play, and can be understood by children
> of three years old ... One lays her head in the lap of the other, in
> such a manner that she can see nothing. Her companion claps
> her several times on the back,[39] holding up one or more fingers,
> saying,

> > "Mingledy, mingledy, clap, clap,
> > How many fingers do I hold up?"'

This nursery sport, familiar in England, too, in the nineteenth century, continues to have life on the Isle of Barra in the Outer Hebrides where it is known in Gaelic as 'Imricean Beag'. The adult sits the child on her lap, and keeping her hand on his head, raises some fingers asking 'Cia meud adhairc air a' bhoc?' (How many horns are upon the buck?) If the child guesses right he is tapped gently ('Is firinneach am boc'), if wrong he gets a harder tap ('Is breugach am boc')—*An Gaidheal*, December 1952, p. 4. This form of the game is, in fact, the usual one in Sweden, and is also known in other parts of Europe. Compare, for instance, the

American formula with that in Silesia:

> Mingeldi, mingeldi, hopp, hurräh,
> Wieviel Finger sind in der Höh?

At Maastricht, on the Dutch border with Belgium, it is said to have been customary for three players to take part, one sitting, one squatting with his face in the first one's lap, and the third striking the back of the guesser and challenging him to tell the number of fingers raised (A. de Cock and I. Teirlinck, *Kinderspel in Zuid-Nederland*, vol. i, 1902, p. 299). This has every appearance of being the game depicted on fol. 52 of 'The Romance of Alexander' (MS. Bodley 264) illuminated at Bruges about 1340.[40] Further, the game as played today in the Hebrides, seems analogous, to say the least, to one of the games depicted in the rock-cut tombs at Beni Hassan in Middle Egypt, which belong to the XII Dynasty. Here, about 2000 BC, a player hides the fingers he is holding up by shielding them with his other hand, which is placed against the guesser's brow, and the inscription reads 'Putting the *Atep* on the forehead' (Edward Falkener, *Games Ancient and Oriental*, 1892, pp. 104–5).

How far to London?

In this game, which is played mostly by girls, one child who is blind-folded tells the others where they must go, and then has to guess the identity of the person with whom she happens to come into contact. As played in Liverpool the blindfolded girl stands facing the wall on one side of the street, while the others go to the wall on the other side and shout 'How far is it to London?' The blindfolded girl tells them perhaps 'Six miles forward', and everyone has to take six paces forward. She then might say 'Five miles to the left' and 'Two miles back', and 'Four miles to the left again', and the players carry out these instructions. Then the girl who is blindfolded is led across the road to the spot where the others started, and she must herself carry out the directions she gave the others, and, when she thinks she has reached London, try to touch some-body. The players are not allowed to move their feet while she tries to touch someone, but are allowed to sway about or bend down to avoid her touch. When she finds someone, she 'feels all over', and makes a guess who the person is. If her guess is correct that player becomes 'man'; but if her guess is incorrect she has to be 'man' again herself.

The exact procedure in this game varies in different places. Sometimes the blind player calls out the number of miles the children are to walk but they may go in whichever direction they like; sometimes she gives each player individual instructions; and sometimes she gives no instructions, but turns round fourteen times while the players take up positions wherever they like (Wolstanton), or she has to wait until the players call 'Coo-ee', while they go off and actually hide themselves (Durham). Just occasionally (a single account) there is no guessing of identity when she finds someone, and whoever she touches automatically becomes the new blind man. In Oxford and Headington, although there is guessing, it does not seem to matter whether she guesses correctly or not, for when she has found someone, and thinks she knows who the person is, she calls out her name, opens her eyes, and dashes to the starting-place. The person she has caught must run too, and whichever of them arrives first makes the other player the next blind man.

Names: 'Cuckoo' (Durham), 'Lion's Den' or 'How Many Miles to the Lion's Den' (Oxford), 'London' or 'How Far to London?' (Liverpool), 'Number Fourteen' (Wolstanton). In Indiana, 'Fourteen, Stand Still' (Brewster). In Edmonton, Alberta, 'Bee Find Honey'.

§ This game has been recollected by only one of our older correspondents (at Midgley, near Halifax, about 1895, where it was called 'How Many Miles to London?'), yet the form of the game apparently belongs to classical times.

Pollux, in his *Onomasticon* (ix. 113), has a rather obscure passage under 'Muinda' (Blindman), in which he seems to describe three games, or three versions of a game, that feature a player who has his eyes shut. In the first: 'One of the players shuts his eyes, cries "Look out!" and begins to chase the others. The one he catches takes his place and shuts his eyes in his turn.' Such a game, to be successful, would have to be played in a confined space, and would seem to be a game like 'Blind Man's Buff' (q.v., especially for the reference to Pollux, and the description he gives of the old form of 'Blind Man's Buff', which bears no relation to 'How Far to London'). In the second: 'One of the players shuts his eyes and the others hide themselves. The blind man searches for them until he finds one of them.' Commentators on this passage have not been able to decide whether, as appears from the Greek, this means that the child kept his eyes closed even when searching for the hidden players; or whether it means, as seemed practical, that he opened his eyes when he began searching. On the evidence, just given, of our report of 'Cuckoo' played today in Durham, the first hypothesis seems the more likely. In the third of Pollux's descriptions: 'The blind man, whether he touches one of his comrades, or whether he points at him, must guess what his name is.'

If these three accounts, written about AD 180–90, are taken in conjunction, particularly the last two, it may be felt that they are a not unreasonable description of the versions children play today of 'How Far to London?'

11. Acting Games

The difference between pretending games and acting games is that in pretending games children make-believe they are other people, and extemporize; in acting games they are allotted parts, they enact a particular story, and for the most part they repeat the words that were spoken when the game was last played. Thus the content of the acting games, as well as their style, is traditional; and children may be preserving for us, in however vestigial form, some of the most genuine folk-plays performed in Britain. Certainly their playlets are no new compositions. Similar passages of dialogue are to be heard repeated in different corners of Britain, and in the different languages of Europe. And at no time, it appears, have the plots been modified to suit the changing susceptibilities of the adult world. Indeed the scenes which oral tradition and the juvenile mind have thought fit to perpetuate over the years are strange to observe. In these playlets children are stolen to be eaten, mutilation is accepted almost as commonplace, and the supernatural is ever-present and constantly interfering with workaday activities. Time and again it is apparent that children either have a need to act out their fears, or actually enjoy the pretence of being frightened. The younger ones, in particular, can be seen relishing these games (they do not think of them as plays), and lingering over the more beastly details. Yet it will be noticed that, as in adult folk-drama, the suspense or horror never piles up without relief. There are repeated interludes for slapstick, when parental or ghostly authority is flouted, when children get spanked (there is much glee in this), or when pure nonsense is spoken. And it seems that these interludes are very necessary. Children of a certain age enter into their parts so intensely that they will, as it were, 'double-live' them. They will know from the story that, for instance, a witch is about to knock at their door to beg matches; and they will act beautifully the role that they are unconcerned and do not know. Yet a close observer will perceive that for all the bold face they are putting on, they are shivering with fright just as if a real witch were approaching.

Old man in the well

The best version of this acting game was collected in Swansea. The characters are a Mother, her Children, and an Old Man. The Old Man goes off and secretes himself in some suitably dark and mysterious place which is designated 'the well'. Thereupon a set dialogue takes place.

> Children to Mother: 'Please, mother, can we have a piece of
>   bread and butter?'
> Mother: 'Let me see your hands.'

The children hold out their hands for inspection.

> Mother: 'Your hands are very dirty. Go to the well and wash
>   them.'

The children go to the well, where they spy the Old Man crouching down. They rush back to the Mother screaming: 'Mother! Mother! There's an Old Man in the well.'

> Mother: 'Don't be silly, children. There isn't an Old Man in the
>   well.'
> Children: 'But we saw him.'
> Mother: 'It's only your father's under-pants. I hung them
>   out to dry. Go again.'

The children go again, see the Old Man, and again come back screaming: 'Mother! Mother! There's an Old Man in the well.'

The Mother again reassures them (repetition is a feature of these playlets), and they go to the well perhaps twice or three times more, until they persuade the Mother to come herself. She sends one of the children to fetch a candle (a twig), lights it, and goes to the well with the children. When they reach the well, and she is about to look in, the Old Man blows the candle out.

Mother to child nearest her: 'What did you want to blow out my candle for?' She cuffs the child who sets up a howl.

The Mother relights the candle, holds it over the well, and the Old Man blows it out again. Mother to another child: 'What did you want to blow out my candle for?' A second child is cuffed and sets up a howl.

This happens three or four times, so that three or four children, or perhaps all of them, are crying at once, which gives a fine opportunity for dramatics.

Eventually the Mother manages to look in the well. The Old Man jumps up with a horrible shriek and gives chase. Whoever he catches is the next Old Man.

The game is also known as 'Frog in the Well' and 'Ghost in the Well'.

§ Previous recordings include: *Folk-Lore Journal*, vol. v, 1887, p. 55, 'Ghost at the Well' described by 'a little girl in west Cornwall in 1882'; *Traditional Games*, 1894–8, 'Ghost in the Copper' (London), 'Mouse and the Cobbler' (Deptford), and 'Deil amo' the Dishes' (Aberdeen); *Games of Argyleshire*, 1901, p. 215, 'Ghost in the Garden'; and *London Street Games*, 1916, pp. 45–7, 'White Shirt', 'Old Devil in Fire', and 'Light Mother's Copper Fire'.

The following additional dialogue, lacking in the Swansea version or in the above recordings, has long been traditional in Devon (Macmillan MSS.):

Mother, on seeing the Old Man in the well: 'What are you doing here?'

> Old Man: 'Picking up sand.'
> Mother: 'What do you want sand for?'
> Old Man: 'To sharpen my needles.'
> Mother: 'What do you want needles for?'
> Old Man: 'To make a bag.'
> Mother: 'What do you want a bag for?'
> Old Man: 'To keep my knives in.'
> Mother: 'What do you want knives for?'
> Old Man: 'To cut off your heads.'
> Mother: 'Then catch us if you can.'

This additional dialogue was also part of 'Ghost in the Garden' played in Dunedin from *c.* 1900 until anyway 1949 (*Games of New Zealand Children*, 1959, pp. 32–3). It was known in Adelaide, South Australia, *c.* 1900 (Howard MSS.). And it was a common component of the game 'Fox and Chickens', described below, e.g. in the Lincolnshire version called 'Pins and Needles', the Galloway 'Auld Grannie', and the Belfast 'Grannie's Needle' (*Traditional Games*, vol. i, 1894, pp. 201–2; vol. ii, pp. 404–5).

The dialogue also occurs in the game 'Die Hexe im Keller' which is said to be much played today in Upper Austria (Kampmüller, *Oberösterreichische Kinderspiele*, 1965, pp. 166–9). Here one child says she wants some bread and butter. The mother says the butter is in the cellar. The child goes down the steps into the cellar and is shoved by the witch who says 'Huuuu'. The child runs back: 'Mother, there is somebody down the steps.' 'Who then?' 'An old witch.' The mother sends a second child with her, who is similarly treated, and then a third and a fourth. Eventually she goes down into the cellar herself. She shakes the witch by the head, saying to the children, 'Isn't this the butter churn?' Then she asks the witch: 'Was tust du denn da?'

> The witch replies: 'Steine klauben!'
> Mother: 'Was tust du mit den Steinen?'
> Witch: 'Messer wetzen!'
> Mother: 'Was tust du mit dem Messer?'
> Witch: 'Leut abstechen!'
> Mother: 'Stichst mich auch ab und meine
> 　　Kinder auch?'
> Witch: 'Ja.'

A correspondent, recalling the English game from her childhood, commented: 'The queer thing was that we were all *really* terrified by the Old Man in the well. We knew he was a playmate, we had even been him ourselves, and we played many jumping-out games and were not frightened by them. But the Old Man was terrifying. He was the personification of evil. In fact we seldom played the game, it scared us too much.'

Ghosties in the garret

In this game, as played in Forfar, and also in Whalsay, Shetland, under the name 'Ghost', one player goes away to be the ghost, as in 'Old Man in the Well', but the mother sends only one of her children, the eldest, to fetch her shirt from the garret. When the eldest child does not return she sends the next eldest, and so on, one child after another, until she sends the last and youngest child. When the last and youngest does not return she goes to the garret herself, and she, too, is captured by the ghost. The ghost then says he intends to eat them, but first he will fetch a friend to share the feast. While he is away the children start escaping; suddenly the ghost reappears, and the chase begins.

In a game called 'Old Man' played at Matching Green in Essex the chaser has similar carnivorous inclinations. After the Old Man has succeeded in catching all the children, he sets about eating them, but finds, to their unconcealed delight, that they 'taste of horrible things like frogs, snakes, and slugs'.

Old Mother Grey

This game, which was highly popular in the nineteenth century, remains fairly general today among younger children (accounts from seventeen schools) and it is the only playlet in which the dialogue is humorous throughout. Usually one child is appointed 'Grandmother Grey' or 'Granny, Granny Grey' or 'Old Mother Grey', and the other children gather round her chorusing:

> 'Old Mother Grey, may we go out to play?'
> Mother Grey: 'No, it's raining.'
> Children: 'No it isn't, the sun's shining.'
> Mother Grey: 'All right, you may go out to play.'

The children rush off, and play around, perhaps moving out of sight.

> Old Mother Grey calls: 'Children, it's dinner time!'
> Children: 'Coming, mother.'
> Mother: 'Where have you been?'
> Children: 'We've been to London to see the Queen.'
> Mother: 'What did she give you?'
> Children: 'A loaf of bread as big as our head, a piece of
>   cheese as big as our knees, a lump of jelly as big as
>   our belly, and a teeny weeny sixpence.'
> Mother: 'Where's my share?'
> Children: 'Up in the air.'
> Mother: 'How shall I get it?'
> Children: 'Stand on a chair.'
> Mother: 'What if I fall?'

Children all laugh, and shout out: 'We don't care.'

Old Mother Grey runs after them, and whoever she catches becomes the next Mother.

In another version, also widespread (current alike in Bristol and Aberdeen), the children sing:

> 'Granny, Granny Grey, may we go out to play?
> We won't go near the water and shoo the ducks away.'
> Granny Grey: 'No, it is my washing day.'

The children plead a second time:

> 'Please, Granny Grey, may we go out to play?
> We won't go near the water and shoo the ducks away.'
> Granny Grey: 'No, it is my ironing day.'

The children plead a third time, with even greater earnestness:

> '*Please*, Granny Grey, may we go out to play?
> We *won't* go near the water and shoo the ducks away.'

Granny Grey relents:

> 'Yes, you may go out to play.
> But don't go near the water and shoo the ducks away.'

The children run off, generally to the other side of the road, and immediately start shooing the ducks away.

Granny Grey, very angry, shouts at them to come back at once.

The children shout back impudently: 'We can't come across the water.'

> Granny: 'Swim across.'
> Children: 'We can't swim.'
> Granny: 'Come by boat.'
> Children: 'We haven't got a boat.'
> Granny: 'Paddle across.'
> Children: 'Yes, we can paddle across.'

One child is then usually caught and spanked for his disobedience. 'It seems senseless,' one teacher remarked, 'but they play it over and over again.'

§ Previous recordings: *Folk-Lore Journal*, vol. v, 1887, pp. 55–6, 'Mother, Mother, may I go out to play?' 'No child! no, child! not for the day', etc.—'I thought this game was a thing of the past, but I came on some children playing it in the streets of Penzance in 1883.' *Yorkshire Folk-Lore Record*, vol. i, 1888, pp. 214–15, 'I saw today three little girls, aged 3, 5, and 7, play a new game, or, at least, a new one to me.'—'Please, mother, may I go out to play?' 'No, my loves, it is a very wet day', etc.; *Folk-Lore Journal*, vol. vii, 1889, pp. 219–22, two Dorsetshire versions; *Traditional Games*, 1894, pp. 390–6. *London Street Games*, 1916, p. 101; *Games of American Children*, 1883, p. 172.
The game has been described with affection by a number of our older correspondents, the following being a Hampshire text of about 1910:

> 'Please, Mother, can we go out to play?'
> 'No, it's wet and cold.'
> 'Please, Mother, can we go out to play?'
> 'No, it's wet and cold.'
> 'Please, Mother, can we go out to play?'
> 'Go then!'

(The children go off, and after a while return.)

> 'Where have you been?'
> 'Grandmother's wedding.'
> 'What did she give you?'
> 'Cake and wine.'
> 'Where's mine?'
> 'On the shelf.'
> ''Tisn't there.'
> 'Cat's got it.'
> 'Where's the cat?'
> 'Behind the stack.'
> 'Where's the stack?'
> 'On fire.'
> 'Where's the fire?'

'Water's quenched it.'
'Where's the water?'
'Fox has drunk it.'
'Where's the fox?'
'Behind the churchyard cracking nuts and
    you can eat the shells.'

(On this the children ran away and were chased by the Mother with a stick.)

§ This is another game that is not confined to English-speaking children. In Bremen in the nineteenth century girls had an amusement which they called 'Der Hühnerhof'. One girl was Grandmother, and the others asked: 'Grotmooder, wat makst du dar?'

> Grandmother: 'Ich spinne.'
> Children: 'Wo is denn din Mann?'
> Grandmother: 'Open Hönerhof.'
> Children: 'Wat makt he dar?'
> Grandmother: 'He futtert de Höner.'
> Children: 'Könt wi denn nig ok en beten
>   hen gaan?'
> Grandmother: 'Ja, awert jagt se mi nig
>   weg!'

The children scampered into the poultry-yard, and immediately began chasing the hens, shooing them with their aprons. The Grandmother ran after them, and, as in England, the child she caught became the next Grandmother (F. M. Böhme, *Deutsches Kinderspiel*, 1897, p. 592).

Fox and chickens

In this playlet, unlike the others, the catching is an integral part of the game and, except in places where the words have been passed on by an adult, the drama is becoming a speechless shadow of its former self. In 1922, when the dialogue was still a feature of the game, A. S. Macmillan could write: 'It is no exaggeration to say that scores of young people have sent me descriptions ... all very much alike but called by many different names, such as "Old

Woman, What's the Time?", "Polly (or Betsy), What's o'Clock?", "The Wolf and the Sheep", "The Fox and the Hen", "Hen and Chickens" etc.'

In the standard game one of the bigger children is the fox, another the hen, and the rest make up the hen's brood. The chickens form up in single file behind the hen, each holding on to the waist or garment of the one in front. They march up to the fox, who is crouching on the ground, and chant:

> Chickany, chickany, crany crow,
> I went to the well to wash my toe,
> When I came back a chicken was dead.

They stop in front of the fox, and the hen asks: 'What are you doing, old fox?'

> Fox, in a gruff voice: 'Picking up sticks.'
> Hen: 'What for?'
> Fox: 'To make a fire.'
> Hen: 'What do you want a fire for?'
> Fox: 'To cook a chicken.'
> Hen: 'Where will you get it?'
> Fox: 'Out of your flock.'

The fox springs up, and tries to seize the last chicken in the line. The hen, with the chickens hanging on behind her like a tail, does her best to guard them, swinging round to face the fox whichever way he goes, and holding out her wings to prevent him slipping past. This active part of the game is now popular in gymnasiums, where the sport is usually called 'Fox and Geese', and the turnover in foxes is frequent, for 'when the end person is touched he becomes the fox, and the game continues until everyone has had a turn at being fox'. In the traditional game, however, the fox has to catch each of the chickens in turn, and take them away to his den. Thus, as the line of chickens diminishes, his predatory activities become more difficult, and it needs a determined fox to succeed in catching the last ones.

§ There is good reason to think that this game was current in Queen Anne's time. Up to a generation or so ago it was played not only under the names 'Fox and Chickens', 'Fox and Goose', 'Wolf and Sheep', and 'Hen and Chickens', but under such curious denominations as 'Chicken come Clock' in Kiltubbrid, Co. Leitrim (Gomme, vol. ii, 1898, pp. 410–11), 'Chickamy, Chickamy, Chany Trow' in Surrey (George Bourne, *William Smith*, 1920, pp. 33–4), 'Wigamy, Wigamy, Waterhen' (*Old Surrey Singing Games*, 1909, p. 11), and 'I'm going to the Pippen to water my chickens' in Wales, *c.* 1915. It is thus likely that 'Chicken a Train Trow' listed amongst children's games in William King's *Useful Transactions in Philosophy*, pt. i, 1708/9, p. 43, is this game, as also 'Come water my chickens, come clock' in 'The Nurse's Song' in *The Tea-Table Miscellany*, vol. iv, 1740; and 'Water my chickens come clock' in Brooke's *The Fool of Quality*, 1764–70 (1859, vol. i, p. 272). It was certainly the 'singular game played at country schools' in Galloway under the name 'Gled Wylie' for it is well enough described in Mactaggart's *Gallovidian Encyclopedia*, 1824; as also in Jamieson's *Scottish Dictionary, Supplement*, 1825, under 'Shue-Gled-Wylie' (Fife), and 'Shoo-Gled's Wylie' (Teviotdale). (A *gled* is a kite, compare continental 'hawk' versions.) In addition J. O. Halliwell, *Popular Rhymes*, 1849, p. 132, gives an 'Old Dame' version in which the children start by singing:

> To Beccles! to Beccles!
> To buy a bunch of netties!
> Pray, Old Dame, what's o'clock?

The Dame replies 'One, going for two', and the game does not proceed until the old dame replies 'Eleven going for twelve'—another detail that has continental and American parallels.

Indeed the game is a favourite in the United States (referred to at least ten times in the *Journal of American Folklore*), the usual name being 'Chickamy Chickamy Craney Crow'. It was described as long ago as 1835 in the American *Girl's Book of Diversions*, pp. 27–8; and Newell, *Games of American Children*, 1883, pp. 155–8, gives interesting accounts in which the predators are variously a fox, an 'Old Buzzard', and a witch. He reports that in Georgia the game began with the rhyme:

> Chickamy, chickamy, crany, crow,
> I went to the well to wash my toe,
> And when I came back my chicken was
> 　gone;
> What o'clock, old witch?

The witch named an hour, and the children repeated their question until the witch replied 'Twelve o'clock'.

> 'What are you doing, old witch?'
> 'I'm making a fire to cook a chicken.'
> 'Where are you going to get it?'
> 'Out of your coop.'
> 'I've got the lock.'
> 'I've got the key.'
> 'Well, we'll see who will have it.'

The witch tried to get past the hen, and seize the last of the line; the mother, spreading out her arms, barred the passage. The witch cried, 'I must have a chick.' The hen retorted, 'You shan't have a chick.' Each child caught dropped out, and, as Newell remarks, 'as the line grows shorter the struggle becomes desperate'.

The similarity of continental and British versions can scarcely be coincidental. In Denmark, where the predator is a hawk, the game (recorded almost a century ago), began as in England with the bird crouching down and scratching in the earth.

> Hen: 'What are you scratching for?'
> Hawk: 'For an old rusty needle.'
> Hen: 'What are you going to do with it?'
> Hawk: 'Mend my pots and pans.'
> Hen: 'What are you going to use them
>   for?'
> Hawk: 'Boiling chickens.'
> Hen: 'Where will you get the chickens?'
> Hawk: 'From you!'

And the hawk tried to seize the chickens who were hanging on behind the hen (*Bfrness Musik og Sange, samlede of en Moder*, 1879). In Yugoslavia, Czechoslovakia, Romania, and Hungary, the pattern, according to Brewster, is similar. Thus in Hungary:

> 'Hawk, hawk, what are you doing?'
> 'Making a fire.'
> 'What's the fire for?'

'To warm water.'
'What's the water for?'
'To scald a chicken.'
'From whose?'
'From yours.'
'I'm their mother; I won't let them.'
'I'm a hawk; I'll get them!'

'Then the hawk dashes for the chickens, and the hen spreads out her arms to protect them' (*American Nonsinging Games*, 1953, pp. 71–6).

The game is also traditional amongst German-speaking peoples. Kampmüller says it continues to be played in Austria, where it is called either 'Henne und Geir' or 'Fuchserl und Hahnl', the game starting with the predator crouching on the ground, and stirring with a stick (*Oberösterreichische Kinderspiele*, 1965, pp. 139–40). In Germany, too, the game generally starts with the predator squatting down and scratching in the earth. 'Was grabst?' asks the hen. 'Ein Löchle,' replies the fearsome bird. 'A hole.'

'What are you looking for in the hole?'
'A stone.'
'What will you do with the stone?'
'Sharpen a knife.'
'What will you do with the knife?'
'Kill all your chickens.'

Zingerle, who speaks of the vulture game ('Geierspiel') as being beloved throughout Germany, remarks that the number of times it was named in the sixteenth and seventeenth centuries proves it to have been well known in the past. One description, cited by Böhme, occurs in Ammann's *Kinderspiele*, 1657 (a rendering of Cats's *Kinder-spel*), where such familiar details are noted as that the vulture's part is taken by the boldest player, the clucking hen's by the most intelligent (*Deutsches Kinderspiel*, 1897, pp. 569–71). In France, unlike in Germany, the predator is usually a wolf. The game is best known as 'La Queue du loup', and the version recorded by Rolland (*Rimes et jeux de l'enfance*, 1883, p. 156) follows the familiar pattern:

La mère: 'Que fais-tu là?'
Le loup: 'Je ramasse des bûchettes.'
La mère: 'Pour quoi faire ces bûchettes?'
Le loup: 'Pour allumer mon feu.'
La mère: 'Pour quoi faire ce feu?'
Le loup: 'Pour chauffer mon eau.'
La mère: 'Pour quoi faire cette eau?'
Le loup: 'Pour affiler mon petit coutiau.'
La mère: 'Pour quoi faire ce petit coutiau?'
Le loup: 'Pour couper la langue à tes
petits agneaux.'

However, there is also a version called 'L'Émouchet', in which the players are 'un émouchet, une poule, et des poussins'; and it seems that both forms of the game have coexisted in France for some centuries. In *Les Trente-six figures contenant tous les jeux*, published in 1587, two groups of youths are separately depicted playing versions of the game, the one called 'poussinets', the other *vulgairement* 'la queuë leu leu'. Rabelais listed 'la queue au loup' in 1534, as one of the games played by Gargantua; and it appears that the game was known in France in the Middle Ages, for around 1380 Froissart, recalling the pleasures of his childhood in 'L'Espinette amoureuse', wrote:

Puis juiens à un aultre jeu
Qu'on dist, *à la Kevve leu leu*.

In fact, the distribution of the game is probably world-wide. Further countries in which it is known to have been played, either with or without the preliminary dialogue, include Italy, Sicily, Sardinia, Spain, Sweden, Russia, Poland, Cuba, Haiti, Ceylon, and China. See, e.g., M. M. Lumbroso, *Giochi*, 1967, p. 73, 'Il lupo, il pastore e gli agnelli'; K. L. Bates, *Spanish Highways and Byways*, 1900, pp. 5–7 (chief players kite, mother, and smallest girl); Caroline Crawford, *Folk Games*, 1908, p. 38 (chief players in Sweden are a fox and geese); *Folklore*, vol. lxv, 1954, p. 69, 'Les Petits Oiseaux' in Haiti; Shufang Yui, *Chinese Children at Play*, 1939, 'Eagle Catch the Chicks'.

Johnny Lingo

The players stand in a ring with one child within the ring and one child outside. Those forming the ring are said to be sheep, chickens, or pigs (each of these pretences is traditional), while the child outside the ring has a name such as 'Johnny Lingo', 'Bobby Bingo', or 'Jacky Jingle'. The child within the ring is a farmer, and begins the game by chanting: 'Who's that walking round my stoney wall?'

Child outside the ring: 'Only little Johnny Lingo.'

Farmer: 'Don't you steal any of my fat sheep or I shall make you tingle.'[41]

Child outside: 'I stole one last night, and I'll steal another tonight', or, 'Neither shall I do so, except I take them one by one', and he touches one of the children on the back, saying 'Come on', or 'Come on little chick, chick, chick' (Matching Green), or 'Come whip' (Roe, Shetland), and the child joins on behind him, holding his waist.

'Who's that walking round my stoney wall?' demands the farmer again, and both children reply, 'Only little Johnny Lingo'.

'Don't you steal any of my fat sheep', cries the farmer.

'I stole one last night, and I'll steal another tonight,' reply the pair, padding round the outside and touching another member of the circle on the back.

So the game proceeds until everybody in the ring has joined behind Johnny Lingo, the challenges and warnings being repeated over and over again, which presumably accounts for the preservation of their archaic wording. There follows a chase in which, usually, the farmer tries to regain his sheep one by one from the end of the line, as in 'Fox and Chickens', while Johnny Lingo does his best to prevent him.

The game is known either by the name of the principal character, or as 'Who Goes Round my Stoney Wall?'

§ This game was clearly popular in the nineteenth century. A writer in *Blackwood's Magazine*, August (pt. ii), 1821, p. 36, reported that in Edinburgh 'the little actors' spoke the following by way of question and answer:

> Who goes round my house this night?
> None but bloody Tom;
> Who stole all my chickens away?
> None but this poor one.

Washington Irving in *Bracebridge Hall*, vol. ii, 1822, p. 37, recorded almost the same words:

> Who goes round the house at night?
> None but bloody Tom!
> Who steals all the sheep at night?
> None, but one by one.

Robert Chambers said that the game 'Bloody Tom' was common among boys 'all over Scotland' (described in *Popular Rhymes of Scotland*, 1842, pp. 62–3); and J. O. Halliwell, the same year, said the children called it, in the slang of the time, 'a regular tearing game' (*Nursery Rhymes*, 1842, pp. 122–3). The thief, and hence the game, has also been known as Johnny Jingo, Johnny Ringo, Johnny Nero, Johnny Able, Johnny Winkle, Jack and Jingle, Jack and Jingo, Jackie Lingo, Daddy Dingo, Jack the Lentern (*sic*), Jenny Langal, Tommy Jingle, Limping Tom, Poor Old Tom, King Sailor, and, in Tasmania, Old Black Joe.

Several of our older correspondents have described the game as played fifty or sixty years ago, sometimes with additional dialogue. At Bridgwater in Somerset a shepherd took part, as well as a farmer and wolf. The wolf approached the shepherd and said, 'Sheep, sheep, sheen-o'.

> The shepherd replied, 'What's want here-o?'
> The wolf: 'A good fat sheep.'
> Shepherd: 'Take the best and leave the worst and come
> again tomorrow.'
> The farmer, who had not seen the wolf, inquired: 'What's
> that? What's that?'
> Shepherd: 'Only calling the dog, sir.'

The farmer turned away, and the wolf dragged off one of the sheep, although not without a struggle, for the Bridgwater sheep resisted being taken. When the last sheep had gone the farmer looked in the fold, found it empty, and 'with much abuse' sacked the shepherd.

In the west country, too, the farmer or master of the flock sometimes had words with the thief ('Bobby Bingo') after the sheep had been stolen, and while they were clinging on behind his back.

> Master: 'What's that behind your back?'
> Bobby Bingo: 'Only a bundle of straw.'
> Master: 'What do you want a bundle of straw for?'
> Bobby: 'To light a fire.'
> Master: 'What do you want to light a fire for?'
> Bobby: 'To boil my kettle.'
> Master: 'What do you want to boil a kettle for?'
> Bobby: 'To make myself a cup of tea.'
> Master: 'Let me look through your key-hole.'

Bobby placed one hand on his hip, and the master looked through the space between his arm and body.

Master: 'I see my sheep.'

The sheep bleated 'Baa, baa', and the master tried to regain them by catching the hindermost in the line.

This action and dialogue links the game, not only with 'Fox and Chickens' and 'Old Man in the Well', but with 'Mother, the Cake is Burning' described below.[42]

Versions of the game are also well known in Austria where it is called 'Lamperlstehln' or 'Wer geht? Wer geht?' (Kampmüller, *Oberösterreichische Kinderspiele*, 1965, pp. 162–4); and in Italy where it is 'Mamma Polleone' (Lumbroso, *Giochi*, 1967, pp. 223–4). The French game 'Le Boucher et les moutons' is similar, but the butcher first weighs the sheep, agrees with the shepherd to buy them, and then finds he has a business to take them, for they are in a line behind the ram (*200 Jeux d'enfants, c.* 1892, pp. 125–6).

Mother, the cake is burning

This pantomime of a game contains enough myth and madness to gratify both folklorists and 9-year-olds. Briefly the plot is as follows: A mother goes to market, leaving her seven children in the care of a maid or eldest daughter. While she is away an evil visitor comes to the door, enters the house on some pretext, and snatches one of the children ('the young-est child' or 'the most precious child'). The mother returns, beats the maid or eldest daughter for allowing the child to be stolen, and goes off again. While she is away the second time, a second child is stolen. The mother, who seems to be simple-minded, returns and again beats the girl in charge, and again leaves home. This occurs seven times until all the children have been stolen. The mother then seeks out the kidnapper who, it is becoming clear, is a magical person. For a while the kidnapper obstructs the mother's entry into his house, but she becomes indomitable: she will even, in some versions, cut off her feet to gain admittance, and eventually succeeds, only to find that her children are now disguised, or renamed, or turned into pies or other delicacies, and about to be eaten. Nevertheless, by skill or luck, she identifies and releases them. Usually the game ends in a chase.

When little girls, dressed in T-shirts and jeans, are seen playing this acting-game at the end of the street, it is difficult to believe that they are not making up the incidents as they go along. Only when comparison is made, scene by scene, with nineteenth-century recordings, does it become apparent that they are following an old and international script dictated by folk memory. It seems best, therefore, with this game, to bring past and present descriptions together; and the following report is based on fifty-nine English-language accounts: twenty-seven contemporary, and thirty-two old, mostly nineteenth century, including eight from the United States (Newell, 1883, 1890, and 1903), and three from Australia (Howard MSS.).[43]

Manuscript versions in our files, other than present-day accounts, are quoted with the date when the game was played.

In most accounts the principal character is a mother who is going to market or 'going washing' or, in the present day, 'going shopping'. Occasionally she asks the children what they would like her to bring home, for instance in Cornwall, 1887: 'The mother says she is going to market and will bring home for each the thing that she most wishes for. Upon this they all name something.' These presents can have significance in the story, for when the mother is handing them out on her return she finds that she has one more present than she has children, and it is then that she realizes one of her children is missing. Ordinarily she knows how many children she has by naming them after the days of the week, 'Monday, Tuesday, Wednesday ...' (e.g. Northumberland, 1846; Liss, 1964). Before she goes out she counts them by reciting the days of the week, or gets the maid or eldest daughter to do so. In the nineteenth century it was usually the 'eldest daughter', sometimes named 'Sue', who was put in charge; today, although this may seem unrealistic, the person who looks after them for her is 'the maid', but the whole play is unrealistic. Thus it was in verse that the mother used to caution her children before she went out:

I charge my daughters every one
To keep good house while I am gone.
You and you, but specially Sue,
Or else I'll beat you black and blue.
1849. Similar Sussex, 1882

Now all you children stay at home,
And be good girls while I am gone ...
Especially you, my daughter Sue,
Or else I'll beat you black and blue.
Hertford, Connecticut, 1883

I am going into the garden to gather
    some rue,
And mind old Jack-daw don't get you.
Especially you, my daughter Sue,
I'll beat you till you're black and blue.
Ipswich, 1893

Go down the garden and get a bit of rue,
Mind old Jack-a-Bed don't take you:
Especially you, my daughter Sue,
Or I'll beat you black and blue.
Wrecclesham, Surrey, c. 1897

Today, after counting them, she merely warns the maid not to lose them, or, pointing to 'Sunday' (who is usually the special child), says, 'That's my very best chicken, and don't you let her go' (Stromness), 'Don't you let my Sunday go' (Alton), or, pointing to a child who is kneeling to represent the youngest one, says, 'Don't you dare lose my best Blacking Topper' (West Ham).

The evil visitor who comes to the door is often a witch. In the United States in 1883 she was sometimes called 'Old Mother Cripsy-crops' or 'Old Mother Hippletyhop'. At Crickhowell in Breconshire, in the present day, she is named 'Heckedy Peg', a lame old woman who announces herself 'I'm Heckedy Peg, I've lost my leg'. In Langholm, today, she is 'Jenny from o'er the hill' a wicked old woman who hobbles along supported by a stick. In 1849 she was a gipsy, as also in east Devon in 1922. In Derbyshire, 1910, she was a 'Peggy Woman' (i.e. a seller of pegs, traditionally a gipsy), and in Somerset, 1922, a 'Pins and Needle-Woman'. The child-snatcher may also be a 'Bogie-man' (Taunton, 1922), 'Black Man' (Hanley, 1890), 'Old Man' (South Elmsall, 1935); and in the present day a 'Tramp' (Westerkirk, Dumfriesshire), a 'Beggar' (Swansea), a 'Baker' (Dublin), a 'Funnyman' (Burslem), 'Black Jack' (Whalsay), 'Jack in the Chimney' (Roe). In the south and west the thief may be a fox or wolf (Cornwall, 1898; Chard, 1922; Abergavenny, *c.* 1930; Alton and St Peter Port in the present day). In the west country the 'children' were often 'sheep'. They may also, even today, be 'chickens', 'scones', or 'pots of jam' (cf. the game 'Jams', p. 136).

It is noticeable that in four out of the ten contemporary accounts in which the visitor begs at the door, he or she asks for something connected with fire. For instance in Oxford the witch asks for a match; in Alton the fox begs a box of matches, in Radnorshire the children are called 'Matchsticks'. This accords with the nineteenth century. At Deptford, in 1898, the witch begged politely, 'Please you, give me a match'; in London, in the same period, the Old Woman promised the eldest daughter a gay ribbon if she would give her a light; in Boston, Massachusetts, 1890, the witch begged 'Give me fire; I'm cold', and when refused, tempted the eldest daughter with a necklace, offering it 'All for one lighted sod and one fat child'.[44]

In the St Thomas district of Swansea, today, the 'Man' asks, 'Can I light my pipe?' The maid at first says 'No'. The man spits on the 'carpet'. 'How dare you dirty my carpet!' exclaims the maid, and rubs the spit in the ground. 'Look the cake's burning', says the man. The maid goes to look at the cake, and while she is away the man steals a child. This incident, too, accords with nineteenth-century practice. In Dronfield, Derbyshire, 1894, the Old Witch begs, 'Please, can I light my pipe?' Children: 'Yes, if you won't spit on t'hearth.' The witch pretends to light her pipe, but maliciously spits on the hearth, and this seems to give her the necessary power, for only then does she run off with the girl called Sunday. Likewise at Sneyd Green, Stoke-on-Trent, in the present day, the 'funnyman' who has begged a drink of water, does not attempt to enter the house and seize a child until he has smashed the cup which holds the water. Similarly at Whalsay in Shetland, in the present day, Black Jack is apparently able to seize the 'youngest child' without hindrance after he has spilt water on the hearth and ruined the bland.[45] There may also be significance and a connection between the ruined bland, the burning cake, and the boiling kettle. At Knighton the witch comes in and says to the maid, 'Quick, the kettle's boiling', and when she goes to see runs off with a 'matchstick'. Formerly the cry was that the pot was boiling over. Among the *dramatis personae* in London in 1894 was a child who played the part of the pot, and at the appropriate time made a 'hissing and fizzing' noise.[46] Sometimes, when the mother was supposed to be a washer-woman, and worked outside the house but within hailing distance, the daughter called out: 'Mother, Mother, the pot boils over' (London, 1894).

> The mother replied: 'Take the spoon and
>   skim it.'
> Daughter: 'Can't find it.'
> Mother: 'Look on the shelf.'
> Daughter: 'Can't reach it.'
> Mother: 'Take the stool.'
> Daughter: 'The leg's broke.'
> Mother: 'Take the chair.'
> Daughter: 'Chair's gone to be mended.'
> Mother: 'I suppose I must come myself.'

This dialogue was also reported in 1846 as known in Northumberland, one girl saying, 'Mother, Mother, the pot's boiling over', the mother answering, 'Then get the ladle and keel it'; and the girl objecting successively that the ladle was 'up a height', that the 'steul' wanted a leg, and that the joiner was either sick or dead.

In some versions the maid appears to deserve the chastisement that is coming to her. In Alton, when the fox knocks at the door and says 'I want a box of matches, please', the maid says 'Take one', and the fox takes Sunday. This may be a contraction of the story, but at Westerkirk in Dumfriesshire, where the children are said to be scones, the maid actually summons the tramp and gives him the best ones. This is precisely as the game was played in Forfar about 1910. The servant had been told to watch all the bannocks and 'pey affa gude attention tae this ane. O' a' my bannockies, this is my favourite'. No sooner is the mistress away than the servant goes to the 'Deil's' hiding-place and cries:

> 'Deil, Deil, come doon the lum,
> And wash yer face afore ye come.'

The maid is also clearly an accomplice in the game played today in Stromness. When the mistress goes out for a short walk the maid pushes 'the best chicken' to the Old Woman, who hides it behind her back. When the mistress returns, and demands in a rage, 'Where is my best chicken?' the maid replies she does not know, and when the maid is told she must go 'up the lane and down the lane' until she finds it, she only pretends to look for it.[47] In Dublin, too, in the present day, the children themselves seem to entice if not summon the evil visitor. As soon as the mother is absent they give notice of it by singing out all together, 'I am stirring my chicken, my chicken', and the villain comes running to take one of them.

In many versions the mother's return to her family provides moments of comic suspense. Everyone knows that a child is missing, and that the maid is about to be smacked for her negligence. But the mother acts as if nothing was wrong until the children have been counted, or their names recited, 'Monday, Tuesday, Wednesday ...', or until she has handed the children their presents and there is one present too many. It almost seems that this repeated counting before and after the loss of each child is to ensure that a primitive audience shall understand what has happened. In Scalloway, when the mother asks where the missing child has gone, the other children say 'She has gone to the well', 'She has gone to a dance', 'She has gone for a walk', and the mother at first believes them. At Evenjobb in Radnorshire, when the 'matches' have been counted, and one of them is found missing, the master cross-examines the maid, 'Where is the other one gone?' The maid replies, 'I don't know.'

> 'Where was you?'
> 'Down the cellar.'
> 'What doing?'
> 'Making leather.'
> 'What for?'
> 'To tie your nose and mine together',
>   replies the maid.

Whereupon the master gives the maid 'a good whacking', although whether for her cheekiness or her carelessness in allowing a match to be stolen is not clear.[48] In London, in 1898, the daughter in charge of the children made them promise not to tell their mother. When the mother returns and asks 'Are all the children safe?' the eldest daughter says

'Yes'. 'Then let me count them.' The children stand in a row, and the mother, who is blind, counts them by placing her hands on their heads. When the eldest daughter has been counted, she runs to the other end of the line to be counted again, and the mother does not at first realize that a child is missing. A similar ruse is attempted today in West Ham. When the maid finds that the favourite child, 'Blacking Topper', is missing, she puts herself in the line with the children to make up the right number. However the mother discovers her trick. 'Where's my Blacking Topper?' she cries. 'I don't know', says the maid. Then the mother spanks the maid for losing her 'Blacking Topper'. This spanking is one of the high-lights of the game, and takes place six or seven times. Yet in some places when the mother asks about the missing child there is no prevarication. The children shout 'The witch has took her' (or, in Hanley, 1890, 'The Black Man took her for a basin of broth'), and the maid is promptly spanked. But whatever the form of the kidnapping and its discovery, it is ritualistically repeated for each child. In West Ham, for example, a new 'Blacking Topper' (or 'Mackintosh') is chosen each time, and kneels down to be the littlest one, so that each time when the mother returns she can make the same complaint, 'Where's my Blacking Topper?', and each time, even on the seventh occasion, the maid tries to hide the fact that another 'Blacking Topper' is missing.[49]

When the last child has been stolen, and sometimes the maid too, or she has run away, or has accepted the fox's invitation to a party (Alton), the mother seeks out the evil visitor's house. At Alton the mother says to the fox, 'Where's my children gone?' The fox says 'Up the road and round the corner.' The mother goes and looks and, of course, she does not find them. In Whalsay, Shetland, she asks Black Jack if he has seen any children. Black Jack says he saw one go to the bridge, and carefully describes one of the children, as he is well able to do. The mother goes there and cannot find the child, so she comes back and Black Jack tells her another place where he says he saw another child. In Cornwall in 1887, when the Old Witch was asked if she had seen the children, she said 'Yes, I think by Eastgate.' The mother went and looked by Eastgate, and not finding them, the witch suggested 'I think by Westgate', and sent the mother on another futile search. In London in 1894 the mother met the witch and asked, 'Is this the way to the witch's house?' The witch replied 'There's a red bull that way'. The mother said 'I think I'll go this way', and the witch warned, 'There's a mad cow that way'. This is echoed today in Dublin. When the mother asks the Baker (who has run

off with the children) where they are, the Baker gives her false directions. Then the children, who are hidden in the Baker's 'den', set up a
cry 'There are snakes over there', and the mother comes running back.
At Taunton, in 1922, the 'Bogie' declared that the children were gone
to London. 'How many miles?' asked the mother. 'Forty-two' (or some
such number), replied the Bogie, and the mother took forty-two steps
for miles and then came back: 'They're not there.' So the Bogie named
further towns, stating their distance. In Swansea today, when the mother
demands of the kidnapper 'Where are the children?' the 'Man' replies:
'Gone to school.'

> Mother: 'How many miles?'
> Man: 'Eight' (or any number).

The mother, and the maid who is with her, take eight steps backwards.

> Mother: 'They are not here.'
> Man: 'They've gone to bed.'
> Mother: 'I want to see them.'
> Man: 'Your shoes will dirty the carpet.'
> Mother: 'I'll take them off.'
> Man: 'The wool will come off your
>   stockings.'
> Mother: 'I'll take off my stockings.'
> Man: 'Your feet are dirty.'
> Mother: 'I'll cut them off.'
> Man: 'The blood will go on the carpet.'
> Mother: 'I'll fly up.'

And in one Swansea version, while man and mother have their strange
altercation, the stolen children stand in a row, swaying from side to side
as if trying to work a magic spell, chanting 'Mother, the cake is burning!
Mother, the cake is burning!'

Similar dialogues were recorded in the south and west of England
in the nineteenth century, and also in the United States. For instance
in 1883, when the mother asked to be let into the witch's house, the
witch refused in exactly the same style, saying, 'No, your shoes are too
dirty.'

> Mother: 'But I will take off my shoes.'
> Witch: 'Your stockings are too dirty.'
> Mother: 'Then I will take off my stockings.'
> Witch: 'Your feet are too dirty.'
> Mother: 'I will cut off my feet.'
> Witch: 'That would make the carpet all
> bloody.'[50]

Dialogues such as this, in which the formalities of polite speech are maintained despite the desperateness of the situation, are not uncommon in folk humour. In the Cornish version of 1898, social decorum is observed even when the shepherd has arrived at the wolf's house and smelt meat being cooked. He says, 'May I go up and taste your soup?' and the wolf blandly replies, 'You can't go upstairs, your shoes are too dirty.' Likewise at Chaffcombe, Somerset, in 1922, after a horrifying argument between the Old Man and the mother, in which it is finally agreed that a million blankets will staunch the blood from the mother's bleeding stumps (she has cut off her feet), the Old Man says 'I have some lovely jam for sale', and the mother inquires, as any housekeeper might be expected to do in other circumstances, 'What kind have you?' 'Some plum and apple', he replies. 'Can I have 4 lb. please?' she says. However, the mother may here be showing presence of mind. In several accounts it is apparent that the kidnapper is an ogre, and has cooked or intends to cook the children, and turn them into pies, jams, or other confections in which the ingredients are transformed. In New York, in 1883, the children were made into pies which were actually served up to the mother to eat. She tries one and exclaims: 'This tastes like my Monday.' This reanimates Monday, who is then spanked and sent home. In London in 1898 the children had their faces covered when their mother arrived (little girls' faces could easily be covered at this time by having their pinafores pulled over them), and they were served to the mother as various kinds of meat: beef, mutton, or lamb. In Langholm, today, the mother or shopkeeper arrives in the nick of time to save the children from being put into Jenny's pot. In South Elmsall, c. 1935, where the Old Man who stole the children was a butcher, the mother went to the butcher's shop and asked for a leg of mutton. One of the children stuck her leg through the Old Man's legs, and the mother exclaimed, 'That's not mutton, that's one of my children.' In Stoke-on-Trent, today, after the mother has been sent a 'hundred miles' in one direction, and 'fifty miles' in another, and found her children are not there, she says 'What's that between your legs? Why, it's one of my children's legs!' Thereupon the kidnapper cuts off the child's leg, and cuts off the legs of the other children too, and they all cry out 'Oh mother, I've lost my leg!' In Guernsey, too, where juvenile lore is largely derived from the north country (owing to evacuation during the war), the children line up behind their captor, the wolf, and the first child puts a leg forward between the wolf's legs. The mother has to recognize whose leg it is, and say correctly 'That's my Wednesday', or whatever is the name of the child. 'Of course she can see who they are', remarked an informant, aged 9. 'She can see them sticking up behind the wolf.' Again at Westerkirk in Dumfriesshire, the children seem to be renamed (as they were in the United States in 1883), for the mistress does not recognize her scones, and calls them by the names of animals, until the quisling maid runs out of the witch's house, whereon 'the mistress calls her something nasty and she hits her'.

Indeed the game can end in a number of ways, most of them incongruous. In some places the mother merely asks for the children, and they are handed over. At Waunerllwyd, near Swansea, the mother has to buy her children from the Beggar with kisses, one kiss for each child and two for the maid. ('It is best if the beggar can be a boy.') In several places the mother chases the children. In others, mother and children chase the thief, and when he is caught, put him in jail. This was the mildest of the fates awaiting the malefactor in former times, when wolves had their heads chopped off, old men were hung, and witches burned. It is recorded for instance in Cornwall, in 1887, that when the Old Witch had been caught the children pretended to bind her hand and foot, and put her on the pile, and then they burnt her, 'fanning the imaginary flames with their pinafores'.

Names in present day: 'Mother, the Cake is Burning' (Swansea and district); 'Amy and Witchie' (Scalloway); 'Fairies and Witches' (Liss); 'Jenny Came O'er the Hill' (Langholm); 'Heckedy Peg' (Crickhowell); 'Jack in the Chimney' (Roe, Shetland); 'Black Jack' (Whalsay, Shetland); 'Blacking Topper' (West Ham); 'Mackintopper' (Isle of Wight); 'Mackintosh' (West Ham);[51] 'Got a Match, Jack?' (Oxford); 'Boxes of Ma ches' (Alton and Herriard); 'Matchsticks' (Knighton and Evenjobb); 'Black Ram' (Chudleigh, south Devon); 'Scones' (Westerkirk); 'Chickens' (Stromness, Orkney); 'I am Stirring my Chicken' (Dublin); 'Run Away Children' (Berry Hill, Forest of Dean); 'Days of the Week' (Swansea).

Names previously current: 'Limpie, limpie, the pot's boiling owre' (listed by Robert Chambers, *Popular Rhymes*, 1826, p. 299); 'Keeling the Pot' (Northumberland, 1846); 'Mother, Mother, the Pot Boils Over' (London and Dronfield, 1894); 'Mother, the Kettle's Boiling' (Abergavenny, *c.* 1920); 'Witch' or 'Old Witch' (Cornwall, 1887; Dartmouth, 1894); 'Pins and Needle Woman' (Somerset, 1922); 'Shepherd and Sheep' (Oswestry, 1883); 'Count my Sheep, Jack' (Luppitt, near Honiton, 1922); 'Black Ram' (Dalwood and Alfington, east Devon, 1922); 'Steal the Pigs' (Fraserburgh, 1898); 'The Children' (Chaffcombe, 1922); 'Box of Matches' (Taunton, 1922); 'Bannockies' (Forfar, 1910).

In Australia: 'Mother, Mother, the Kettle's Boiling' (Powelltown, Victoria, *c.* 1935); 'Blackie, Blackie, Come Here' (Footscray, Victoria, *c.* 1915); 'Diggley Bones' (Toowoomba, Queensland, *c.* 1905). In New Zealand: 'Old Digley Bones (Bay of Plenty, 1885); 'Blacksmith' (Kaitaia, Westland, 1949)—Sutton-Smith, *Games of New Zealand Children*, 1959, pp. 33–5.

§ The absence of any recordings of this farce before the nineteenth century is disappointing, but hardly lessens the likelihood of its being old. Games are played throughout Europe in which children are stolen, begged, or bought one by one; in which passages of comic dialogue occur closely matching the British texts; and in which the child-taker limps with a defective foot, as did the man-eating hag Empusa, whose name scared little children in classical times. In the German acting game 'Lange Elen', described in 1836, before any account in English of 'Mother, the Cake is Burning', a mother goes off leaving her children (or lengths of cloth) in one person's care, and a thief comes to the house and snatches one of them. Immediately the guardian's cry is not that there has been a thief but that the broth boils over: 'Moder, Moder, de Brei kaakt aver!' The mother calls back, 'Throw a bit of salt in it', and, as in Britain, the guardian protests her inability to carry out a simple action, so that the mother is induced to return and learn what has really happened (H. Smidt, *Kinderund Ammenreime in plattdeutscher Mundart*, 1836, cited Böhme, 1897, pp. 583–4). In the game 'Stoff Verkaufen', played today in Austria, that part of the English text is enacted where the evil visitor gains each child by a trick. The witch's response each time her plea for a length of cloth is refused, is to say to the mother: 'Run quickly to your neighbour, her cow has calved and she needs help'

(Kampmüller, *Kinderspiele*, 1965, pp. 164–5). Likewise in the cloth-stealing game played in post-war Berlin, the thief obtains each length of cloth by saying, for instance, 'Your milk is boiling over'; and the human personality of the cloth becomes apparent as the game proceeds, for when the thief makes a suit out of the cloth, the suit scolds the thief saying 'You are bad, you are bad', or 'Wicked Emma, Wicked Emma' (Peesch, *Berliner Kinderspiel*, 1957, pp. 47–8). In the game 'Moder o Moder wo ist Kindken bliewen?' described about 1820 in a letter to the Grimm brothers, two buyers come to the mother again and again to buy a lamb, and it is significant that the child they ask for each time, and which the mother most strenuously refuses them, is the youngest child. In this game when the last and youngest child has eventually been obtained, the buyers hide him. Then the other children cry out 'O Mother, O Mother, where is the little child that has eaten the snakes and toads?' and the mother goes off to search for him (*Zeitschrift für Volkskunde*, N.F., vol. ii, 1931, p. 147). In the once widely popular game 'Frau Rose' or 'Mutter Rose' (a source of recreation, also, to German mythologists), it is noticeable that the evil character who approaches with the intention of obtaining the children (whether in the guise of chickens, flowers, or plasters for a sore foot) walks with a limp, and that although the mother gives her children away, the evil character has to wheedle them from her, one by one, with stories that are palpably false. In this game, however, the fun lies in the struggle which follows when the mother has to wrest the children from the witch's grasp by sheer strength (Böhme, *Deutsches Kinderspiel*, 1897, pp. 539–41). Likewise, in the game 'Brot backen' or 'Backofenkraucher', only that part of the play is enacted where the children, in the guise of loaves or buns, are cooked or overcooked in an oven, and the point of the game is the strenuous action which ensues when the loaves are pulled from their place, as in the old game in England of 'Drawing the Oven' or 'Jack, Jack, the Biscuit Burns', much described in the nineteenth century.[52]

Thus, despite the fact that many individual points of similarity occur between 'Mother, the Cake is Burning' and the games played on the Continent, it appears that nowhere is the full drama preserved so effectively as in Britain. On the Continent the acting is often of comparatively short duration, it merely sets the scene for a physical contest; and the games are the equivalents not so much of 'Mother, the Cake is Burning' as of 'Honey Pots', 'Jams', 'Limpety Lil', and 'Cripple Christy' (qq. v.). Yet there is one exception. In Sicily, and in the foot of Italy, playlets are enacted whose similarity to the British witch-play are such that they would scarcely seem out of place if found being performed in the Scilly Islands or in Cornwall.

In the game 'Le galline', played today at Forenza, near Potenza, in Basilicata, one child is a fox, another an old dame, a third a cock, and the rest are hens. The old dame tells the cock to look after the hens while she goes to church, and warns him about the fox. As soon as she has gone the cock calls the fox and gives him a hen. The other hens cry out 'Coccodè, coccodè', and the old dame comes running back. 'Is the fox here?' 'No', replies the cock. 'Beh', says the old dame, 'pruvamm a cuntà'. The old dame counts the hens, and cries 'There's one missing!' 'How, one,' replies the cock, 'let me count them.' The cock counts them and cheats as he counts, so that the number comes right. The old dame is pacified, and sets off again to church, repeating her previous injunction about the fox. This goes on until there are no hens left and the cock can no longer trick the dame into thinking that she still has the right number. Yet the dame goes again to church, telling the cock to be careful or the fox will get him too; and this, of course, is what happens. She returns from church to find the cock has gone. Only now does she set out in search of her hens. On the road she meets some neighbours who tell her that various things have happened to her hens: some have been lamed, some have gone blind, some lost a wing. The children who are playing the parts of the hens then show themselves in the distance: some limp, some shut an eye, some bend an arm. The old dame thinks she recognizes them and scatters chicken food, calling 'Cosc, cosc, cosc mei'. But when the chickens follow her, and she sees the pitiful state they are in, she no longer thinks they are hers, and shouts 'Sciò, sciò, sciò, sciò, ca nun sit le mei'. However, the hens recover, and the old dame takes them back, calling 'Cosc, cosc, cosc, sit le mei' (you are mine).

Likewise, in the game 'Mamma caduta dal monte' played at Paceco in Sicily, a mother puts her children in the charge of her eldest daughter while she goes to buy vegetables. While the mother is away an old woman comes and tells the eldest daughter that her mother has fallen from a balcony. When the eldest daughter goes to see the old woman takes a child; and she repeats this trick for each child, telling the eldest daughter that her mother has fallen from one high place and then another. When the mother returns home from shopping she asks the eldest daughter where the children are, and the eldest daughter confesses that the old woman has taken them. The Sicilian mother, however, is apparently as simple-minded as the British mother; she leaves the eldest daughter and goes to buy some *pasta*. This time the old woman snatches the eldest daughter. The theft of the last child, as in Britain, seems to bring the mother to her senses. When she returns from her shopping, she realizes *subito* that the old woman is to blame. She goes to the old woman's house and asks her not whether she has her children, but (as in Britain, apparently realizing that they are to be eaten) whether she has a hen. The old woman replies that she has a hen, but only one, which she is going to eat herself. The mother implores her to give it up, and makes her way into the hen-house. The children who are in the hen-house cry out, and, in the words of the child who gave this description to Signora Maroni Lumbroso, 'the old woman is going to finish badly because mother and daughter give her so many blows that she will remember them all her life' (*Giochi*, 1967, pp. 143–4 and 188–9).

Thus do children in Sicily, and the Shetland Isles, although separated by race, language, and history, not to mention about two thousand miles, apparently share a common heritage.

12. Pretending Games

'Some times I kill Some One and Some One kills me but my
men release me and I release them Back.'
Boy, c. 6, Peckham Rye

Children, as Stevenson observed, 'take their enjoyment in a world of moonshine'. Each day, when the spell is upon them, they skip through a labyrinth of pretendings, and we suppose them to be imaginative, ignoring the evidence that the young do not commonly invent, merely imitate. We overlook, perhaps, when they amuse us with their oddities, that what passes as original is due not to art but to artlessness, to mishearings, to imperfect understanding, to the three-foot-high viewpoint which sees a palace roof in a table top, and fears a thunderstorm when the dog snores. Thus their pretending games turn out to be little more than reflections (often distorted reflections) of how they themselves live, and of how their mothers and fathers live, and of the books they read, and the TV programmes they watch. Whatever has latest caught their fancy is tested on their perpetual stage.

A class of 10-year-olds are taken round a post office, and the craze for the next week is playing 'Telephone Exchange'. A teacher uses the John o' Groats to Land's End walking race in a geography lesson, and the children arrive home from school breathless and bedraggled because they, too, have been walking from John o' Groats. They re-present, as if they were newsreels, the more spectacular national events: Coronations and rescues at sea; the climbing of Mount Everest, Princess Alexandra's wedding, and the Great Train Robbery. In Berlin, when the wall was built (1961), West German children began shooting at each other across miniature walls. In the United States, after the death of President Kennedy (1963), children were found playing 'Assassination'. Throughout time, it seems, juvenile performances have varied only as their surroundings have varied. In classical Rome, where the law was administered in public, Seneca observed Roman boys playing at judges and magistrates, 'the magistrates being accompanied by little lictors with fasces and axes' (*De constantia sapientis*, xii). In the sixteenth century Bruegel, in his painting of children amusing themselves in the street, shows one group playing at weddings, another group at christenings, and a third group taking part in a pretence religious procession. In eighteenth-century France Noël-Antoine Pluche noted:

'Children mimick by Turns the Processions of the Church, the March of Soldiers, the Attack of Places, the driving of a Coach, the several Attitudes of Trades-People, in short, whatever they see.'

(*Spectacle de la Nature*, vol. vi, 1748, p. 97). At the beginning of the twentieth century Norman Douglas came upon the smaller boys and girls in the streets of London playing:

'Mothers and Fathers, for instance, and Teachers, and Schools, and Soldiers, and Nurses, and Hospitals, and Carts and Horses, and Shops, and Convicts and Warders, and Railway Stations, and games of that kind.'

And during the Second World War children in Auschwitz concentration camp, well aware of the reality, were seen playing a game that proved the most terrible indictment ever made against man, a game called 'Going to the Gas Chamber'.

Mothers and fathers

The 6-year-old child who plays 'Mothers and Fathers' re-enacts the common incidents of his everyday life with what seems tedious exactness, until one realizes that there is a thrilling difference: he has promoted himself, he is no longer the protesting offspring being scrubbed to bed, but is the father or mother; and the 6–month-old doll is the one being scolded for not getting into the bath.

> The little actor cons another part;
> Filling from time to time his 'humorous stage'
> With all the persons, down to palsied age,
> That life brings with her in her equipage;
> As if his whole vocation
> Were endless imitation.

Even beyond Infant School the girls sometimes play 'Mothers and Fathers', and 'Houses' and 'Tea Parties' and 'Shopping' and 'Supermarkets' and 'Brides'. ('When I play "Brides",' says a 7-year-old, 'and pretend to be married I have to make my husband's tea and find his slippers'); and sometimes the boys cannot resist the fascination of the game. They ask teacher 'Can I go over and play with the girls?' and are usually welcome. In domestic dramas the male role is not a popular one; in some young eyes (an East Dulwich 10-year-old's, for example) the father is little more than a figure of fun:

> 'My friend and I play "Husband and Wife". I am the wife,
> I have to wash-up, and wash the floor or clean the
> windows, while my friend sleeps.'

This revealing drama is apparently also stock repertory in the United States where, according to Brian Sutton-Smith, the domestic hero enters the home, clasps the 'mother' in his arms, gives her a loud kiss, stretches, and says 'Well, I guess I'll take a nap'. Indeed it seems to be traditional for the breadwinner to be portrayed as self-indulgent. In 1903 Edwin Pugh reported in *Living London* that in the game 'Mothers and Fathers' it was not uncommon for the boys to 'reel about the pavement in a dreadful pantomime as "father" '.

The marvellous pleasure of playing 'Houses' lies first in making the house:

'We make little squares with dead grass,' writes a Scots girl in the Border Country, 'and leave a little doorway in one side. We put dead grass in a circle against one wall as a fire and put rowans in it for burning coal. We hunt stones to serve as sideboards and dressers. A piece of heather and brown bracken is put in a corner as an ornament. We take up our old dolls as babies. Then we pretend a baker arrives in a van. We go out and buy a cake, bread, and biscuits. Sometimes we go and visit one of our neighbours, make up a row, and not speak for a few days.'

Idyllic surroundings are not, however, essential to their make-believe. City children are fully competent, when the desire is upon them, to lay their hands on boards, wire netting, old curtains, and packing-cases, for building material. In 1962 amidst the dust of demolition in the University area of Manchester little girls were seen being very busy round a 'house' made of a large plush Victorian armchair. We asked them (7–9 years old) what they were playing, and their proud reply was 'Bombed Houses'.

When children speak of dressing-up their accounts become long and detailed. Ankle-length dresses, large hats, veils, high heels (one youngster thought they were 'high hills'), cigarettes, powder and make-up, represent the joys of adulthood. 'One of my favourite tricks to get my mother's make-up out of the house,' recalls a 14-year-old, 'was to shout and tell my mother that my little sister was crying. When she went to see, I would sneak out of the back door. My friends thought that I was the best rouger in our street. They all wanted me to put on their rouge, which was a very great honour. The powder they liked to put on themselves.' However, when rouge and mascara are not to be had, coal dust, blackboard chalk, and tomato sauce seem to do as well. A group of girls running a 'Beauty Salon' were seen to be quite happy (in January) dipping their fingers in puddles for lotions and putting real mud-packs on their foreheads. To be like teenagers they loosen their hair, adopt affected voices, and push their fists inside their jerseys to make bosoms, for the emphasis is on realism as they see it. Northerner II in *The Yorkshire Post* (November 1965) reported a kindly old gentleman watching some children in the street playing 'Mums and Dads'. Across the road, with his feet in the gutter, sat a lonesome 2-year-old. 'Why isn't he playing with you?' asked the old gentleman. 'Oh he is', said a 10-year-old Mum. 'He's a baby waiting to be born.'

Playing schools

Perhaps the most popular of the mundane pretences is playing 'Schools'. Boys as well as girls play 'Schools' when they get home from school, and on Saturdays when they do not go to school, and even in playtime at school.

> 'The most favourite game played in school is "Schools", says an Edinburgh 9-year-old. 'Tommy is the headmaster, Robin is the school-teacher, and I am the naughty boy. Robin asks us what are two and two. We say they are six. He gives us the belt. Sometimes we run away from school and what a commotion! Tommy and Robin run after us. When we are caught we are taken back and everybody is sorry.'

Clearly playing 'Schools' is a way to turn the tables on real school: a child can become a teacher, pupils can be naughty, and fun can be made of punishments. It is noticeable, too, that the most demure child in the real classroom is liable to become the most talkative when the canes are make-believe.

Playing schools has, in fact, long been ritualized. In the following game called 'Johnny Green', described by a Langholm 12-year-old, the cheeky replies are traditional, and this game is quite as much an 'acting game' as mimicry:

'You are all supposed to be in school when the teacher comes in. She says to Johnny Green, who was absent yesterday, "What was wrong with you yesterday, Johnny Green?"

He says, "I killed a fly and had to go to its funeral."

Johnny Green gets a thrashing and while he is still out on the floor after his thrashing, she says, "What was wrong with you the day before yesterday?"

Johnny Green replies, "My mother made an apple tart and I had to stay at home and get a piece."

He gets another thrashing for that. After giving him the thrashing the teacher sends him to his seat. "Who will go for some caramels for me?" she asks.

Johnny Green says he will. He comes back and says "The camels' humps won't come in the door."

There are roars of laughter. He gets another thrashing and gets the rest of the children into trouble for laughing.'

We have also been audience to this act in Glasgow; and in J. T. R. Ritchie's *The Golden City*, 1965, pp. 15–16, there is an account of the game as known in Edinburgh. A similar mad playlet, which seems to be a perennial in Aberdeen, concerns a child named 'Silly Sally', who is continuously unhelpful when her mother receives guests, answering the telephone instead of the front door, putting washing powder into the biscuit mixture, tripping over the visitor's legs and pouring tea on their heads.

Road accidents

Some pretending games portray events which might happen, but have not happened yet. As a child grows older he becomes increasingly aware of the world around him, and needs to explore its possibilities. 'He is not sure how one would feel in certain circumstances; to make sure, he must come as near trying it as his means permit' (Stevenson again). Thus all over Britain children play 'Road Accidents':

> 'When we run about the playground pretending that we are driving cars', writes a 10-year-old boy, 'we pretend that we are drunk, and go wobbling about the roads we make out of shingle. When someone crashes we sent out a breakdown lorry. Sometimes the girls make a hospital in the G.P. room, and we get an ambulance to come out to fetch the injured drivers.'

Similarly when girls play 'Hospitals', as all little girls seem to do at one time or another, they are not being morbid (as an adult would be, acting such a fantasy), they are expressing healthy and commendable emotions: the feminine urge to soothe, to put right, to have everybody happy; and they are looking for reassurance that should they themselves happen to be stricken they, too, will be looked after and made well. Over and over again it is evident that 'Hospitals' is a comforting and even joyful game.

> 'I play hospitals when I have some time to spare. I pretend I am a very strict Matron, and make the nurses work hard. When my friends come to play with me, we become surgeons and do operations and make blood out of red paint and water. We use imaginary instruments and use small sweets for pills. Sometimes mummy lets us take some orange juice to the hospital, which we have outside. Mummy is making me a nurse's uniform, and when it is finished I shall play hospitals much more often.'
>
> *Girl, 10, Whetstone*

Not infrequently their patients are their dolls:

> 'I sometimes pretend in my tent with my dolls that I am a nurse in a far away country. I had a hospital set for Christmas once, so I give my dolls operations. My two favourite dolls are Josephine and Peggy-Sue. Josephine

has blonde coloured hair and Peggy-Sue has a blouse and
skirt because she is a "teenage" doll. She has high heeled
shoes and stockings. When my dolls get better, I give
them a tea-party, so on a sunny day I think I am one of the
happiest girls in the world.'

Girl, 10, Finchley

The boys seem to prefer causing injuries, or being injured, to being those
who heal. In the playground they pretend to be jeeps, trains, buses, fire
engines, motorbikes, jets, or ships.

'Me and David play "Jeeps" in the playground every day.
We bash through people knocking them over and tripping
them over. We have lots of fun together.'

Boy, 9, Ipswich

They play 'Trains', forming up in lines and holding on to each other's
coat-tails:

'Last Friday i and my friend played trains and we keep
braking them other trains to peses and wen we have dun
one train we go and do a nuther.'

Boy, 8, Ipswich

Except in the game of 'Cops and Robbers' (see below), only girls seem
to think it fun to be upholders of the law:

'My Friend and I play "Police Women". We go around the
streets petending to tell people off. We say for exampiall
stop brarking bottels or get that child off your cross-bar.'

Girl, 10, Fulham

Playing horses

Amongst little girls 'Playing Horses' is almost as popular as playing
'Hospitals', and popular with some boys too. Whether or not the game
can be associated with the sense of animism which W. H. Hudson experienced when about 8 years old is for the analysts to say; and depends

on whether a child is pretending to possess a horse (the common dream-wish), or to be a horse himself. When a child pretends to be a horse or other animal he often becomes, as in no other pretending game, almost unconscious that he is pretending. 'There is something mystical about the game', a professor observed, recalling his youth. 'I remember once when I was playing horses with the other boys, I was serving a mare, and a grown-up came over and stopped me, he said I was being indecent.' And the professor, fifty years later, still clearly resented the charge, adding—as if the plea was necessary—'I was completely innocent.'

This confusion between horse and self is often evident in the children's accounts:

> 'I play horses with two other girls, I am the horse and the other two are the masters. First we find a hook in the wall. Then one of the girls takes off her belt and fixes one end to me and the other to the hook. When the horse wants her master she must neigh. When the master comes she puts the belt round my waist and takes me round the playground and brings me back to the stable and ties me up again. Then I am ready for the next trip.'
>
> *Girl, 7, Wilmslow*

If children's pretending is extrovert, they speak of it readily; if the pretending is introvert they will not admit to it under any circumstances. One of us remembers when she was a rabbit, being astonished at her nurse's stupidity when the nurse chided her for lagging behind on a walk. How could a little rabbit be expected to keep up? And even less, how could a rabbit explain that rabbits did not keep up?

Yet in most make-believe games, for instance when children are playing with toys, it is apparent that they are fully aware of the difference between play and reality. Korney Chukovsky, in his book *From Two to Five* (translated by Miriam Morton, 1963, p. 26), tells of a 4-year-old playing with her wooden horse who whispered: 'The horsie put on a tail and went for a walk.' Her mother overheard and interrupted, saying: 'Horses' tails are not tied to them; they cannot be put on and taken off.'

'How silly you are Mommie!' replied the child, 'I am just playing!'

A child is likewise 'just playing' when he mounts a hobby-horse. He is not deceived by the stick between his legs into thinking that he is actually riding. He is content to be pretending. He is engaged upon one of the oldest of juvenile pastimes, and one of the most frequently depicted in previous centuries; and it is interesting to find that despite the superior mobility of bicycles, pedal cars, and roller-skates, the appeal remains today.

> 'My way for passing the time is playing with my home-made hobby-horses. I have three horses, two grey ones and one white horse. The grey ones are called Pixie and Frosty, the white one is Snowball. My friend and I made our hobby-horses by collecting all the old, worn-out socks, and stuffing them with rags. After that, we sew buttons on for eyes and then we make ears with white or grey cloth. We then find quite a short stick and put it in the sock, then we tie string or wool around it to make it secure. Then our horses are nearly finished but not quite, we have still the bridles to make. This is done by getting wool (and sometimes plaiting it to make it strong). Then we tie the wool to form a bridle and put it on the horse.'
>
> *Girl, 10, Weybridge*

Storybook world

Some of the children's attempts to project themselves into special situations are so prosaic that only natural affection restrains us from terming them ludicrous.

> 'We play "Hotels". When we play "Hotels" you have a room, and one person goes round and collects the money for staying in the room.'
>
> *Girl, 9, Camberwell*

Often, however, the story enacted is beyond ordinary experience; it is a vision of improbable possibility, a tale from contemporary mythology. They pretend, for example, to be giving a concert or a fashion show, and 'stars' are discovered during the performance; or it is a beauty contest, and there are judges who 'pick the first, second, and third, and tell them what their prizes are, like a weekend in Paris'. There are also the games in which, while still being themselves, they allow their circumstances to alter—usually for the worse:

> 'We play "Runaways". We pretended our father was horrible
> and made us work like slaves. One night we ran away with
> only a few shillings and a sackful of food taken from the
> pantry, and took a ride in the back of a hay lorry.'
>
> *Girl, 12, Oxford*

They seem to have a particular predilection for being orphans ('We play sisters who are very poor, and have no mother and father and nobody to love them'), although it is noticeable that they are not unwilling to triumph over their misfortunes, either by their own exertions or Cinderella-wise, or by a judicious compound of both.

> 'My favourite game is to play at circuses. I play at starting
> with being poor. We are orphons. Then we find wild
> animals and train them. Then we get a present from our
> uncle which is a lot of money.'
>
> *Girl, 9, Wilmslow[53]*

Girls also pretend to be princesses, or Red Riding-Hood, or a film star, or a fairy queen ('The fairies have wings and flutter about. I like this game because it does not end up in a fight or a battle'). The boys have mock adventures, rather formless games of 'Pirates and Castaways', 'Deep Sea Diving', or 'Tarzan in the Trees'. Groups of two or three may be seen crossing deserts, searching for hidden treasure (girls as well as boys), and exploring unknown jungles: a game that adults, less fancifully minded, usually know as 'going for a walk'.

> 'My best friend and I often play at explorers in the
> Hermitage of Braid. We pretend to hack our way through
> the undergrowth with broad knives. After that we pretend
> to be attacked by savage natives and when one of us is
> wounded we often start an argument. Then we make our
> way down to the stream and try to jump across.'
>
> *Boy, 9, Edinburgh*

'If we were always to judge from reality,' Tolstoy commented, 'games would be nonsense. But if games were nonsense what else would there be left to do?'

War games

There is a noteworthy difference between playing at 'Soldiers', and playing at 'War' with two opposing sides. Many old prints show children playing at soldiers, dressing up in uniforms and drilling with pretence muskets, or marching in procession with a little officer or sergeant strutting in front; but they do not, as far as we know, show children having mock battles. Pugh, in *Living London*, 1903, tells how during the Boer War wonderfully drilled regiments of juvenile soldiers were to be seen parading the streets: 'It was a memorable spectacle to see these bands of little ones, to whom some tiny *vivandières* were usually attached, marching along in perfect step through the mire and dust of the road, wearing their helmets and tunics, carrying their weapons, also an "ambulance", beating their drums and blowing their toy trumpets, with that dignified gravity of which only children know the secret.' Such a parade (a photograph of a back street shows a troop with flags flying and rifles shouldered) would be improbable today, and not only because soldiers are less often seen on parade. Children today are nearer to the realities of war: there is no parading and much killing.[54]

Occasionally when they play a war game there is only one side, the enemy is non-existent, the battle an illusion:

> 'Some nights in the summer the boys in our avenue go in and fetch their guns and war helmets, and go to the dark field and make a camp. When we are ready two boys go off, and when they are coming back they start running, and when they get to us they say there is an enemy convoy going over the warren and we get our guns, fill the pistols with caps, and put on our helmets. Then we go to the warren and put old hairnets over our helmets and stick ferns in them. When we have done that we start firing our guns, and some of us reckon to be killed.'
>
> *Boy, 10, Annesley*

Usually, however, the fighting is only partially make-believe.

> 'First you pick two sides, one English and one German. One side which is always the English creeps up to the camp of the Germans, and one person which is usually me goes behind a German guard and hits him on the head. Then

we take the leader of the Germans so that they won't have
a leader to show them what to do. I myself have been
captured but have always got away. I have been wounded
and been taken to hospital.'

Boy, 8, Wilmslow

And sometimes the game is more rules and planning than imagination. The players 'dip' to see who shall be the commanders of the opposing forces; the commanders pick their sides; an agreement is made on
how many stones each soldier may carry for grenades; and a coin is
tossed to decide which side shall go out first. 'There is much fighting in
this game therefore girls cannot play, but if you have had enough you
say "I'm quitting" and then you have to go back to the headquarters
of your side' (Boy, 11). In other accounts, however, action and fantasy
merge into Walter Mitty heroics, and an adult scarcely knows whether
the young historian is more concerned with the facts of the game or with
self-aggrandizement.

'My game is cowboys. Now I am Cheyenne, I play it in
the school yard I am fighting the indians with my gun, I
killed 20 of them and the chief, that's why all the others
ran away, but if their chief was not dead they would keep
charging till they kill me so that when I was just ready to
get on my knees all the troops came then all the other
indians came but not from the same camps they had
funny faces they were like lions like in yellow stone kelly so
we all had a fight they had lots of indians but we still killed
them they was only about 40 of us left.'

Boy, 9, York

Some boys manage to be both romantic and down-to-earth at the same
time. Outside the Students' Union in Bristol a lad aged about 10 was
organizing his playfellows for a battle and trying to be fair to both sides.
When one player demurred at not being on the English side, the leader
was overheard saying emphatically: 'I tell you none of us is English, the
English always wins, that's why!'

Names: The following are some of the battles that are regularly fought
on British soil in the second half of the twentieth century, 'Germans
and English', 'British and Reds' (Chinese), 'Commandoes and Japs',

'Nips and Yanks' ('Nips and Yanks' explained a 10-year-old 'is really another game of "Germans and British" '), 'Foreign Legion and Arabs', 'Redcoats and Scottish Highlanders', 'Greeks and Romans'.

'Cowboys and Indians' remains an outstanding favourite (as also on the Continent[55]), and according to the TV programme of the moment, may be named: 'Raw Hide', 'Wagon Train', 'Pony Express', 'Totem Pole', 'Cavalry and Indians', 'Gun Law', 'Apache Warpath' ('If you kill the cowboys the game is finished'), 'Cheyenne', 'Laramie', 'Wells Fargo', 'Lone Ranger', or 'Cisco Kid'. (' "Cowboys and Indians" does not obey any set of rules and as often as not ends up in a free fight.')

Surprisingly popular (TV influence again) are 'Knights in Armour', 'Knights of Old', 'King Arthur and His Knights', 'Sir Lancelot', 'Medieval Men', 'Robin Hood', 'Ivanhoe', and 'William Tell'.

Of a slightly more domestic character, but mostly TV inspired, are 'Cops and Robbers' (see below), 'Biggles and Crooks', 'Z-Cars', 'Highway Patrol' (on bikes), 'Black Riders', 'Stage Coaches and Robbers' (at Hounslow, once a notorious district for highwaymen), 'Russian Spies', 'Dangerous Mission', 'Security Police', and 'Man from U.N.C.L.E.'

Amongst the fantastical: 'Super Car', 'Superman', 'Batman', 'Captain Marvel', 'Thunderbirds', 'Robots' ('They pretend to be robots gone mad', reports a headmaster), 'Daleks' and 'Spacemen'. But spacemen are not as popular as they were in the 1950s, when astronauts were still fabulous, and, led by Dan Dare of *Eagle*, they had to contend in outer space with green-hued foes of mighty intellect. By the mid-sixties spacemen had become commonplace, and the scope for the wonderful seems to have been correspondingly reduced.

Cops and robbers

Of all the perennial characters which 9-year-olds adopt to enliven a chase or give point to a brawl, the most popular are cops and robbers. Year in and year out boys enact the battle between crime and the law, passionately engaging themselves to whichever side they find themselves on, without apparent preference for right or wrong. On occasion the game is an elaborate make-believe, with stones for gold, pieces of paper for bank notes, guns, handcuffs, stocking masks, and almost a story.

> 'You have a bank and a bank manager and the robbers rob
> the bank. Then the cops chase the robbers, the robbers
> go to their hide-out until the cops have gone. Then the
> robbers rob another bank and the cops chase the robbers
> and they go to their hide-out, and it goes on like that until
> the cops find the robbers hide-out and catch them.'

Sometimes the make-believe is no more than an occasion for a fight. 'The robbers knowk the cops out and the cops knok the robbers out and so on. If anybody falls out we call them big babys.' 'When a convict is caught he can struggle until he is put into the den. When he is in the den he is tied to a pole and is asked who the leader is. If he does not talk with this method he is tied to the merry-go-round.' (The merry-go-round is a type of swing placed in the recreation ground by the local council.) Quite often the game is played on bikes. 'You are on fast bicks. Every person must have a spud gun and a packet of caps. You must not hit the Robber with the spud but you must hit just in frunt of his bick. When he is caught you have a jail. You have to give him a chance to get away and if he does you start all over again.' And, popularly, the game is played at night, and the chasing side has torches. As a practical-minded 12-year-old remarked:

> 'You have to play in the dark because torches are no good
> in the daytime. It is more exciting also. Because if they
> chase you through the gardens they can see where you go
> but at night they need torches to find you. You can easily
> give them the slip (nip into the gardens) and lose them.'

Indeed when the game is played at night, in the unrestricting darkness, it often takes on the form of 'Release' or 'Relievo' (q.v.), the den being the jail, the seeking side the cops, and if 'the free robbers touch the caught ones without being caught themselves they can release them'.

Names: 'Bobbies and Thieves', 'Convicts', 'Cops and Burglars', 'Cops and Robbers' (much the most common name), 'Escaped Prisoners', 'Kidnappers', 'Policemen and Robbers', 'Prisoners and Warders'. In Wilmslow, 'River Police and Smugglers'. In the Outer Hebrides 'Smugglers and Customs'.

§ In the past highwaymen and press-gangs were amongst the *dramatis personae*. Edward Moor, *Suffolk Words*, 1823, p. 238, gives simply

'Robbers'. *Notes and Queries*, 18 June 1910, p. 483, gives 'Robbers and Travellers' and 'Robbers and Policemen', as played by children at London elementary schools. In Forfar, *c.* 1910, it was 'Snouts and Robbers' and 'Takkies and Thieves'. Norman Douglas, *London Street Games*, 1916, p. 36, gives 'Robbers and Coppers' and he, too, equates the game with 'Release'.

Fairies and witches

In the war games that the girls play the protagonists are almost invariably supernatural. They are fairies and witches, roles which give 5– to 8-year-olds infinite scope for pantomime: the fairies flapping their arms and quickly frightened, the witches who pursue them holding their fingers as if they were claws, bending their bodies as if they were aged, and having coats or pieces of cloth flowing from their shoulders for cloaks. The witches generally emerge from a den, and the fairies too sometimes have a palace or place of safety. Often 'there are not as many witches as there are fairies because we do not like being witches'. And they like to play in the dark. In Langholm the fairies dance round together in the darkness until a voice cries 'Witches!' and the fairies flutter off into the night. In Bristol the fairies sing in small shrill voices:

> Wicked old witch are you hungry today?
> If you are then we will all run away.

In Radnorshire the witch has a magic wand that 'turns us into a frog, or something like that'. In fact the enjoyable part of the game is what happens to the fairies after they have been caught. Generally, as in Accrington, 'they are put in a stewpot and eaten for the witches' tea'. The more grisly the details, the more the girls enjoy the game. On the outskirts of Gloucester we found the boys playing conkers, studiously ignoring a group of giggling screaming little girls playing, as they informed us, 'Fairies and Witches'.

> 'How do you play that?' we asked.
> 'There's a witch and she catches you,' they said.
> 'And then?'

'*Takes you to her corner.*'
'And then?'
'*Stews you.*'
'And then?'
'*Eats you.*'
'And then?'
'*Throws the bones away.*'

Hence 'Fairies and Witches' is sometimes known as 'Stewpot' (Camberwell) and 'Witches' Cauldron' (Knottingley). In some places the evil one is a wizard, a wolf, or a ghost, but the fate of those caught is the same, to be boiled in a stewpot and eaten. Even when they play 'Invisible Man', as girls do in Wolstanton, those unlucky enough to be caught end up in the pot:

> 'The first person the Invisible Man touches becomes cook.
> The cook pretends to stir a cauldron of boiling water. In
> the meantime the Invisible Man is still catching other
> people. When all the players are caught the cook goes in
> the pot. Then, when the people in the pot are supposed to
> be cooking nicely the Invisible Man does all kinds of horrid
> things to you like hanging you or putting you in a fridge at
> freezing point. Thus the game goes on.'
>
> *Girl, 9*

And in the fields around Liss, where they play 'Dragons', and 'you are not allowed to run out of the field when the dragon chases you', the fate of those caught is equally unpleasant and final:

> 'The dragon takes the person he has caught to the
> haunted tower where he chains them to the wall, and
> then he presses a button. Suddenly a whole lot of spiders
> drop down on the prisoner and make him scream. When
> the spiders have woven cobwebs all over the prisoner the
> dragon puts the prisoner in the fire and burns him. This
> game is nearly always played in Autumn and Winter.'
>
> *Girl, 9*

At this point, it seems, we reach the boundary of juvenile invention.

Endnotes

1. Thus, too, at the turn of the century: 'On nights when, as boys, we used to thread its dim streets playing "Jock, Shine the Light" ... [Langholm] had an indubitable magic of its own.' — Hugh MacDiarmid, *The Listener*, 17 August 1967, p. 204.

2. See *Oxford Dictionary of Nursery Rhymes*, 1951, pp. 69–70, where the rhyme is shown to have been current in George III's day. Cf. also J. O. Halliwell, *Nursery Rhymes*, 1844, p. 124: 'The following is used by schoolboys, when two are starting to run a race. One to make ready, And two to prepare; God bless the rider, And away goes the mare.'

3. An informant recalls that in her day in Bath, c. 1905, it was customary to say 'Sunlight Soap is the best in the world'. It seems that advertizers were as able then, as now, to have their slogans adopted by children. Indeed, in the period before the First World War, commercial advertizers had a number of amusing devices for attracting juvenile attention which are unknown today.

4. 'Giant's Treasure' is more often the name of a related Scout game in which the person in front, who is blindfold or has his back turned, guards a knife, bottle, or other object, which the players try to snatch from him without being heard. This game also goes under the names: 'Blind Knife', 'Blind Pirate', 'Sleeping Pirate', 'Sneaking Pirates', 'Blue Peter', 'Stalking', 'Creeping', 'Crack-a-nut', 'Farmer's Apples', 'Stealing the Honey Pot', 'The Bear and the Honey', 'Doggie and the Bone', and 'Princess in the Tower'.

5. In Accrington, where the game itself is called 'Lucy Locket', the song is exactly as in *The Oxford Dictionary of Nursery Rhymes*, p. 279.

6. Several styles of combat are known as 'Cock Fighting'; in fact the terms 'cock' and 'cock fight' are recurrent in children's speech, continuing testimony to the place the 'royal diversion' once held in British life. It has been prohibited since 1849.

7. However inappropriate the term 'flying angels' in this context, it is traditional. See James Greenwood, *Odd People in Odd Places*, 1883, p. 45 and Norman Douglas, *London Street Games*, 1916, p. 19, ' "Horse Soldiers" (also called "Flying Angels") is rather rough'. In Aberdeen to ride on someone's shoulders is termed 'cocksie coosie', hence the game 'Cocksie Coosie Fight'.

8. It is scarcely necessary to confirm that little boys have jousted in play ever since the days when their elders jousted in earnest. A representation of two small boys riding poles, by way of hobby-horses, and jousting with sticks, is reproduced by Strutt plate xv, from a fourteenth-century manuscript book of prayers. An early sixteenth-century Flemish Calendar in the British Museum shows a group of boys likewise engaged, carrying whirligigs for lances (MS. Adds. 24098, fol. 23b). William Fitzstephen, in his account of the sports of Londoners in the twelfth century, refers to the lay-sons of citizens coming out into the fields on Sunday afternoons in Lent equipped with lances and shields, and adds that there were also present 'the younger sort with pikes from which the iron head has been taken off, and there they get up sham fights'.

9. A duel between camel riders is shown in Bruegel's picture of children's street games, painted 1560. Here the two riders are shown holding either end of a loop of rope, and are attempting to pull each other across a line marked by two bricks.

10. When we tried the game ourselves we were at first uneasy, and justifiably so, about where the knife was going to land. But after some practice we found that our determination not to be humiliated by our opponent was such that we had developed an icy coolness: we were concentrating on the flight of the knife from the point of view of the game rather than of our own or our 'partner's' safety.

11. 'Vicarage grounds, chestnut trees in autumn, "conkers" and children — what more could a parish priest want?' Correspondent to *The Times*, 13 October 1962, p. 9. One 10-year-old in our survey delightfully confessed, 'My granny sends me all my conkers'.

12. All children questioned in Oxford gave this formula, as did a correspondent recalling his Oxford schooldays in the 1880s.

13. 'Isn't that rather a mouthful?' we asked. 'Oh no, you just say it quickly', and the boy gabbled it like one-o'clock. Compare the following which Mrs Chamberlain records in *West Worcestershire Words*, 1882, p. 15, as 'written down for me by a National School boy'—'Hobley, hobley, Honcor, My first conkor. Hobley, Hobley ho, My first go. Hobley, hobley, ack, My first smack.'

14. It is a fixed belief with schoolboys, and some adults too, that horse chestnuts are poisonous, and should on no account be put in the mouth, a superstition probably arising from their bitter taste. Formerly, however, they were considered beneficial to horses with the cough (hence their name?); and instructions for making a 'strictly edible and agreeable flour' for human consumption may be found in *Household Words*, 24 December 1881, p. 176. In Yorkshire, where chestnut trees are not as common as in southern England, boys continued to contest with hazel nuts anyway up to the Second World War, and possibly do so still.

15. *The Life and Correspondence of Robert Southey*, vol. i, 1849, p. 55. Southey continues with a nice illustration of the schoolboy ethos, showing it to have been as particular in the eighteenth century as today. Southey, at this time a little fellow, came one day upon a boy whom he considered to be cheating. He 'had fallen in with a great number of young snails, so recently hatched that the shells were still transparent, and he was besmearing his fingers by crushing these poor creatures one after another against his conqueror, counting away with the greatest satisfaction at his work. He was a good-natured boy, so that I, who had been bred up to have a sense of humanity, ventured to express some compassion for the snails, and to suggest that he might as well count them and lay them aside unhurt. He hesitated, and seemed inclined to assent till it struck him as a point of honour, or of conscience, and then he resolutely said, no! that would not do, for he could not then fairly say he had conquered them'.

16. The victim on these occasions does not attempt to resist. He curls up to protect himself, and takes what comes, consoling himself that the next person to be given ten seconds to run will be the one who caught him.

17. ' "King of the Castle" and "No Man Standing" are just red savagery set to rules', remarked Edwin Pugh in *Living London*, vol. iii, 1903, p. 267. 'King of the Castle'—in the United States generally known as 'King of the Mountain' or 'King of the Hill'—is included amongst the games in Bruegel's picture of children at play, painted in 1560. 'No Man Standing' or 'No Time for Standing' is a game in which every player tries to uproot every other by grasping at his ankles.

18. 'Tuck yer napper in, I'm a-coming' was the cry in London streets sixty years ago, and before that (*vide* 'The Gondoliers') it was 'Tuck in yer Tuppenny'.

19. The 'baneful trick' of stooping without warning, just as a player is making his leap, used to be known as 'fudging', and, declared *The Boy's Handy Book*, 1863, deserved 'whatever punishment playground justice may award ... We have heard of a collar-bone broken through *fudging*'.

20. Today leapfrog is chiefly the sport of the younger boys and, judging by the number of accounts received from girls, is becoming a feminine pastime. Probably its image has not been enhanced by its inclusion amongst gymnasium games, along with the vaulting-horse. As a Spennymoor girl remarked, 'The boys play a rougher game on the same idea as leapfrog called "Hum-a-dum-dum" ' (see below).

21. This terminology is traditional. The Rev Walter Gregor, born 1826, recalled that in his boyhood at Keith, Banffshire, 'the boy that stooped his back was called "the bull" pronounced *bill*' (Gomme, vol. ii, 1898, p. 440). In Wigan the game is called 'Cutter', which is the cry of the leader when determining where the boy making the back shall move to next. This term, too, is old, being recorded in *The Boy's Own Book*, 1855, p. 25 (see below). At King's School, Canterbury, *c.* 1875, the game was called 'Cut Throat'; in Canning Town, *c.* 1910, it was 'Cut Lump'; in *London Street Games*, 1916, it was 'Cut-a-Lump' or 'Cutter'; and in Dundee today it is 'Cut Foot and Guide'.

22. In France 'Le Saute-Mouton à la Semelle', the sheep similarly moving forward 'la longueur de son pied droit, posé en équerre au milieu du gauche' (*200 Jeux d'enfants, c.* 1892, p. 140).

23. The writer concluded with a warning, necessary for boys in the middle of the nineteenth century: 'Whenever you play at "Foot and an O'er", always loosen the straps at the bottom of your trousers, if any you wear; because if you don't, you may very easily do them a serious injury, by tearing them.'

24. H. E. Bates has said it was a game of which 'I can hardly speak without emotion'. Howard Spring imagined it the splendid invention of his own boyhood gang in Cardiff. Readers of *The Times*, January-February 1951, wrote more letters about it to the editor than could be printed.

25. The question whether or not part of a boy's anatomy has touched the ground can be the subject of urgent debate. A writer in the London *Evening News*, 21 December 1931, p. 11, reported the following dialogue when a member of the mounted side had lost his seat, and was clinging on desperately underneath his mount:

> 'Steve's touched!'
> 'Garn, I 'aven't!'
> 'Just look at yer!'
> 'All right—look!'
> 'Yer back's on the ground!'
> 'Ye're blind!'
> 'Wait till ye're up, an' I'll give yer a claht on the jaw!'

As a Walworth boy confessed to us (1961): 'The reason why I like Jump Jimmy Knacker is because it is not always a fair game and it gets very exciting.'

26. Although not in Camborne and Helston when we were there in 1961. The boys said they used indeed to play it, but someone at school had broken an arm (or leg), the game had been banned, and this had, for the time being, dissipated enthusiasm.

27. Written by John Stanford and published 18 May 1878. Edward Moor, 1823, listed 'Hie Cocolorum Jig' amongst the sports of his Suffolk childhood. 'High-cock-a-lorum' was the name known to Tom Brown before he started his *School Days* (1857, p. 63). The children down 'Deadman's yard' devoted their energies to 'Hi Cockolorum' (*Illustrated London News*, 7 January 1860, p. 24). So did Michael Ernest Sadler at his Winchester prep school in 1871; also the boys of St Paul's School, *c.* 1885; of Repton College, *c.* 1905; of Cheltenham College, *c.* 1935; and the choir boys of Westminster Abbey, *c.* 1930.

28. For a summary of door-knocking pranks and their names see *The Lore and Language of Schoolchildren*, pp. 377–92.

29. This may be equated with the 'game' (so styled) known as 'Confessions', where a person is tortured until he reveals something considered sufficiently shameful to justify his release; and for it to be someone else's turn to be made to confess.

30. *Venereal Disease and Young People*, BMA, 1964. The rules of this unseemly game appeared in greater detail in the *Daily Express*, 6 March 1964, p. 8.

31. The name 'Cappers' apparently comes from *cap*, meaning to emulate, to surpass, in the way schoolboys used to *cap verses*. 'In puritanical times of old,' remarks Forby in his *Vocabulary of East Anglia*, 1830, '*capping of texts* was a favourite, and doubtless very edifying, sort of pious pastime. With us at large, the word is used on a great variety of profane occasions. An idle boy leaps a ditch, or climbs a tree, and if his play-fellow cannot equal or out-do him, it is a *cap*; he has *cap'd* him.' In Westmorland two generations ago the game was known as 'King Cappers' (*EDD*).

32. Since no game, worthy of the name, could be more innocuous than this one, Mr Smith provides an interesting example of the dedicated adult's inability to leave well alone. Having been shown how to play. 'Time' by his young daughter, he not only felt it necessary to alter the game to make it suitable, as he considered, for a schoolroom, but recommended that the teacher should take part, should indeed take the principal role, and should retain the principal role throughout the course of the game. For example: 'When one of the players finally guesses the time decided upon, the teacher says to the fortunate guesser, "which do you like better, pears or apples?" ' Such small amusement as the game

possesses is thus effectively monopolized by the teacher.

33. In the United States this last dialogue is so common it gives the game its usual name, 'Lemonade'. Indeed the ridiculous words have been repeated times without number, for as long ago as 1903 Newell set down the following from the recitation of a 12-year-old girl in St Paul, Minnesota: 'Here we come!' 'Where from?' 'Jamestown, Virginia.' 'What's your trade?' 'Lemonade.' 'Give us some.' (*Games of American Children*, 1903, pp. 249–50.)

34. The front man' is elsewhere known as the 'standard', 'post', 'pillar', 'pillow', or 'cushion'. These names are in themselves long established, e.g. the term 'pillow' appeared in a description of the game, under the name 'Ships', in the *Almondbury and Huddersfield Glossary*, 1883.

35. 'Huckey Buck' was in fact also a name for the present game. Children in Suffolk used to cry:

> Huck-a-buck, huck-a-buck,
> How many fingers do I hold up?
> G. F. Northall, *Traditional Rhymes*, 1892, p. 401.

36. *The New Yorker*, 13 November 1937, pp. 32–42.

37. See F. M. Böhme, *Deutsches Kinderspiel*, 1897; pp. 633–4; J. W. P. Drost, *Het Nederlandsch kinderspel*, 1914, pp. 41–6; Stavre Th. Frashëri, *Folk-Lore*, vol. xl, 1929, pp. 370–1 (Albanian account, the game being called 'Raqe, Hypa, Zdrypa'); B. L. Ullman in *Classical Philology*, vol. xxxviii, 1943, pp. 94–102; Paul G. Brewster in *Béaloideas*, vol. xiii, 1943, pp. 40–79, and in *North Carolina Folklore*, vol. i, 1952, pp. 58–9; Roger Pinon, *La nouvelle Lyre Malmédienne*, vol. ii, pt. 3, 1954, pp. 17–25; Brian Sutton-Smith in *Folk-Lore*, vol. xlii, 1951, pp. 329–33 (New Zealand variants); Jeanette Hills, *Das Kinderspielbild von Pieter Bruegel*, 1957, pp. 18–19; R. T. Allen in *Maclean's Magazine*, 22 October 1960, p. 32 (Canadian account); M. M. Lumbroso, *Giochi*, 1967, p. 55 ('Quanti corni' played in Lombardy). In Istanbul it is 'Çatti Patti Kaç Atti'. In the Moscow district of Vnukovo, a boy told our correspondent he called the game 'Kozyol' (Goat).

38. In 1942 English members of the Eighth Army in the Western Desert were surprised to see South African troops playing an apparently juvenile leap-frog game which, when they joined in, was found to be 'not a game for weaklings'. The game has, in fact, been banned in South African schools owing to the number of girls as well as boys who have been injured while playing it.

39. Cf. Petronius: 'manuque plena scapulas eius subinde verberavit'. Also 'Old Johnny Hairy, Crap in!' in *Traditional Games*, vol. ii, 1898, pp. 449–50; and 'Hurly-burly, Thump on the Back' listed as a standard name in *A Handbook of Irish Folklore*, 1942, p. 673.

40. Sometimes thought to be 'Hot Cockles', a game more obviously depicted at fol. 97.

41. Or, as a small stolid lad in Somerset was heard warning, 'Don't yew come stealing my gurt hog'.

42. A further connecting link is apparent in the game 'Cripple Chirsty' played in the Lorne district of Argyllshire (*Folk-Lore*, vol. xvi, 1905, p. 220). Cripple Chirsty came limping along leaning on a stick, and the protecting player, a hen, addressed her: 'Hey, Cripple Chirsty, what do you want with me today?'
'A beck and a bow and I would thank you for your eldest daughter.'
The hen gave the witch a curtsy and a bow, but refused to give up her eldest daughter, or any other of the children who were hanging on in a line at her back. The witch then attacked the hen, trying to reach the furthermost player.

43. Printed sources: Brockett, *North Country Words*, 1846, under *Keeling*; Halliwell, *Popular Rhymes*, 1849, p. 131; *Folk-Lore Record*, vol. v, 1882, p. 88; *Shropshire Folk-Lore*, 1883, p. 520; Newell, *Games of American Children*, 1883, pp. 215–21, and 1903, pp. 258–63; *Folk-Lore Journal*, vol. v, 1887, pp. 53–4; *Journal of American Folk-Lore*, vol. iii, 1890, pp. 139–48 (Newell); Northall, *Folk Rhymes*, 1892, p. 391; *County Folk-Lore: Suffolk*, 1893, p. 62; Gomme, *Traditional Games*, vol. i, 1894, pp. 396–401 and vol. ii, 1898, pp. 187–9, 215, 391–6, 449; Rodger, *Lang Strang*, 1948, pp. 43–4 (Forfar, 1910).

44. In *The Journal of American Folk-Lore*, vol. iii, 1890, pp. 142–4, Newell deduces from parallel Swedish, Italian, and Catalan games, and by references to superstition in Ireland, that 'a demand for fire, or for a light, on the part of a stranger, constitutes ground for suspicion of witchcraft, and that such a request must not be complied with'.

45. Bland, made with equal parts of hot water and whey, remains a popular drink in Shetland, although not drunk perhaps to the extent it was in 1701, when it was reported to be so ordinary there were 'many people in the countrey who never saw ale or beer all their lifetime'.

46. Just as the boys did who represented burning biscuits in the game called 'Jack, Jack, the Biscuit Burns'—*School Boys' Diversions*, 1820, pp. 10–12.

47. This appears to be in accord with the game as played in Sweden. There, the old woman, who also hobbles on a stick, points at one of the children and asks 'May I have a chicken?' Although at first refused she is eventually given each of the 'chickens' and does not have to steal them—A. I. Arwidsson, *Svenska Fornsånger*, vol. iii, 1842, p. 437. In Spain the Mother leaves Marquilla in charge of the brood, with directions, if the wolf comes, to fling him the smallest chicken—K. L. Bates, *Spanish Highways and Byways*, 1900, p. 317. In German versions of the game, under the name 'Frau Rose', the children are begged rather than stolen—Wilhelm Mannhardt, *Germanische Mythen*, 1858, pp. 273–83. The plot may here have been influenced by the otherwise unrelated European game of 'Rich and Poor' in which children are begged.

48. 'I call this a very interesting game', stated our informant, a girl aged 12.

49. It was no surprise when one small girl remarked, 'Sometimes we never get to the end of this game.'

50. Little girls, today, in Krombach, Westphalia, skip to a similar fancy:

'Aprikose Liese, geh' mal auf die Wiese.'
'Mutter, ich hab' kein Schuh.'
'Zieh des Vaters Pantoffl'n an.'
'Mutter, die sind zu klein.'
'Schneid' ein Stück von der Ferse ab.'
'Mutter, dann gibt es Blut.'

'Apricot Liz, go to the meadow.'
'Mother, I have no shoes.'
'Put your father's slippers on.'
'Mother, they are too small.'
'Then cut a bit off your heel.'
'Mother, then it will bleed.'

51. A 10-year-old girl told us confidently 'Blacking Topper or Mackintosh is a foreign name for a favourite child, and this is how the game gets its name'. The name 'Blacking Toppers' (also spelt 'Topas' and 'Topa') appeared in 1910 as the name of a game played by children in London elementary schools (*Notes and Queries,* 11th ser., vol. i, p. 483). Norman Douglas, *London Street Games,* 1916, p. 48, listed 'Black In Topper'. Our own records show the game being called 'Blacking Topper' in London c. 1930, c. 1947, and 1960.

52. In this game Idle Jack and his master, after some playful preliminaries, had to go up to the oven and draw out each of the loaves, who were boys seated on the ground in single file, each boy holding on to the one in front. Descriptions appear in *School Boys' Diversions,* 1820, pp. 10–12; *Boy's Own Book,* 4th ed., 1829, p. 37; *Every Boy's Book,* 1841, p. 30; *Alphabet of Sports,* 1866 ('Draw the Batch'); and Seán O Súilleabháin's *Irish Wake Amusements,* 1967, p. 82 ('Drawing the Bonnavs'). Northall, *English Folk-Rhymes,* 1892, p. 390, states that in Warwickshire the baked bread used to attract attention by chanting:

Jack, Jack, the bread's a-burning,
All to a cinder,
If you don't come and fetch it out,
We'll throw it through the winder.

53. Psychologists doubtless equate such make-believe with playing 'Hospitals'. The child wishes to assure herself that even if something disastrous occurred in her home-life she would still be able to manage. The gifted Ann and Jane Taylor, towards the end of the eighteenth century, were other little girls who indulged in these fancies. 'We most frequently personated two poor women making a hard shift to live; or we were "aunt and niece", Jane the latter and I the former; or we acted a fiction entitled "the twin sisters", or another, the "two Miss Parks". And we had, too, a great taste for royalty, and were not a little intimate with various members of the royal family. Even the two poor women, "Moll and Bet", were so exemplary in their management and industry as to attract the notice of their Royal Highnesses the Princesses ("when George the Third was King").'— *Autobiography of Mrs Gilbert, formerly Ann Taylor,* vol. i, 1874, p. 29.

54. Boys are shown parading as soldiers in Jacob Cats's *Emblemata,* 1622; in Stella's *Jeux de l'enfance,* 1657; and frequently in juvenile literature, for instance in *A Little*

Pretty Pocket-Book, 1744. Husenbeth recalled that when he was at Sedgly Park School during the Napoleonic Wars, the boys formed a troop of soldiers, each paying nine pence for a wooden gun, and three pence for his pasteboard cap, so that they made a fine show on parade (*History of Sedgley Park*, 1856, pp. 109–10). Thomas Miller, born 1807, played at 'French and English', enlisting his recruits with broken bits of white pot to represent the King's Shilling (*Country Year Book*, 1847, p. 18). There is a tale that when Elizabeth I was concerned about the effects of her policies on the Scottish nation, she would inquire how the boys were amusing themselves. If they were playing soldiers, she took it as a warning that it was time for her to arm.

55. In France children play 'Le Cowboy et l'Indien', in Germany 'Cowboy und Indianer', in Italy 'Caw-boys e Indiani'.

Acknowledgments

A work of this kind cannot be accomplished by two people on their own; and it has again been our good fortune that many perceptive and energetic people, strategically placed in different parts of Britain, and indeed in different parts of the world, have been willing to help us. Our hope is that they have never felt we were taking their assistance for granted, any more than have they, we hope, taken for granted our ability to do justice to the wealth of material they have made available to us.

The following are the chief schools, together with the teachers responsible at the time, who, in addition to those listed in *The Lore and Language of Schoolchildren*, pp. xi–xiv, have contributed to this work or who have made further contributions since then.

ABERDEEN	Powis Secondary School (Mr H. W. Valentine, Head Teacher; Miss Netta Y. Dick, Woman Adviser)
ACCRINGTON	Peel Park County Junior School (Mr John Heaton)
BACUP	St Saviour's County Primary School (Mrs Margaret Dearden)
BANBURY	Easington School for Girls (Miss M. H. Dawson, Head Mistress)
BARROW-IN-FURNESS	St Aloysius Roman Catholic Secondary School (Miss M. Morris)
BERRY HILL	Berry Hill Secondary School (Mr K. R. E. Farmer, Head Master)
BISHOP AUCKLAND	Cockton Hill Junior School (Mr Harold Guthrie, Head Master)
BRIGHTLINGSEA	St James' Junior School (Mr W. Wilcox, Head Master)
BRISTOL	Embleton Junior School (Mr W. H. James, Head Master)
	Portway Secondary Girls' School (Miss B. O. Draper, Head Mistress)
	Westbury Park Junior Mixed and Infants' School (Mr W. J. Lander, Head Master)
BUTE	Kingarth School (Miss C. M. McFarlane)
CRICKHOWELL	Crickhowell Junior School (Miss Joyce Short)
CUMNOCK	Cumnock Academy (Mr A. L. Taylor; Dr John Strawhorn; Mr Charles McLeod)
CUMNOCK, NEW	Bank Junior Secondary School (The English Staff)
DUNOON	Dunoon Grammar School (Mr Alasdair J. S. Sinclair)
EDINBURGH	James Gillespie's Boys' School (Miss Ella Henderson)
	John Watson School (Miss A. M. Ireland)
ENFIELD	Grange Park Primary School (Mrs Olive Sellick)
	Ponders End Boys' School (Mr A. H. Sellick, Head Master)
	Ponders End Secondary School (Mr A. H. Sellick, Head Master)
FRODSHAM	Frodsham Church of England Junior School (through Mrs L. R.

	Stanton)
GLASGOW	The Grammar School, Uddingston (Mr Ian C. MacLeod)
GLASTONBURY	St John's Boys' School (Mr G. C. White)
GRIMSBY	Harold Secondary Modern Boys' School (Mr D. H. Potts, Head Master)
GUERNSEY	Castel Primary School (Mr Laurence Adkins, Head Master; Mr R. J. Gill)
	The Grammar School for Boys, St Peter Port (Mr Laurence Adkins)
	Vale Junior School (Mr Laurence Adkins)
HELENSBURGH	Hermitage Senior Secondary School (Dr Ian J. Simpson)
HELSTON	Helston County Primary School (Miss J. Martin)
INVERNESS	Dalneigh Primary School (Miss Katherine Mackintosh)
IPSWICH	Priory Heath Junior School (Mr H. A. James, Head Master)
	Rushmere St Andrew County Primary School (Miss Helen Southgate, Head Teacher)
	Springfield Junior School (Mr Leslie Stow, Head Master)
JERSEY	The Convent F.C.J., St Helier (Miss Lynda Hodkinson)
KINLOCHLEVEN	Kinlochleven Junior Secondary School
KNIGHTON	Knighton County Secondary School (Mr Frank Noble; Mr and Mrs H. J. Williams)
LANGHOLM	Langholm Academy (Miss Eva Smart)
LEWIS	Nicholson Primary School, Stornoway (Mr John Angus Maciver)
LISS	Liss County Junior School (Mr D. M. Dolman, Head Master, and successively Mr I. W. Cutler, Head Master)
LIVERPOOL	Waterloo County Secondary School (Mr G. H. Roberts)
LONDON	Beaufort House Junior Mixed School, Fulham (Mr J. R. Bevan, Head Master)
	Godwin County Primary School, West Ham (Mr R. S. Richards, Head Master)
	Munster Junior Mixed School, Fulham (Head Master, Mr I. H. W. Haines)
	Netley Junior Mixed School, Camden Town (Mr D. D. Mackay, Head Master)
	St John's Parochial School, Kilburn (Mr A. Kinsman, Head Master)
	Walworth Secondary School (Miss Valerie J. Avery)
LYDEARD ST LAWRENCE	Lydeard St Lawrence County Primary School (Miss Mona Penny, Head Mistress)
MANCHESTER (SALE)	Sale Grammar School (Dr G. G. Urwin)
MARKET RASEN	The Modern School (Mr S. B. Vickers, Head Master)
MIDDLETON CHENEY	Middleton Cheney County Primary School (Mr George Stevens, Head Master)
NORWICH	Colman Junior School (Miss Antonia Steedman)
OFFHAM	Offham County Primary School (Mrs E. M. Melville, Head Mistress)
ORKNEY	Kirkwall Grammar School (Mr H. G. MacKerron, Rector)
	The Academy, Stromness (Mr W. Groundwater, Rector)
OXFORD	Headington Secondary Modern School (Miss Margaret

	Hornsey)
PERTH	Kinnoull School (Mr J. S. Soane, Head Master)
PLYMOUTH	Pennycross Primary School (Mr F. Uglow, Head Master)
ST ANDREWS	Madras College (Dr J. Thompson, Rector)
ST LEONARDS-ON-SEA	St Mary Star of the Sea School (through Mrs L. R. Stanton)
SCARBOROUGH	Gladstone Road Junior School (Miss R. Horsman; Mr H. Weale)
SHETLAND	Livister School, Whalsay (Mrs J. Grant Wood, Head Teacher)
	Scalloway Junior Secondary School (Mr Robert N. Hutchison, Head Master, and successively Mr John Gray, Head Master)
SPENNYMOOR	Spennymoor Grammar Technical School (Mr D. Cockburn, Head Master; Mr Matthew Walton; Mr E. W. Ashton)
SWANSEA	Brynmill Junior Mixed School (Mr Reginald Gammon)
	Glanmor Secondary School for Girls (Miss Joyce A. Terrett)
	Waunarlwydd Infants' School (Miss Dorothy Lloyd, Head Mistress)
TWICKENHAM	Twickenham Technical School (Mr T. P. Stanton)
WELSHPOOL	Ardwyn Nursery and Infant School (Miss L. N. Griffiths, Head Mistress)
	The High School (Miss F. H. Rosser)
	Welshpool Secondary Modern School (Mr J. Spergeon)
WIDECOMBE-IN-THE-MOOR	Widecombe-in-the-Moor County Primary School (Mr F. A. Baldock, Head Master)
WIGAN	St Cuthbert's Junior School (Mr B. J. Murphy, Head Master)
WILMSLOW	Chancel Lane Church of England Controlled School (Mr Roy H. Couchman, Head Master)
WINDERMERE	Windermere Endowed School for Girls (Miss Brakewell, Head Mistress)
WOLSTANTON	Ellison Street County Primary School (through Miss Fay Prendergast)
YORK	Tang Hall Primary School (Miss Theodora Ross)

Moreover, Mrs L. R. Stanton, Head of the Education Department, Maria Assumpta College of Education, encouraged her students to acquire information for us in more than forty schools, chiefly but not exclusively in the Greater London area. Miss A. E. Osmond and students of Bedford College of Education again went to much trouble on our behalf tackling specific problems; and Mr P. C. Sheppard of Brentwood School, Miss E. M. Wright, Head Mistress, Huyton College Preparatory School, and Mr Alex Helm of Congleton followed up particular lines of inquiry.

A number of teachers other than those named above have either allowed us to visit them and their pupils, or have supplied us with tape recordings or other information, amongst them: Mr Harvey Macpherson (to whom we are also grateful for a copy of Dean's *Alphabet of Sports*) when at St Leonard's Primary School, Banbury; Mr K. Bumstead, Bramford Primary School; Mr Bryn Jones, Fairfield Grammar School, Bristol; Mr K. M.

Allan, Head Master, Ellesmere County Primary School; Mrs Margaret Hope Luff, Milton House School, Edinburgh; Miss G. R. Brooker, Head Mistress, Greatham County Primary School; Mr Herbert Brelsford, Head Master, St Martin's School, Guernsey; Mr F. H. Le Poidevin, Head Master, Amherst Junior Mixed School, Guernsey; Mr J. I. H. Fleming, successively Head Teacher of Flotta Public School, and Head Master of Stenness Public School, in Orkney; Miss Anita Colquhoun, Sand School, Garderhouse; Mrs Inga I. A. Thomson, Skeld Public School, Shetland; Miss G. L. Landon, Sneyd Green Junior School; and Mr and Mrs Frank L. Pinfold, Swine Church of England School. No tally has been kept of the number of children spoken to in the street when we have been travelling around, but we would like to remark on the courtesy children have always shown us when we approached them, and on the way they have never seemed surprised by our questions.

Individual adults who have answered queries, or who have provided us with specialist, background, or local information, have included: Mr F. O'Brien Adams (recollections of Bembridge, Isle of Wight); the late Mrs Barbara Aitken (who also collected for Lady Gomme); Mrs Cornelia Baké (assistance with Dutch material); Mrs Barbara Bagshaw (Bristol); Miss Gertrude M. Black (Stornoway); Miss Theo Brown, Folklore Recorder, The Devonshire Association; Mrs Aldyth M. Cadoux, who collected for us in Moscow; Miss Kathleen Crawshaw, who sent Gillington's *Hampshire Singing Games*; Miss K. H. Crofts (Kennington); Mr Gilbert H. Fabes (recollections of Vauxhall Bridge Road); Mr Alec Forster (Anglesey); Mrs Gande (Luccombe); Mr and Mrs Fritz Gasch; Mr H. W. Harwood of Halifax, whose passing was a sad loss to us; Mr G. E. Hawkins (recollections of Hull); Miss M. Hewson (Louth); Mr G. H. Hobbs (Petersfield); Mr Philip Howell (Birmingham and Cheltenham); Mrs Kathleen Hunt (Bicester and Newcastle upon Tyne); Mrs C. C. Hurst (recollections of Earl Shilton, Leicestershire); Mr P. G. Inwood (Wrecclesham in the nineteenth century); Mr Chris Kilkenny (Newcastle upon Tyne); Mr John MacInnes (translations of children's papers written in Gaelic); Miss Maureen MacMillan (Ballachulish); Miss H. Milne; Mr Pat Page (Dundee); Mr Julian Pilling (Nelson); Mrs Vivien Pope; Mrs Lilian M. C. Fandall (references to games in medieval manuscripts); Dr and Mrs Rossell Hope Robbins; Mr F. C. Rowlands (Eccleshill); Mr Stewart Sanderson; Mr Frank Shaw (Liverpool); Mrs Margaret Smallwood (recollections of Salisbury); Mr Alexander L. Stark (Stirling); Mr George Stratton (Birkenhead); Miss Wendy Twine (Liss); Mr Andrew Weir of *The Yorkshire Post*; Miss Dora M. Wild (Douglas,

Isle of Man); and The Rev J. Stafford Wright.

We are also indebted to well-wishers in different places who have often been to much trouble arranging that the survey should have a good coverage, amongst them: Miss R. Beresford; Mrs Kate Bone; Miss J. B. T. Christie; Mr and Mrs L. Gilbert; Dr Hugh Marwick; Mr Roger Mayne; Mr Dennis Potter; Mrs Bruce Proudfoot; Mr R. U. Sayce; Mr J. H. Spence, Director of Education, Zetland; Miss K. I. Stevenson; Miss Ruth L. Tongue; Mr R. A. Wake; Mr D. Woodward; and Mrs Michael Young (Sasha Moorsom). In addition, we would like to put on record that it is no coincidence that references are numerous in this volume to the localities where Mr Laurence Adkins, Mr Roy H. Couchman, Mr Robert S. Richards, Miss Yvonne K. Rodwell, Mr A. H. Sellick, Mr Alasdair J. S. Sinclair, Mr A. L. Taylor, Mr S. B. Vickers, and Mr and Mrs Matthew Walton have been active; while many as are the references to Swansea we can be certain there would have been yet more had it not been for the untimely death in 1965 of Miss Joyce A. Terrett who had been collecting for us continuously for fourteen years.

Our information has also been supplemented, most happily, by some extensive collections of games made independently of our survey. We are indebted to Mrs Violet Brewser for presenting us with the important collection of children's manuscripts and related material on games formed in Somerset in the early twenties by her father, the late A. S. Macmillan; to Dr Francis Celoria for the folklore record sheets concerning games assembled under his auspices in the Department of Extramural Studies, Keele University; to Mr Cuthbert Graham and *The Press and Journal*, Aberdeen, for the large collection of games and bairns' rhymes contributed by readers in 1959; to Mr David Holbrook for kindly giving us the safe-keeping of Lady Gomme's manuscripts subsequent to the publication of her book; and to Miss G. Johnson, Chief Librarian and Curator, Camberwell Public Libraries, for a further 489 children's essays, this time on 'Games I play with my friends', entered for the annual essay competition sponsored by the Libraries Committee.

A feature of this work which has given us particular pleasure has been the amount of contemporary material we have had for comparative purposes through the co-operation of collectors and correspondents overseas. We are grateful to Larer Helge Bfrseth for her book *Min mann Mass*, and for other Norwegian material; Dr Paul G. Brewster for his invaluable *American Nonsinging Games*; Mrs Kenneth Carpenter (Patricia Evans) of Reno for her book *Rimbles* and other help; Miss Nina Demurova for a report from Moscow; Professore and Signora

V. Gargiulo for assistance in and around Capri; Miss Joan Hunt of Edmonton, Alberta, and through her Mr F. W. Wootton, The Principal, Hazeldean Elementary School, Edmonton, for the contributions of 130 pupils; Signora Matizia Maroni Lumbroso, La Presidente, Fondazione Ernesta Besso, Rome, for her invaluable books *Giochi descritti e illustrati dai bambini* and *Conte, cantilene e filastrocche*, and other kindnesses; Mrs Philip Martin and Miss Barbara Martin for information and demonstrations of games played in Montreal; Miss Elisabeth Nielsen for Danish games; Professeur Roger Pinon for the further parts as they appeared of his great work *La Nouvelle Lyre Malmédienne*; Professor Brian Sutton-Smith of the Teachers College, Columbia University, for his volume *The Games of New Zealand Children*, and for numerous off-prints; Mme M.-M. Rabecq-Maillard, Conservateur du Musée d'Histoire de l'Education, Paris, for following up inquiries; Mme H. A. Rasheed for descriptions of games played in Egypt; Dr Ian Turner of Monash University, Victoria, for Australian material collected in preparation for his book *Cinderella Dressed in Yella*; Mr Carl Withers, editor of the Dover edition of Newell's *Games and Songs of American Children*, for many books and kindnesses; Frl. Barbara Zeller for information from Zurich; and Dr Dorothy Howard, editor of the Dover edition of Lady Gomme's *Traditional Games*, whose manuscript collections of games in Australia and the United States we have again consulted. Further, Mrs Cecily Hancock (Storrs, Connecticut), Miss Myra Iwagami (Chicago), Mr and Mrs Nelles (Ottawa), and Professor Morris Silverman (New York), have kept continually alert to our interests sending books, press cuttings, and other materials; while Professor Archer Taylor of Berkeley, who remains at the centre of the folklore scene, has not only kept us informed of new European publications, but has presented us with a number of valuable works including Otto Kampmüller's *Oberösterreichische Kinderspiele*.

Likewise friends in Britain such as Lady Archibald, Miss Joan Ford, Miss Joan Hassall, Miss Carrol Jenkins, Mr Roland Knaster, Miss B. A. Kneller, Mrs Margaret Opie, Miss Jean C. Rodger, and Mr and Mrs Tom Todd, have continually kept their eyes open for us, sending press cuttings, children's books, and playthings; and just because Mr James Opie, Mr Robert Opie, and Miss Letitia Opie are our children, we should not, and do not, take for granted their continued collaboration now they are away from home.

We have also to thank Father Damian Webb OSB, the vividness of whose photographs is the result not just of technical skill, but of a deep understanding of children and their games; Mrs Robert Berk (when Miss

Jenny King) whose strenuous year on the survey was as good for our morale as it certainly was for our files; Mrs Gillian Davies who, during her free time, was also industrious at our third desk; and Miss Gwen Twine who could not be with us a day let alone eight years without being a friend to this work.

Finally we are, as ever, deeply indebted to Miss F. Doreen Gullen of Scarborough who as our mentor examined our pages as they were written, and who as our friend somehow made it so much easier that they should be written.

Index of Games